GIVE PEOPLE MONEY

GIVE PEOPLE MONEY

**HOW A UNIVERSAL BASIC INCOME
WOULD END POVERTY, REVOLUTIONIZE WORK,
AND REMAKE THE WORLD**

Annie Lowrey

CROWN
NEW YORK

Published in the United States by Crown,
an imprint of the Crown Publishing Group, a division
of Penguin Random House LLC, New York.
crownpublishing.com

CROWN and the Crown colophon are registered trademarks
of Penguin Random House LLC.

Chapter Four is adapted from "The Future of Not Working" by
Annie Lowrey, which appeared in *The New York Times Magazine*
on February 23, 2017. Chapter Six is adapted from "The People
Left Behind When Only the 'Deserving' Poor Get Help" by Annie
Lowrey, which originally appeared in *The Atlantic* on May 25, 2017.

Library of Congress Cataloging-in-Publication Data
Name: Lowrey, Annie, author.
Title: Give people money : how a universal basic income would end
poverty, revolutionize work, and remake the world / Annie Lowrey.
Description: New York : Crown, [2018]
Identifiers: LCCN 2017060432 | ISBN 9781524758769
(hardcover) | ISBN 9781524758776 (pbk.)
Subjects: LCSH: Guaranteed annual income. | Poverty—
Government policy.
Classification: LCC HC79.I5 .L69 2018 | DDC 331.2/36—dc23
LC record available at https://lccn.loc.gov/2017060432

ISBN 9781524758769
Ebook ISBN 9781524758783

Printed in the United States of America

Book design by Elina Nudelman
Jacket design by Elena Giavaldi

1 3 5 7 9 10 8 6 4 2

First Edition

FOR EZRA

CONTENTS

Wages for Breathing

ONE OPPRESSIVELY HOT AND MUGGY DAY IN JULY, I STOOD AT A military installation at the top of a mountain called Dorasan, overlooking the demilitarized zone between South Korea and North Korea. The central building was painted in camouflage and emblazoned with the hopeful phrase "End of Separation, Beginning of Unification." On one side was a large, open observation deck with a number of telescopes aimed toward the Kaesong industrial area, a special pocket between the two countries where, up until recently, communist workers from the North would come and toil for capitalist companies from the South, earning $90 million in wages a year. A small gift shop sold *soju* liquor made by Northern workers and chocolate-covered soybeans grown in the demilitarized zone itself. (Don't like them? Mail them back for a refund, the package said.)

On the other side was a theater whose seats faced not a movie screen but windows looking out toward North Korea. In front, there was a labeled diorama. Here is a flag. Here is a factory. Here is a *juche*-inspiring statue of Kim Il Sung. See it there? Can you make out his face, his hands? Chinese tourists pointed between the diorama and the landscape, viewed through the summer haze.

Across the four-kilometer-wide demilitarized zone, the North Koreans were blasting propaganda music so loudly that I could hear not just the tunes but the words. I asked my tour guide, Soo-jin, what the song said. "The usual," she responded. "Stuff about how South Koreans are the tools of the Americans and the North Koreans will come to liberate us from our capitalist slavery." Looking at the denuded landscape before us, this bit of pomposity seemed impossibly sad, as did the incomplete tunnel from North to South scratched out beneath us, as did the little Potemkin village the North Koreans had set up in sight of the observation deck. It was supposedly home to two hundred families, who Pyongyang insisted were working a collective farm, using a child care center, schools, a hospital. Yet Seoul had determined that nobody had ever lived there, and the buildings were empty shells. Comrades would come turn the lights on and off to give the impression of activity. The North Koreans called it "peace village"; Soo-jin called it "propaganda village."

A few members of the group I was traveling with, including myself, teared up at the stark difference between what was in front of us and what was behind. There is perhaps no place on earth that better represents the profound life-and-death power of our choices when it comes to government policy. Less than a lifetime ago, the two countries were one, their people a polity, their economies a single fabric. But the Cold War's ideological and political rivalry between capitalism and communism had ripped them apart, dividing families and scarring both nations. Soo-jin talked openly about the separation of North Korea from the South as "our national tragedy."

The Republic of Korea—the South—rocketed from third-world to first-world status, becoming one of only a handful of countries to do so in the postwar era. In 1960, about fifteen years after the division of the peninsula, its people were about as wealthy as those in the Ivory Coast and Sierra Leone. In 2016, they were closer income-wise to those in Japan, its former colonial occupier, and a brutal one. Citigroup now expects South Korea to be among the most prosperous countries on earth by 2040, richer even than the United States by some measures.

Yet the Democratic People's Republic of Korea, the North, has faltered and failed, particularly since the 1990s. It is a famine-scarred pariah state dominated by governmental graft and military buildup. Rare is it for a country to suffer such a miserable growth pattern without also suffering from the curse of natural disasters or the horrors of war. As of a few years ago, an estimated 40 percent of the population was living in extreme poverty, more than double the share of people in Sudan. Were war to befall the country, that proportion would inevitably rise.

Even from the remove of the observation deck— enveloped in steam, hemmed in by barbed wire, patrolled by passive young men with assault rifles—the difference was obvious. You could see it. I could see it. The South Korean side of the border was lush with forest and riven with well-built highways. Everywhere, there were power lines, trains, docks, high-rise buildings. An hour south sat Seoul, as cosmopolitan and culturally rich a city as Paris, with far better infrastructure than New York or Los Angeles. But the North Korean side of the border was stripped of trees. People had perhaps cut them down for firewood and basic building supplies, Soo-jin told me. The roads were empty and plain, the buildings low and small. So were the people: North Koreans are now measurably shorter than their South Korean relatives, in part due to the stunting effects of malnutrition.

South Korea and North Korea demonstrated, so powerfully demonstrated, that what we often think of as economic circumstance is largely a product of policy. The way things are is really the way we choose for them to be. There is always a counterfactual. Perhaps that counterfactual is not as stark as it is at the demilitarized zone. But it is always there.

• • •

Imagine that a check showed up in your mailbox or your bank account every month.

The money would be enough to live on, but just barely. It might cover a room in a shared apartment, food, and bus fare. It would save you from destitution if you had just gotten out of prison, needed to leave an abusive partner, or could not find work. But it would not be enough to live particularly well on. Let's say that you could do anything you wanted with the money. It would come with no strings attached. You could use it to pay your bills. You could use it to go to college, or save it up for a down payment on a house. You could spend it on cigarettes and booze, or finance a life spent playing Candy Crush in your mom's basement and noodling around on the Internet. Or you could use it to quit your job and make art, devote yourself to charitable works, or care for a sick child. Let's also say that you did not have to do anything to get the money. It would just show up every month, month after month, for as long as you lived. You would not have to be a specific age, have a child, own a home, or maintain a clean criminal record to get it. You just *would,* as would every other person in your community.

This simple, radical, and elegant proposal is called a universal basic income, or UBI. It is universal, in the sense that every resident of a given community or country receives it. It is basic, in that it is just enough to live on and not more. And it is income.

The idea is a very old one, with its roots in Tudor England and the writings of Thomas Paine, a curious piece of intellectual flotsam that has washed ashore again and again over the last half millennium, often coming in with the tides of economic revolution. In the past few years—with the middle class being squeezed, trust in government eroding, technological change hastening, the economy getting Uberized, and a growing body of research on the power of cash as an antipoverty measure being produced—it has vaulted to a surprising prominence, even pitching from airy hypothetical to near-reality in some places. Mark Zuckerberg, Hillary Clinton, the Black Lives Matter movement, Bill Gates, Elon Musk—these are just a few of the policy proposal's flirts, converts, and supporters. UBI pilots are starting or ongoing in Germany, the Netherlands, Finland, Canada, and Kenya, with India contemplating one as well. Some politicians are trying to get it adopted in California, and it has already been the subject of a Swiss referendum, where its reception exceeded activists' expectations despite its defeat.

Why undertake such a drastic policy change, one that would fundamentally alter the social contract, the safety net, and the nature of work? UBI's strange bedfellows put forward a dizzying kaleidoscope of arguments, drawing on everything from feminist theory to environmental policy to political philosophy to studies of work incentives to sociological work on racism.

Perhaps the most prominent argument for a UBI has to do with technological unemployment—the prospect that robots will soon take all of our jobs. Economists at Oxford University estimate that about half of American jobs, including millions and millions of white-collar ones, are susceptible to imminent elimination due to technological advances. Analysts are warning that Armageddon is coming for truck drivers, warehouse box packers, pharmacists, accountants, legal assistants, cashiers, translators, medical diagnosticians, stockbrokers, home appraisers—I could go on. In a world with far less demand for human work, a UBI would be necessary to keep the masses afloat, the argument goes. "I'm not saying I know the future, and that this is exactly what's going to happen," Andy Stern, the former president of the two-million-member Service Employees International Union and a UBI booster, told me. But if "a tsunami is coming, maybe someone should figure out if we have some storm shutters around."

A second common line of reasoning is less speculative, more rooted in the problems of the present rather than the problems of tomorrow. It emphasizes UBI's promise at ameliorating the yawning inequality and grating wage stagnation that the United States and other high-income countries are already facing. The middle class is shrinking. Economic growth is aiding the brokerage accounts of the rich but not the wallets of the working classes. A UBI would act as a straightforward income support for families outside of the top 20 percent, its proponents argue. It would also radically improve the bargaining power of workers, forcing employers to increase wages, add benefits, and improve conditions to retain their talent. Why take a crummy job for $7.25 an hour when you have a guaranteed $1,000 a month to fall back on? "In a time of immense wealth, no one should live in poverty, nor should the middle class be consigned to a future of permanent stagnation or anxiety," argues the Economic Security Project, a new UBI think tank and advocacy group.

In addition, a UBI could be a powerful tool to eliminate deprivation, both around the world and in the United States. About 41 million Americans were living below the poverty line as of 2016. A $1,000-a-month grant would push many of them above it, and would ensure that no abusive partner, bout of sickness, natural disaster, or sudden job loss means destitution in the richest civilization that the planet has ever known. This case is yet stronger in lower-income countries. Numerous governments have started providing cash transfers, if not universal and unconditional ones, to reduce their poverty rates, and some policymakers and political parties, pleased with the results, are toying with providing a true UBI. In Kenya, a U.S.-based charity called GiveDirectly is sending thousands of adults about $20 a month for more than a decade to demonstrate how a UBI could end deprivation, cheaply and at scale. "We could end extreme poverty right now, if we wanted to," Michael Faye, GiveDirectly's cofounder, told me.

A UBI would end poverty not just effectively, but also efficiently, some of its libertarian-leaning boosters argue. Replacing the current American welfare state with a UBI would eliminate huge swaths of the government's bureaucracy and reduce state interference in its citizens' lives: Hello UBI, good-bye to the Departments of Health and Human Services and Housing and Urban Development, the Social Security Administration, a whole lot of state and local offices, and much of the Department of Agriculture. "Just giving people money is a very natural solution," says Charles Murray of the American Enterprise Institute, a right-of-center think tank. "It's a way of cutting the Gordian knot. You don't need to be drafting ever-more-sophisticated solutions to our problems."

Protecting against a robot apocalypse, providing workers with bargaining power, jump-starting the middle class, ending poverty, and reducing the complexity of government: It sounds pretty good, right? But a UBI means that the government would send every citizen a check every month, eternally and regardless of circumstance. That inevitably raises any number of questions about fairness, government spending, and the nature of work.

When I first heard the idea, I worried about UBI's impact on jobs. A $1,000 check arriving every month might spur millions of workers to drop out of the labor force, leaving the United States relying on a smaller and smaller pool of workers for taxable income to be distributed to a bigger and bigger pool of people not participating in paid labor. This seems a particularly prevalent concern given how many men have dropped out of the labor force of late, pushed by stagnant wages and pulled, perhaps, by the low-cost marvels of gaming and streaming. With a UBI, the country would lose the ingenuity and productivity of a large share of its greatest asset: its people. More than that, a UBI implemented to fight technological unemployment might mean giving up on American workers, paying them off rather than figuring out how to integrate them into a vibrant, tech-fueled economy. Economists of all political persuasions have voiced similar concerns.

And a UBI would do all of this at extraordinary expense. Let's say that we wanted to give every American $1,000 a month in cash. Back-of-the-envelope math suggests that this policy would cost roughly $3.9 trillion a year. Adding that kind of spending on top of everything else the government already funds would mean that total federal outlays would more than double, arguably requiring taxes to double as well. That might slow the economy down, and cause rich families and big corporations to flee offshore. Even if the government replaced Social Security and many of its other antipoverty programs with a UBI, its spending would still have to increase by a number in the hundreds of billions, each and every year.

Stepping back even further: Is a UBI really the best use

of scarce resources? Does it make any sense to bump up taxes in order to give people like Mark Zuckerberg and Bill Gates $1,000 a month, along with all those working-class families, retirees, children, unemployed individuals, and so on? Would it not be more efficient to tax rich people and direct money to poor people through means-testing, as programs like Medicaid and the Supplemental Nutrition Assistance Program, better known as SNAP or food stamps, already do? Even in the socialist Nordic countries, state support is generally contingent on circumstance. Plus, many lower-income and middle-income families already receive far more than $1,000 a month per person from the government, in the United States and in other countries. If a UBI wiped out programs like food stamps and housing vouchers, is there any guarantee that a basic income would be more fair and effective than the current system?

There are more philosophical objections to a UBI too. In no country or community on earth do individuals automatically get a pension as a birthright, with the exception of some princes, princesses, and residents of petrostates like Alaska. Why should we give people money with no strings attached? Why not ask for community service in return, or require that people at least try to work? Isn't America predicated on the idea of pulling yourself up by your bootstraps, not on coasting by on a handout?

As a reporter covering the economy and economic policy in Washington, I heard all of these arguments for and objections against, watching as an obscure, never-before-tried idea became a global phenomenon. Not once in my career had I seen a bit of social-policy arcana go viral. Search interest in UBI more than doubled between 2011 and 2016, according to Google data. UBI barely got any mention in news stories as of the mid-2000s, but since then the growth has been exponential. It came up in books, at conferences, in meetings with politicians, in discussions with progressives and libertarians, around the dinner table.

I covered it as it happened. I wrote about that failed Swiss referendum, and about a Canadian basic-income experiment that has provided evidence for the contemporary debate. I talked with Silicon Valley investors terrified by the prospect of a jobless future and rode in a driverless car, wondering how long it would be before artificial intelligence started to threaten my job. I chatted with members of Congress on both sides of the aisle about the failing middle class and whether the country needed a new, big redistributive policy to strengthen it. I had beers with European intellectuals enthralled with the idea. I talked with Hill aides convinced that a UBI would be a part of a 2020 presidential platform. I spoke with advocates certain that in a decade, millions of people around the world would have a monthly check to fall back on—or else would make up a miserable new precariat. I heard from philosophers convinced that our understanding of work, our social contract, and the underpinnings of our economy were about to undergo an epochal transformation.

The more I learned about UBI, the more obsessed I became with it, because it raised such interesting questions about our economy and our politics. Could libertarians in the United States really want the same thing as Indian economists as the Black Lives Matter protesters as Silicon Valley tech pooh-bahs? Could one policy be right for both Kenyan villagers living on 60 cents a day and the citizens of Switzerland's richest canton? Was UBI a magic bullet, or a policy hammer in search of a nail? My questions were also philosophical. Should we compensate uncompensated care workers? Why do we tolerate child poverty, given how rich the United States is? Is our safety net racist? What would a robot jobs apocalypse actually look like?

I set out to write this book less to describe a burgeoning international policy movement or to advocate for an idea, than to answer those questions for myself. The research for it brought me to villages in remote Kenya, to a wedding held amid monsoon rains in one of the poorest states in India, to homeless shelters, to senators' offices. I interviewed economists, politicians, subsistence farmers, and philosophers. I traveled to a UBI conference in Korea to meet many of the idea's leading proponents and deepest thinkers, and stood with them at the DMZ contemplating the terrifying, heartening, and profound effects of our policy choices.

What I came to believe is this: A UBI is an ethos as much as it is a technocratic policy proposal. It contains within it the principles of universality, unconditionality, inclusion, and simplicity, and it insists that every person is deserving of participation in the economy, freedom of choice, and a life without deprivation. Our governments can and should choose to provide those things, whether through a $1,000-a-month stipend or not.

This book has three parts. First, we'll look at the issues surrounding UBI and work, then UBI and poverty, and finally UBI and social inclusion. At the end, we'll explore the promise, potential, and design of universal cash programs. I hope that you will come to see, as I have, that there is much to be gained from contemplating this complicated, transformative, and mind-bending policy.

CHAPTER ONE

The Ghost Trucks

THE NORTH AMERICAN INTERNATIONAL AUTO SHOW IS A GLEAM-
ing, roaring affair. Once a year, in bleakest January, carmak-
ers head to the Motor City to show off their newest models,
technologies, and concept vehicles to industry figures, the
press, and the public. Each automaker takes its corner of the
dark, carpeted cavern of the Cobo Center and turns it into
something resembling a game-show set: spotlights, catwalks,
light displays, scantily clad women, and vehicle after vehicle,
many rotating on giant lazy Susans. I spent hours at a recent
show, ducking in and out of new models and talking with
auto executives and sales representatives. I sat in an SUV as
sleek as a shark, the buttons and gears and dials on its dash-
board replaced with a virtual cockpit straight out of science
fiction. A race car so aerodynamic and low that I had to
crouch to get in it. And driverless car after driverless car after
driverless car.

The displays ranged in degrees of technological spectacle
from the cool to the oh-my-word. One massive Ford truck,
for instance, offered a souped-up cruise control that would

brake for pedestrians and take over stop-and-go driving in heavy traffic. "No need to keep ramming the pedals yourself," a representative said as I gripped the oversize steering wheel.

Across the floor sat a Volkswagen concept car that looked like a hippie caravan for aliens. The minibus had no door latches, just sensors. There was a plug instead of a gas tank. On fully autonomous driving mode, the dash swallowed the steering wheel. A variety of lasers, sensors, radar, and cameras would then pilot the vehicle, and the driver and front-seat passenger could swing their seats around to the back, turning the bus into a snug, space-age living room. "The car of the future!" proclaimed Klaus Bischoff, the company's head of design.

It was a phrase that I heard again and again in Detroit. We are developing the cars of the future. The cars of the future are coming. The cars of the future are here. The auto market, I came to understand, is rapidly moving from automated to autonomous to driverless. Many cars already offer numerous features to assist with driving, including fancy cruise controls, backup warnings, lane-keeping technology, emergency braking, automatic parking, and so on. Add in enough of those options, along with some advanced sensors and thousands of lines of code, and you end up with an autonomous car that can pilot itself from origin to destination. Soon enough, cars, trucks, and taxis might be able to do so without a driver in the vehicle at all.

This technology has gone from zero to sixty—forgive me—in only a decade and a half. Back in 2002, the Defense Advanced Research Projects Agency, part of the Department of Defense and better known as DARPA, announced a "grand challenge," an invitation for teams to build autonomous vehicles and race one another on a 142-mile desert course from Barstow, California, to Primm, Nevada. The winner would take home a cool million. At the marquee event, none of the competitors made it through the course, or anywhere close. But the promise of prize money and the publicity around the event spurred a wave of investment and innovation. "That first competition created a community of innovators, engineers, students, programmers, off-road racers, backyard mechanics, inventors, and dreamers who came together to make history by trying to solve a tough technical problem," said Lt. Col. Scott Wadle of DARPA. "The fresh thinking they brought was the spark that has triggered major advances in the development of autonomous robotic ground vehicle technology in the years since."

As these systems become more reliable, safer, and cheaper, and as government regulations and the insurance markets come to accommodate them, mere mortals will get to experience them. At the auto show, I watched John Krafcik, the chief executive of Waymo, Google's self-driving spin-off, show off a fully autonomous Chrysler Pacifica minivan. "Our latest innovations have brought us closer to scaling our technology to potentially millions of people every day," he said, describing how the cost of the three-dimensional light-detection radar that helps guide the car has fallen 90 percent from its original $75,000 price tag in just a few years. BMW and Ford, among others, have announced that their autonomous offerings will go to market soon. "The amount of technology in cars has been growing exponentially," said Sandy Lobenstein, a Toyota executive, speaking in Detroit. "The vehicle as we know it is transforming into a means of getting around that futurists have dreamed about for a long time." Taxis without a taxi driver, trucks without a truck driver, cars you can tell where to go and then take a nap in: they are coming to our roads, and threatening millions and millions of jobs as they do.

In Michigan that dreary January, the excitement about self-driving technology was palpable. The domestic auto industry nearly died during the Great Recession, and despite its strong rebound in the years following, Americans were still not buying as many cars as they did back in the 1990s and early aughts—in part because Americans were driving less, and in part because the young folks who tend to be the most avid new car consumers were still so cash-strapped. Analysts have thus excitedly described this new technological frontier as a "gold rush" for the industry. Autonomous cars are expected to considerably expand the global market, with automakers anticipating selling 12 million vehicles a year by 2035 for some $80 billion in revenue.

Yet to many, the driverless car boom does not seem like a stimulus, or the arrival of a long-awaited future. It seems like an extinction-level threat. Consider the fate of workers on industrial sites already using driverless and autonomous vehicles, watching as robots start to replace their colleagues. "Trucks don't get pensions, they don't take vacations. It's purely dollars and cents," Ken Smith, the president of a local union chapter representing workers on the Canadian oil sands, said in an interview with the Canadian Broadcasting Corporation. This "wave of layoffs due to technology will be crippling."

Multiply that threat to hit not just truckers at extraction sites. Add in school bus drivers, municipal bus drivers, cross-country bus drivers, delivery drivers, limo drivers, cabdrivers, long-haul truckers, and port workers. Heck, even throw in any number of construction and retail workers who move goods around, as well as the kid who delivers your pizza and the part-timer who schleps your groceries to your doorstep. President Barack Obama's White House estimated that self-driving vehicles could wipe out between 2.2 and 3.1 million jobs. And self-driving cars are not the only technology on the horizon with the potential to dramatically reduce the need for human work. Today's Cassandras are warning that there is scarcely a job out there that is not at risk.

If you have recently heard of UBI, there is a good chance that it is because of these driverless cars and the intensifying concern about technological unemployment writ large. Elon Musk of Tesla, for instance, has argued that the large-scale automation of the transportation sector is imminent. "Twenty years is a short period of time to have something like 12 [to] 15 percent of the workforce be unemployed," he said at the World Government Summit in Dubai in 2017. "I don't think we're going to have a choice," he said of a UBI. "I think it's going to be necessary."

In Detroit, that risk felt ominously real. The question I wondered about as I wandered the halls of the Cobo Center and spoke with technology investors in Silicon Valley was not whether self-driving cars and other advanced technologies would start putting people out of work. It was when— and what would come next. The United States seems totally unprepared for a job-loss Armageddon. A UBI seemed to offer a way to ensure livelihoods, sustain the middle class, and guard against deprivation as extraordinary technological marvels transform our lives and change our world.

· · ·

It goes as far back as the spear, the net, the plow. Man invents machine to make life easier; machine reduces the need for man's toil. Man invents car; car puts buggy driver and farrier out of work. Man invents robot to help make car; robot puts man out of work. Man invents self-driving car; self-driving car puts truck driver out of work. The fancy economic term for this is "technological unemployment," and it is a constant and a given.

You did not need to go far from the auto show to see how the miracle of invention goes hand in hand with the tragedy of job destruction. You just need to take a look at its host city. In the early half of the twentieth century, it took a small army—or, frankly, a decently sized army—to satiate people's demand for cars. In the 1950s, the Big Three automakers—GM, Ford, and Chrysler—employed more than 400,000 people in Michigan alone. Today, it takes just a few battalions, with about 160,000 auto employees in the state, total. Of course, offshoring and globalization have had a major impact on auto employment in the United States. But advancing technology and the falling number of work hours it takes to produce a single vehicle have also been pivotal. With less work to go around and few other thriving industries in the area, Detroit's population has fallen by more than half since the 1950s, decimating its tax base and leaving many of its Art Deco and postmodern buildings boarded up and empty.

More broadly, the decline of manufacturing in the United States has hit the whole of the Rust Belt hard, along with parts of the South and New England. There were 19.6 million manufacturing jobs in the country in 1979. There were roughly 12.5 million manufacturing jobs as of 2017, even though the population was larger by nearly 100 million people. As a result, no region of the United States fared worse economically in the postwar period than the manufacturing mecca of the Midwest, with its share of overall employment dropping from about 45 percent in the 1950s to 27 percent by 2000.

Even given such painful dislocations, economists see the job losses created by technological change as being a necessary part of a virtuous process. Some workers struggle. Some places fail. But the economy as a whole thrives. The jobs eliminated by machines tend to be lower-paying, more dangerous, and lower-value. The jobs created by machines tend to be higher-paying, less dangerous, and higher-value. The economy gets rid of bad jobs while creating better new ones. Workers do adjust, if not always easily.

In part, they adjust by moving. Millions of workers have left Detroit and the Rust Belt, for instance, heading to the sunny service economy of the Southwest or to the oil economy of the Gulf of Mexico. They also adjust by switching industries. On my way to Detroit, in a moment of Tom Friedman–esque folly, I asked the Lyft driver taking me to the Baltimore airport what he thought of the company's plans to shift to driverless cars and the potential that he would soon be out of a job. "It's worrisome," he conceded. "But I'm thinking of trying to get some education to become someone to service them. You're not going to just be able to take those cars into the shop, with the regular guys who are used to fixing the old models. You're going to need a technician who knows about software."

The point is that economies grow and workers survive regardless of the pain and churn of technological dislocations. Despite the truly astonishing advances of the twentieth century, the share of Americans working rose. The labor market accommodated many of the men squeezed out of manufacturing, as well the influx of tens of millions of women and millions and millions of immigrants into the workforce. When manufacturing went from more than a quarter of American employment to just 10 percent, mass unemployment did not result. Nor did it when agriculture went from employing 40 percent of the workforce to employing just 2 percent.

The idea that machines are about to eliminate the need for human work has been around for a long time, and it has been proven wrong again and again—enough times to earn the nickname the "Luddite fallacy" or "lump-of-labor fallacy." In the early nineteenth century, Nottingham textile workers destroyed their looms to demand better work and better wages. (No need.) During the Great Depression, John Maynard Keynes surmised that technological advances would put an end to long hours spent in the office, in the field, or at the plant by 2030. (Alas, no.) In 1964, a group of public-intellectual activists, among them three Nobel laureates, warned the White House that "the combination of the computer and the automated self-regulating machine" would foster "a separate nation of the poor, the unskilled, the jobless." (Nope.) Three swings, three misses. As the economist Alex Tabarrok, an author of the popular blog *Marginal Revolution,* puts it, "If the Luddite fallacy were true we would all be out of work because productivity has been increasing for two centuries."

Still, over and over again I heard the worry that this time it *really* is different. In his farewell address, President Obama augured, "The next wave of economic dislocations won't come from overseas. It will come from the relentless pace of automation that makes a lot of good, middle-class jobs obsolete." Magazine covers, books, and cable news segments warn that the robots are coming not just for the truck drivers, but Wall Street traders, advertising executives, college professors, and warehouse workers.

In some tellings, the problem is that technology is not creating jobs in the way it once did and is destroying jobs far faster. This is the same old story about technological unemployment, on steroids: Advancing tech might lead to improvements in living standards and cheaper goods and services. But what is so great about having a self-driving car if you have no job, your neighbor has no job, and your town is slashing the school budget for the third time in four years?

What if there is no need for humans, because the robots have gotten so good?

Detroit again offers a pretty good encapsulation of the argument. Cars are undergoing a profound technological shift, transforming from mechanical gadgets to superpowered computers with the potential to revolutionize every facet of transit. Billions of dollars are being spent to rush driverless vehicles into the hands of consumers and businesses. Yet the total employment gains from this revolutionary technology amount to perhaps a few tens of thousands of jobs. Robots are designing and building these new self-driving cars, not just driving them. That same dynamic is writ large around the country. Brick-and-mortar retailing giant Walmart has 1.5 million employees in the United States, while Web retailing giant Amazon had a third as many as of the third quarter of 2017. As famously noted by the futurist Jaron Lanier, at its peak, Kodak employed about 140,000 people; when Facebook acquired it, Instagram employed just 13.

The scarier prospect is that more and more jobs are falling to the tide of tech-driven obsolescence. Studies have found that almost half of American jobs are vulnerable to automation, and the rest of the world might want to start worrying too. Countries such as Turkey, South Korea, China, and Vietnam have seen bang-up rates of growth in no small part due to industrialization—factories requiring millions of hands to feed machines and sew garments and produce electronics. But the plummeting cost and lightspeed improvement of robotics now threaten to halt and even shut down that source of jobs. "Premature deindustrialization" might turn lower-income countries into service economies long before they have a middle class to buy those services, warns the Harvard economist Dani Rodrik. A common path to rapid economic growth, the one that aided South Korea, among other countries, might simply disappear. The tidal shift could "be devastating, if countries can no longer follow the East Asian growth model to get out of poverty," Mike Kubzansky of the Omidyar Network, a nonprofit foundation funded by the eBay billionaire, told me. Mass unemployment would likely hit high-income countries first. But it could hit developing nations hardest.

There is a more frightening story to tell about techno-logical unemployment in the twenty-first century, though— one that implies that today's changes are not just a juiced-up version of what has happened in the past, but a profoundly different kind of disruption. That different kind of disruption relies on smart computing systems to improve themselves, thus truly rendering much human work obsolete.

• • •

Facebook employs a team of artificial-intelligence experts who build software to recognize and tag faces in photographs, answer customer-service complaints, analyze user data, iden-tify abusive or threatening comments, and so on. One of the tasks that this team, called Facebook AI Research, or FAIR, has taken on is programming automated chatbots to perform negotiations, like making a restaurant reservation.

Getting a spot at a local Italian joint involves relatively few and mostly fixed variables. A good outcome might be a table for a party of four at 8 p.m. on Tuesday, not an agree-ment to stop the enrichment of uranium in exchange for an easing of financial sanctions or a new contract with a different pay schedule, better retirement benefits, and fast-vesting shares. In those latter examples, as in much of life, negotiation is as much art as science. It requires evaluating how valuable certain things are, often when it is not obvious. It requires identifying and resolving conflicts and trying to sort out information asymmetries. It goes a lot better with a theory of mind, meaning an understanding that the guy on the other side of the table has different motivations and resources than you do. It is something at which computers are terrible and humans excel.

A Facebook chatbot started off doing simple, formulaic negotiations, asking for two of a given item and agreeing to settle for one, for instance. Then it began analyzing reams of data and trying to refine and improve its own ability to come to a good resolution—teaching itself, in other words. It started to fake interest in a low-value item, conceding it later in a negotiation. "This behavior was not programmed by the researchers but was discovered by the bot as a method for trying to achieve its goals," the Facebook researchers noted. The AI also started writing its own responses to bids, moving past the formulaic ones its engineers had given it.

The AI got so good so fast that it began passing a kind of Turing test. "Most people did not realize they were talking to a bot rather than another person—showing that the bots had learned to hold fluent conversations in English," the Facebook researchers wrote in a blog post. The performance of the best bot negotiation agent matched the performance of a human negotiator. "It achieved better deals about as often as worse deals, demonstrating that FAIR's bots not only can speak English but also think intelligently about what to say."

Perhaps the most striking outcome of the experiment: The bots, coded to communicate in English, eventually developed their *own* language to perform negotiations among themselves:

> BOB: i can i i everything else . . . .
>
> ALICE: balls have zero to me to me to me to me to me to me to me to me to
>
> BOB: you i everything else . . . .

This looks silly to human eyes and sounds silly to human ears, granted. But I was struck by what a beautiful and remarkable technological feat it was, and how human, creative, adaptive those bots could be. The bots determined that it was more efficient and effective to speak in their own shorthand, so they did. They expanded their own capacities, learning and teaching themselves to do not just simple negotiations but complex, almost *human* negotiations. "Agents will drift off understandable language and invent codewords for themselves," one engineer told *Fast Company*. "Like if I say 'the' five times, you interpret that to mean I want five copies of this item. This isn't so different from the way communities of humans create shorthands." (After the bots developed their own language and stopped speaking in English, I would note, Facebook shut them down.)

The Facebook negotiation bots illustrate why so many futurists, technologists, and economists are so concerned about technology's new job-destroying capacity. Up until now, humans were the ones doing the technological innovation, building better machines and making marginal improvements to computing systems. But artificial intelligence, neural networks, and machine learning have allowed such technologies to become self-improving. It is not just driverless cars that have radically progressed in the past few years, due to these advances. Google Translate has gotten dramatically better at interpreting languages. Virtual assistants such as Apple's Siri and Amazon's Alexa have seen the same kind of improvement. Computer systems have gotten better than doctors at scanning for cancer, better than traders at moving money between investments, better than interns at doing routine legal work.

Just about anything that can be broken into discrete tasks—from writing a contract to pulling a cherry off a vine to driving an Uber to investing retirement money—is liable to be taken out of human hands and put into robotic ones, with robotic ones improving at a flywheel-rapid rate. "Could another person learn to do your job by studying a detailed record of everything you've done in the past?" Martin Ford, a software developer, writes in *Rise of the Robots*. "Or could someone become proficient by repeating the tasks you've already completed, in the way that a student might take practice tests to prepare for an exam? If so, then there's a good chance that an algorithm may someday be able to learn to do much, or all, of your job." One recent survey asked machine-learning experts to predict when AI would be better than humans at certain tasks. They anticipated that the bots would beat the mortals at translating languages by 2024, writing high-school essays by 2026, driving a truck by 2027, working in retail by 2031, writing a bestselling book by 2049—*phew*—and performing surgery by 2053. "Researchers believe there is a 50 percent chance of AI outperforming humans in all tasks in 45 years and of automating all human jobs in 120 years," the survey's authors noted.

This prospect is an amazing and a frightening one were it to come to pass. The change to our economy and our lives would be revolutionary. It would all start with ingenuity, innovation, and investment—with new businesses offering fresh software and hardware, and enterprises buying it and making their pricey, flighty, and hard-to-train human workers redundant. Jobs that consisted of simple, repeated tasks would be the first to go. But artificial intelligence is, well, intelligent. In time, commercial companies would begin selling technologies that communicated, negotiated, made decisions, and executed complicated tasks just like people— better than people. These technologies would be forever improving and getting cheaper too. Businesses looking to advertise would find that the banners and television spots tested and produced by AI got better results. Banks would start replacing loan officers with algorithms. Contracts, insurance, tax preparation, anything having to do with paperwork, all those jobs would disappear. "i can i i everything else," indeed, Bob.

If the AI systems got good enough and regulatory reforms allowed it, education and health care—two giant and growing employment sectors commonly considered resistant to productivity improvements and to technological unemployment—might find themselves transformed. Cash-strapped state and local governments might allow students to go to school at home, learning and taking tests on smart, interactive AI systems approved by school boards. Major hospitals have already started to use IBM's Watson technology to help doctors make diagnoses—soon, they might fire doctors to make way for telemedicine, photo-driven diagnostics, and automated care. Little self-commanding robots might start irrigating sinuses and excising moles. Insurers might start giving incentives for patients to speak with AI systems rather than a blood-and-bones doctor. Patients might start to see human doctors as error-prone butchers. Put in economists' terms, advances in AI and automation might finally solve Baumol's cost disease.

Of course, some jobs could never be outsourced to a computer or a machine. Preschools would still need caretakers to help with toddlers. Reiki healing, serving a community as an elected representative, acting as the executive of a corporation, performing archival research, writing poetry, teaching weight lifting, making art, performing talk therapy—it seems impossible for robots to take those jobs over. But imagine a world with vastly fewer shop clerks, delivery drivers, and white-collar bureaucrats. Imagine a world where every recession came with a jobless recovery, with businesses getting leaner and lighter. Imagine a world where nearly all degrees became useless, the wage premium that today comes with a fancy diploma eroded. Imagine millions and millions of jobs, forever gone.

Sure, some people would survive and even thrive in this world. A business that replaces a worker with a robot is often a business becoming more competitive and profitable. The stock market might boom, with shareholders, entrepreneurs, the holders of patents, and so on seeing their earnings and wealth soar. Wealth and income might become more and more concentrated in the hands of fewer and fewer. Inequality, already at obscene levels, might become far worse.

But what of labor, not capital? What of the people left out of the winner-take-all sweepstakes, people struggling with worthless degrees and a hypercompetitive job market? Their contributions to the economy would be less valuable—in many cases, unnecessary—and thus they would earn less. Their wages would stagnate. Periods of joblessness would last longer. Mobility would remain low. To be sure, higher productivity and whiz-bang new technologies would vastly improve the lives of average working folks in many ways. Entertainment might become dazzling and immersive beyond our imagining, with brilliant video games, lifelike AI simulators, and fantastic films and television delivered for cheap or free. Driverless cars would reduce the number of road accidents and save lives, all while making travel less expensive. AI advances in medicine might lead to rapid improvements in health—the end of cancer, the death of communicable diseases.

But America's redistributive policies are not designed to support this kind of world. Unemployment benefits are temporary and often used to encourage workers to move into growing industries. Payments last for half a year, not half a lifetime. The safety net encourages work, as do income supports for the lower-middle class. The Earned Income Tax Credit only goes to people with earned income, meaning people with jobs. The welfare and food stamp programs have work requirements. Our existing set of policies helps people through temporary spells of joblessness and makes work pay. It could not and would not buoy four-fifths of adults through permanent unemployment.

The system would falter and fail if confronted with vast inequality and tidal waves of joblessness. A basic income is the obvious policy to keep people afloat. "Machines, the argument goes, can take the jobs, but should not take the incomes: the job uncertainty that engulfs large swaths of society should be matched by a welfare policy that protects the masses, not only the poor," said the World Bank senior economist Ugo Gentilini, speaking at the World Economic Forum. "Hence, [basic-income grants] emerge as a straightforward option for the digital era."

· · ·

Of late, the Bay Area has become the center of the UBI universe. Musk, Gates, and other tech titans have expressed interest in the policy christened the "social vaccine of the twenty-first century," "a twenty-first-century economic right," and "VC for the people."

Increasingly, that interest is turning into action. There are now "basic income create-a-thons," for programmers to get together, talk UBI, and hack poverty. Cryptocurrency enthusiasts are looking into a Bitcoin-backed basic-income program. A number of young millionaire tech founders are funding a basic-income pilot among the world's poorest in Kenya. The start-up accelerator Y Combinator is sending no-strings-attached cash to families in a few states as part of a research project. And Chris Hughes, a founder of Facebook, has plowed $10 million into an initiative to explore UBI and other related policies, something he is calling the Economic Security Project. "The community is evolving as we speak from a small group of people who say, *This is it,* to a large group of people who say, *Hey, there may be something here,*" he told me.

There might be some irony, granted, in Silicon Valley boosting a solution to a problem it believes that it is creating—in disrupting the labor underpinnings of the whole economy, and then promoting a disruptive welfare solution. Those job-smothering, life-awesoming technologies come in no small part from garages in Menlo Park and venture-capital offices overlooking the Golden Gate and group houses in Oakland. "Here in Silicon Valley, it feels like we can see the future," Misha Chellam, the founder of the start-up training school Tradecraft and a UBI advocate, told me. But it can feel disillusioning when that omniscience yields uncomfortable truths, he said. "When people join start-ups or work in tech, there's an aspirational nature to it. But very few CEOs are happy with the idea that their work is going to cause a lot of stress and harm."

Yet the boosterism also does seem to be ignited by a real concern that we are in the midst of a profound economic and technological revolution. Sam Altman, the president of Y Combinator, recently spoke at a poverty summit cohosted by Stanford, the White House, and the Chan Zuckerberg Initiative, the Facebook billionaire's charitable institution. "There have been these moments where we have had these major technology revolutions—the Agricultural Revolution, the Industrial Revolution, for example—that have really changed the world in a big way," he said. "I think we're in the middle or at least on the cusp of another one."

As it turns out, the idea of a UBI has tended to surface during such epochal economic moments. It first arrived, it seems, at the very birth of capitalism, as medieval feudalism was giving way to Renaissance mercantilism during the reign of Henry VIII. For centuries, England's peasants had toiled as subsistence farmers on common lands held by local lords or by the Catholic Church. (This was called the open-field system.) In the late 1400s, more and more land had become "enclosed," with lords barring serfs from grazing animals, planting crops, or building small homesteads, instead hiring them to pasture their sheep and process their wool. Fields that had once supported families instead supported private flocks. Subsistence farmers became wage workers, and oftentimes became beggars or vagrants.

"Who will maintain husbandry which is the nurse of every county as long as sheep bring so great gain?" complained one sixteenth-century Briton cited in the historical tome *Tudor Economic Problems.* "Who will be at the cost to keep a dozen in his house to milk kine, make cheese, carry it to the market, when one poor soul may by keeping sheep get him a greater profit? Who will not be content for to pull down houses of husbandry so that he may stuff his bags full of money?"

The proliferation of enclosure meant the privatization of public goods, the immiseration of the peasantry, the enrichment of the gentry, and a growing number of vagrants. It meant the upheaval of a centuries-old economic system. It raised the question of what England's lords and Crown owed its citizens. And in 1516, Saint Thomas More felt called to answer that question. In *Utopia,* his work of philosophical fiction, More converses with an imaginary traveler named Raphael Hythloday (in Greek, "nonsense talker"). Hythloday discusses the problems of crime and poverty in England, citing the scourge of sheep as a root cause. These meek animals have come to "devour" men, he says, referring to the plight of peasants affected by enclosure. Hythloday notes that England hangs its thieves, and suggests a better option:

> This way of punishing thieves was neither just in itself nor good for the public; for, as the severity was too great, so the remedy was not effectual; simple theft not being so great a crime that it ought to cost a man his life; no punishment, how severe soever, being able to restrain those from robbing who can find out no other way of livelihood. . . . There are dreadful punishments enacted against thieves, but it were much better to make such good provisions by which every man might be put in a method how to live, and so be preserved from the fatal necessity of stealing and of dying for it.

This "method how to live" is a guaranteed minimum income, one of the first cases made for a UBI-type policy.

The notion resurfaced again during the Industrial Revolution, often as part of a philosophical conversation about rentiers, poverty, rights, and redistribution or as a salve for technology-driven unemployment. In 1797, for instance, Thomas Paine argued that each citizen should get recompense for the "loss of his or her natural inheritance, by the introduction of the system of landed property" at the age of twenty-one, as well as a pension from the age of fifty until death. The British Speenhamland system made certain payments to poor workers unconditional. In the middle of the nineteenth century, the French radical Charles Fourier—a "utopian socialist," as Karl Marx described him—argued that "civilization" owed everyone a minimal existence, meaning three square meals a day and a sixth-class hotel room, as noted in the Basic Income Earth Network's history of the idea. Later, the famed political economist John Stuart Mill made a case for a UBI as well.

During the radical 1960s—the dawn of our new machine age, and the transformative era when women and people of color began to demand entry into and full participation in an economy dominated by and built to enrich white men— the idea emerged again, having a "short-lived effervescence." The Nobel laureate Milton Friedman suggested the adoption of a "negative income tax," using the code to boost all families' earnings up to a minimum level. Martin Luther King Jr. called for a basic income and other radical, universal policies to aid in the causes of racial and economic justice. Both the Republican Richard Nixon and the Democrat Daniel Patrick Moynihan offered support for the idea. But none of these efforts prevailed, in part because pilot studies erroneously indicated that certain forms of support might increase divorce rates. The radical idea was forgotten soon after.

Today, the UBI finds itself in an extraordinary heyday, fueled by tech-bubble money and driven by both the fear of joblessness and hope for a better future. "We're talking about divorcing your basic needs from the need to work," Albert Wenger, a UBI advocate and venture capitalist, has argued. "For a couple hundred years, we've constructed our entire world around the need to work. Now we're talking about more than just a tweak to the economy—it's as foundational a departure as when we went from an agrarian society to an industrial one."

• • •

Still, despite the creation of AI and the concern about the future of human labor, the arguments for implementing a UBI to ward off technological unemployment felt hyperbolic—or at least premature—to me.

If technology were rapidly improving and putting workers out of their jobs, there would be an easy way to see it in our national statistics. It would be evident in something called "total factor productivity," sometimes referred to as the "Solow residual." We would expect a factory to produce more widgets if its owner bought a new widget-pressing machine. We would expect a factory to produce more widgets if it hired more workers, and had them toil for more hours. TFP growth occurs when factory workers figure out how to get more widgets out of their widget presses without buying new machinery or increasing their hours. TFP accounts for ingenuity and human capital. Economists feel that it is our best measure of dynamism in our economy.

If driverless cars were replacing truck drivers and AI systems were replacing translators and robots were replacing doctors, we would expect TFP to be soaring—even if employment was falling and the economy was slowing down as a result. The country would still be doing a lot more with a lot less. But TFP growth has slowed down since the mid-2000s. This is a profound yet scarcely discussed problem. If the average annual rate of productivity growth clocked between 1948 and 1973 had carried forward, the average family would be earning $30,000 more a year. Had inequality stayed at its 1973 level, on the other hand, the average family would be earning just $9,000 more.

So why is there such a profound disconnect between our lived reality, of an underpowered jobs market and stupefying technological marvels and deep fear over the robot apocalypse, and the national statistics, which suggest that the economy is getting less and less innovative?

Some argue that the statistics are not capturing the effect of innovation on the economy and are mismeasuring the rapid pace of technological change. Let's say that a given technological gizmo has gotten five times as good in the past eighteen months, but the government believes it has only gotten twice as good. If such mismeasurements were pervasive, the national statistics might be profoundly flawed. A related argument is that today's computing advances have changed the economy in ways that have reduced the size of the dollars-and-cents economy, and have therefore made it harder to measure their value. Take the music industry. Recorded music sales peaked in the late 1990s, back when you still might get a mix tape from a crush. They have collapsed since then. It is not that everybody stopped listening to music—quite the opposite. It is that technological advances washed away the music industry's longtime cash base.

A yet more dour analysis holds that the technological progress being made simply is not as impressive as people make it out to be. Fruit-picking robots, cancer-screening apps, drones, digital cameras, and driverless cars cannot compete with the transformative power of threshing machines, commercial airliners, antibiotics, refrigerators, and the birth control pill in terms of economic importance. "You can look around you in New York City and the subways are 100-plus years old. You can look around you on an airplane, and it's little different from 40 years ago—maybe it's a bit slower because the airport security is low-tech and not working terribly well," Peter Thiel, a billionaire tech investor and adviser to President Trump, recently mused to Vox. "The screens are everywhere, though. Maybe they're distracting us from our surroundings." (He more famously said, "We wanted flying cars, instead we got 140 characters.")

It could also be that our sluggish rate of economic growth has spurred our sluggish rate of innovation. The economist J. W. Mason of the Roosevelt Institute, a left-of-center think tank, argues that depressed demand for goods and services and crummy wages across the economy have reduced the impetus for businesses to get leaner, more productive, and more creative. Higher wages and a faster-growing economy would boost productivity, he argues, by forcing companies to shell out money on labor-saving technologies.

Or perhaps it is that our latter-day technological advances have not had time to show up in the productivity statistics yet. Gutenberg's printing press is inarguably one of the greatest technologies ever dreamed up by man, revolutionizing the way that information spreads and that records are kept. But it did little to speed up growth or improve productivity in the fifteenth and sixteenth centuries, economists have found. Or take electrification. In the 1890s and early 1900s, American businesses and families started hooking into the power grid, brightening buildings at night and paving the way for an astonishing array of consumer and industrial goods, from door buzzers to space shuttles. Yet, as the economist Chad Syverson has noted, for roughly a quarter century following its introduction, productivity growth was relatively slow. The same is true for the first information technology era, when computers started to become ubiquitous in businesses and homes. As the economist Robert Solow—hence the Solow residual—quipped in 1987, "You can see the computer age everywhere but in the productivity statistics." In most cases, productivity did speed up once innovators invented complementary technologies and businesses had a long while to adjust—suggesting that the innovation gains and job losses of our new machine age might be just around the corner. If so, mass unemployment might be a result—and a UBI might be a necessary salve.

But the argument emanating from Silicon Valley feels speculative and distant at the moment. Those driverless cars are miraculous, and stepping into one does feel like stepping into the future. Those AI systems are amazing, and watching them work does feel like slipping into a sci-fi novel. Yet people remain firmly behind the wheel of those driverless cars. And those AI systems remain far removed from most people's jobs and lives. Opening a discussion about a UBI as a solution to a world with far less demand for human labor feels wise, but insisting the discussion needs to happen now and on those terms seems foolish and myopic.

There are more concrete problems to address, after all.

CHAPTER TWO

Crummy Jobs

THE FAMILY OF SIX AWOKE IN A CRAMPED STUDIO APARTMENT IN A neighborhood not far from downtown Houston, and spent a few minutes together before breaking apart for the day. The kids went to school. The mother, Josefa, headed in for a shift at Burger King. The father, Luis, nursed an injury that has cost him precious hours on the job. The kids got out from school. The mother walked to her second job at a Mexican restaurant. One of the older daughters went to clock in at Raising Cane's, a chicken shack on a bustling commercial street. Her sister decided to take a rare day off to catch up on schoolwork. The girl working got off after 9 p.m., her mother an hour later. Someone in the household was working nearly every waking hour of the day. It was always like that.

A few years ago, I embedded with the Ortiz family, as they seemed to represent a few trends in fast-food work and the low-wage economy more generally. The first is the surprising prevalence of fast-food jobs among older workers. Back in the 1950s and 1960s, burger-flipping gigs really were for teens in the summertime. Now more are being held by middle-aged adults struggling to avoid eviction and to put food on the table, thanks to three decades of wage stagnation. As of 2013, just one in three fast-food workers was a teenager, and 40 percent were older than twenty-five. A quarter were raising children, and nearly a third had at least some college education. In the Ortiz family, everyone old enough to work was working, with the family swinging as many as eight jobs at a time.

The second trend is the way that technology has made jobs more miserable and menial, not less. In many ways, a fast-food kitchen has become a space-age marvel, filled with research-intensive equipment that churns out perfectly identical and compulsively edible burgers, chicken fingers, and fries, at warp speed and minimal cost. That has made fast-food workers' jobs duller and more repetitive, the Ortizes told me. Burger flipping is button pushing, with the pressure of beeping alarms and timer clocks and digital surveillance. Worse, algorithmic "just-in-time" scheduling systems let employers set worker hours according to demand, making schedules and hours unpredictable—a particular problem for parents with young children and households too poor to handle much income volatility. Often, workers do not receive their schedules until shortly before they are due to work. Sometimes, they are even asked to "clopen," both closing down and opening up shop. When I met her, Josefa had been working for nearly three weeks straight.

Third, the Ortizes exemplified the grinding poverty that so many fast-food workers—and millions of others in the modern economy—are facing. The vast majority of employees at places like Sonic and Jack in the Box make less than $12 an hour, hardly enough to keep a family afloat, even with two workers on full-time schedules. Moreover, nearly all fast-food workers lack employer-sponsored health and retirement benefits, and there is scant opportunity to move up in the profession. The Ortizes were struggling to cobble together money from $10-an-hour and $7.75-an-hour and $7.25-an-hour gigs that often started or finished in the dark. The family was living in an apartment that cost $550 a month and continually scrambling to make rent, pay for utilities, keep gas in the car, and buy food. Luis's spell of illness had put them at the brink of homelessness.

I had met the Ortizes through their activism with Fight for $15, a labor-backed movement pushing for raises and union representation for the country's 3.8 million fast-food workers and others. It had kicked off just after Thanksgiving in 2012, when workers for Taco Bell, Burger King, Wendy's, and other establishments walked off the job, with some gathering on New York's Madison Avenue to chant "We demand fair pay!" in front of a McDonald's. The movement quickly became national and then international, spreading to some three hundred cities on six continents. In response, many employers voluntarily boosted their wages, and a dozen states eventually pushed up their minimum wages as well.

Still, the problem of low pay persists. Most families in poverty are dealing with joblessness, but as of 2016, 9.5 million people who spent at least twenty-seven weeks a year in the labor force remained below the poverty line, destitute or perilously close, with no clear pathway to the middle class. The attending problems are financial, physical, and emotional. Luis and Josefa talked about the pressure and the stress of their uncertain schedules, and the strain of knowing their children were growing up deprived. At the end of her shift at Raising Cane's, climbing into Luis's car, one of the Ortiz daughters told me that she often did not eat dinner. "The smell of the chicken fills me up," she said.

The working poor, the precariat, the left behind: this is

modern-day America. We no longer have a jobs crisis, with the economy recovering to something like full employment a decade after the start of the Great Recession. But we do have a good-jobs crisis, a more permanent, festering problem that started more than a generation ago. Work simply is not paying like it used to, leaving more and more families struggling to get by, relying on the government to lift them out of and away from poverty, feeling like the American Dream is unachievable—even before the robots come for all of our jobs.

Look at inequality. Data compiled by the famed economists Emmanuel Saez and Thomas Piketty shows that the bottom half of earners went from making 20 percent of overall income in 1979 to just 13 percent in 2014. The top 1 percent, on the other hand, have gone from making 11 percent to 20 percent. The pie has gotten vastly bigger, and the richest families have reaped bigger and bigger pieces of it. You can also see how serious the problem is by tracking median household income, which has stagnated for the past twenty or thirty years—even though the economy has grown considerably. Yet another way to see it: The middle class is shrinking and its share of aggregate income has plunged. At the same time, the ranks of the poor have grown, and they have seen essentially no income gains at all. Something is tipping the balance in favor of capital and corporations, and away from workers and people.

I spent years reporting on the persistent problems of families in the lower three-quarters of the income distribution, and years debating the ways that policymakers might help them. Democrats want to make health care universal, boost the minimum wage, and make college free, for instance. Republicans want to slash corporate taxes to encourage investment and to reduce red tape to help companies grow. But the SEIU's Andy Stern and others, particularly on the far left, have started arguing that more radical solutions are necessary. Democrats have started talking about bigger wage subsidies, even government-sponsored jobs plans. Among those more athletic, more out-of-the-box proposals is a UBI. This grant to all Americans could provide the strong counterballast the economy needs, and it offers a radical way to recenter the worker in the economy. It could be an urgent policy not just for a robot-filled future, but for right now.

Families like the Ortizes need more, better, immediately, I thought, and UBI might be one way to make sure that they got it.

. . .

Over the past four decades or so, a number of interconnected trends have conspired to push the earnings of workers down and the earnings of the wealthy, the investor class, and corporations up.

There is globalization, washing away millions of good jobs from places like Pittsburgh, Detroit, Gary, Toledo, and South Bend. Most economists see trade as a win-win, to be sure. Rich, high-wage countries like the United States get cheaper imports, and more labor and capital to use on higher-value investments. Poor, low-wage countries like Vietnam get jobs, capital, and a productivity bump. But when it comes to recent history, trade might better be described as a win-win-lose. The economists David Autor, David Dorn, and Gordon Hanson describe what happened to the Rust Belt as the "China Shock." Job losses were deep and local labor markets were "remarkably slow" to adjust. "At the national level, employment has fallen in U.S. industries more exposed to import competition, as expected, but offsetting employment gains in other industries have yet to materialize," they write. Some good jobs are simply gone, and they are not coming back.

The economic, psychological, and political toll of this China Shock is only now being fully understood. It has contributed to phenomena as diverse as political polarization and falling marriage rates. More and more older white people without degrees are dying early "deaths of despair." Mortality rates are actually increasing despite economic growth and advances in health care, the Princeton economists Anne Case and Angus Deaton have found. Their findings illustrate "the collapse of the white, high-school-educated working class after its heyday in the early 1970s, and the pathologies that accompany that decline."

The loss of manufacturing jobs has contributed to the broad decay in the unionization rate among private-sector workers—another major factor leading to stagnant wages and crummier jobs. (Those factories in Detroit and Pittsburgh tended to be heavily unionized.) In the 1950s, one in three workers belonged to a union that could help them bargain for higher wages, better benefits, more family and sick leave, improved working conditions, and so on. Now, just one in twenty has a union card. Had private-sector union density been in 2013 what it was in 1979, workers would have earned an average of $2,704 more per year, according to one estimate.

That is not just because of the direct effects that unions have on the wages of their members. It is also thanks to the indirect effects that unionization has on the whole workforce. If Business A is offering $15 an hour with benefits for a union gig, Business B needs to match that offering in order to attract the same caliber of worker, whether it is offering a union position or not. The decline of unionization, then, has translated into over $100 billion a year in lost wages for men with private-sector, nonunion jobs, and explains about a third of the growth in wage inequality among them. It "is likely the largest single factor underlying wage stagnation and wage inequality" for male middle-wage earners, the left-of-center think tank the Economic Policy Institute has found. Women are not exempt from these trends, of course. They have collectively lost $24 billion a year in wages, and the evaporation of union gigs accounts for a fifth of the growth in wage inequality for them.

Another trend that does primarily impact women is the decline in the value of the minimum wage, given that the typical minimum-wage worker is female. Accounting for inflation, the federal minimum wage of $7.25 an hour as of 2017 is about 8 percent below where it was in 1967. If you add in the skyrocketing cost of health care, child care, and housing, it is far too low to keep workers' families out of poverty, as the struggles of the Ortiz family demonstrate. Erosion in the real value of the minimum wage accounts for about two-thirds of the growth of the wage gap between female workers in the fiftieth and tenth earnings percentiles, meaning workers making between $750 and $1,800 a week nowadays. For all workers, it explains about half of the growth of the gap.

In the past few years, many states and cities have stepped in to lift their local minimum wages, with Fight for $15 helping to ignite a broader, bipartisan push to give workers a raise. Protests, rallies, long-form stories, segments on the nightly news, and Capitol Hill hearings have called attention to this long-standing problem that the recovery has failed to fix, with cities and states acting in turn. "The hours aren't a problem. It's the pay," Sepia Coleman, an activist with the movement and a health worker in Tennessee, told me. She struggles to care for her ailing mother. "I can't work 120 hours a week! If the pay isn't there, the hours aren't going to matter." Four million workers got a raise in 2017 due to minimum-wage increases, and Seattle, Los Angeles, San Francisco, and Washington, D.C., have bumped their floors all the way up to $15. Even so, roughly 3 million workers are still earning the federal minimum, and the wage floor remains perilously low in many big cities where costs are high.

One less heralded and less understood reason workers are not earning as much is the growing dominance of big businesses—companies with monopoly or monopsony power, and the corresponding rise of markets with fewer and fewer competitors. In the early half of the twentieth century, the government viewed monopolies as a potent threat to democracy, and forced the Ma Bells and the Standard Oils of the world to break apart. As Franklin D. Roosevelt put it in an address to Congress in 1938, "The liberty of a democracy is not safe if the people tolerate the growth of private power to a point where it becomes stronger than their democratic state itself. That, in its essence, is fascism." But right around the time that all those jobs were offshored to China, the government started to change its mind on the monopoly threat. In his seminal 1978 book *The Antitrust Paradox,* Robert Bork, the failed Reagan nominee for the Supreme Court, argued that corporate mergers benefited consumers by providing lower prices and promoting greater business efficiency. The government should stop focusing on ensuring competition for competition's sake, he thought, and instead focus on consumer welfare.

Washington concurred, and in time it became easier both for companies to buy up their supply chains and for them to buy up their competitors. As a result of those legal changes and the rise of cash-rich and profit-obsessed Wall Street, any number of major industries—hospitals, agriculture, telecoms, trucking, insurance, airlines, banking, energy—saw significant consolidation. Even pizza delivery has become dominated by a handful of major players, with Pizza Hut, Domino's, Little Caesars, and Papa John's accounting for more than one-third of the national pie.

It might not be obvious, but economists think this has contributed to income inequality and wage stagnation. With fewer companies to work for, workers have fewer potential employers to bid them up—especially given the prevalence of non-compete agreements even in industries as low-wage and menial as fast food. Plus, consolidated industries tend to be dominated by older companies that gobble up their younger and more dynamic competitors. That reduces "job churn," since those old companies expand more slowly and retain their workers for longer periods than newer companies do. Churn—with workers negotiating raises as they jump from firm to firm—is a crucial source of wage growth that has been eroded by the growth of big business.

Increasing concentration has also exacerbated what you might think of as "profit inequality." Over the past forty years, a small number of firms have gotten much richer, their earnings growing far faster than those at less profitable firms. That means people at a few firms are making lots of money, while most people at most companies are not. While top executives at public companies have become part of a superstar economy, with their earnings trajectory diverging wildly from just about everybody else's, income inequality in fact stems mostly from differences among the pay scales at different companies, not the pay scales within companies. The ratio of pay between managers and janitors within a given firm has not really changed much over time.

And yet, it is a lot less likely for companies to employ their janitors anymore. The same years that have seen the rise of profit inequality have also seen a sea change in the relationship between employer and worker, with the effect of depressing wages and reducing benefits for average Joes. A few decades ago, companies began outsourcing jobs that were not related to their "core competencies," things like payroll management, food services, landscaping, travel booking, legal work, and human resources. In some cases, firms stopped employing many workers at all, instead moving to franchise models that lowered corporate liability, increased profits, and pleased Wall Street. This means lots of people supportive of, but not central to, corporate missions have seen their stable, benefit-laden jobs disappear. Gone are the days of pensions, sick leave, and paid vacation for all. Here are the days of hourly compensation with no job security, working for, but not at, a big firm.

All of this has fed the rise of "contingent work," with workers on call, on contract, freelancing, or temping. (Some economists also include part-time employees in this category.) The estimates on such alternative arrangements vary widely, in no small part because the government did not track contingent employment between 2005 and 2017, when it conducted a one-off survey. Still, several studies have concurred that contingent work has grown from not much of anything to a powerful something over the past thirty or forty years—and especially over the past decade. The proportion of workers in "alternative work arrangements" climbed from 10 to 16 percent between 2005 and 2015, according to one estimate. One in three adults "undertook informal paid work activities either as a complement to or as a substitute for more traditional and formal work arrangements," according to a Federal Reserve survey. Of those people, about one in three was selling new or used goods online, with others performing housework, landscaping, acting as assistants, or doing seasonal labor, like picking up shifts at the local mall at Christmas.

One thing is for sure: Contingent workers get a raw deal. They are several times more likely to find themselves unemployed month to month than workers with traditional employment contracts. They earn 11 percent less per hour, and 50 percent less per year. They are more likely to be impoverished. And they are more likely to be on government assistance, with taxpayers picking up the tab that businesses do not pay. "Do these companies deserve all their tax breaks?" one labor activist asked me. "Do they deserve all the subsidies and all the things that we give them and their employees have to still have low-income housing and food stamps and assistance?"

· · ·

On a sunny spring afternoon, I was sitting with a few Uber drivers, talking about the "gig economy" over beers and fries at the back of a Pittsburgh burger joint. All of them had been working with Uber to make ends meet, and in some cases were struggling to do so. They had problems with their cars, problems paying bills, problems accessing medical care, problems with insurance, problems trying to save, problems getting food on the table.

Like many other Rust Belt cities, Pittsburgh was ravaged by the loss of manufacturing jobs. In some ways, Uber has offered the city a salvation, creating thousands of flexible ridesharing gigs and a smallish number of highly compensated positions for scientists and technologists at its local Advanced Technologies Group office. But salvation has seemed chimerical, with those ridesharing jobs paying little and pulling work away from the city's taxi and jitney drivers and those highly compensated positions at the Advanced Technologies Group dedicated in part to eliminating the need for human drivers entirely.

The former problem is the pressing one, the drivers told me. "Their immediate concern is their immediate experience," said Erin Kramer, the executive director of One Pennsylvania, a local community organizing group, who was sharing burgers and beers with us. "These folks are complaining that they're not even considered employees. They're not valued. There's no way to get ahead doing this."

The drivers explained how and why in vivid detail. "There were more and more people jumping on to Lyft and Uber, especially Uber, and then at one point, Uber was doing this special thing to try and get more passengers, where they did a discount or they took out the service charge for passengers," Heather Smith, an Uber and Lyft driver, told me. (I agreed to withhold her real last name, to avoid retaliation by her employers.) "When I would look at my breakdown of payment, I was basically seeing them pay themselves and then take half the service charge and then pay me. I said, 'Fuck it. Good-bye, Uber.'"

She told me that she did make decent money mentoring new drivers for Lyft. "Well, they didn't compensate for me doing the calls and stuff like that, but once I would meet with the person and do a mentor session, which is usually like thirty minutes, forty-five at the max, then I would be paid $35 just for that session," she said.

"That's pretty good money," I said.

"If you can line them up, you can do really well."

"Was that enough to live on in Pittsburgh?"

"No."

Companies like Uber can pay their workers so little because they are often not employees. On-demand, gig-economy firms usually do not hire their drivers or shoppers or delivery workers, instead classifying them as contractors and buying their services. That means that the companies are not subject to minimum-wage rules. They do not need to divert their workers' paychecks into unemployment-insurance funds or Social Security. They are not required to offer health care to workers who spend full-time hours on the clock.

Many Uber and Lyft drivers feel the companies had misled them, promising, if not employment in a traditional sense, a stake in something. "When you sign up, they refer to you as a partner," Seth McGrath, a forty-year-old Uber driver, chimed in, as everyone around the table nodded. "Which is so not true. They keep you at arm's length, right? You can't call anyone. You can't talk to a warm body."

The sudden rise of gig-economy jobs in many ways feels like the apotheosis of the past half century of workplace trends. Private-equity partners and venture capitalists have shunted billions and billions of dollars to start-ups seeking to disrupt brick-and-mortar businesses, vault over workplace protections, pay peanuts, employ close to no one, and offer no benefits or job security. Uber is just the biggest and most visible of these players. Others include the freelance-services marketplace Fiverr, Uber's ridesharing rival Lyft, the grocery delivery company Instacart, and the do-anything handyman service TaskRabbit, now part of Ikea. Nobody quite knows the size of the diverse and chaotic and fast-changing pool of workers serving these businesses, but estimates drift as high as 45 million.

For all these start-ups, the basic business model is the same. The company offers a Web- or mobile-based platform, light and endlessly scalable to new consumers. That platform connects individuals offering a product or service to folks in search of that product or service, whether it be a ride, a sandwich, or a hand to change hard-to-reach lightbulbs. The company hosts the search, allows the match, and then sets up the exchange of goods or provision of services. It settles payment, and takes a cut.

That payment often works out to very little indeed. Uber has touted the statistic that its median full-time driver for its UberX program in New York City makes $90,766 a year. "UberX driver partners are small business entrepreneurs demonstrating across the country that being a driver is sustainable and profitable," the company wrote in a blog post, since taken down. "In contrast, the nation's taxi drivers are often below the poverty line." But drivers themselves have heartily disputed those figures, particularly after Uber cut its rates in 2016. "You have created a culture of expendable drivers," the Uber Drivers Network of New York wrote to the company in an open letter. "You have saturated the company and the industry as a whole with expendable drivers that make it nearly impossible for any one single driver to make a decent income." Some said they were making far less than the minimum wage, as little as $3 an hour.

"On the low end, $150 a night," McGrath told me, explaining how he would put his young daughter to bed and then head out to pick up college kids. After taxes, gas, and car expenses, though, he said, he would only pocket half of whatever he made.

This is not to say that there are not salutary benefits for gig-economy workers, including Uber drivers. Many appreciate the flexibility that working for the car-sharing service allows. And they said that they often used Uber to smooth their income, hitting the road when their other earnings were low and doing less when they were flush. I asked McGrath if there were other options for supplementing his income in Pittsburgh. Why did he decide to work with Uber, as opposed to freelancing or picking up a shift at a local store? "I have a car," he told me. "I'm able to afford the additional insurance. I keep my car relatively clean, which is hard to do with a seven-year-old. For me, it was the flexibility in the time and [the fact] that the barriers to entry were really low."

In public, the firms of the gig economy venerate that flexibility and independence as a way of casting themselves as the champions of today's millennial entrepreneurs, rather than corporations that are stiffing the proletariat. Yet in private, independence is actively discouraged. Uber tells its drivers what kinds of cars they need to have, sets pay scales, instructs them on how to manage customers, fires them if their star ratings go too low, and even tells them what to do if someone vomits in their car. These jobs feel like jobs to many drivers, if not very good ones, rather than freewheeling freelance gigs.

More and more politicians and labor experts are arguing that neither label really fits. The government might need to create a new standard for "dependent contractors," individuals reliant on but not employed by businesses. The government could, for instance, levy a surcharge on businesses using 1099 gig workers. Those funds could pay for unemployment insurance, workers' compensation, and other minimal benefits. At the same time, Uncle Sam could require on-demand businesses to reimburse workers for basic expenses and pay out the local minimum wage for any hours spent on the job. That would require the businesses to better track their workers' hours. It would probably raise prices for consumers too. But it would ameliorate one of the worst problems with the gig economy—namely, pay that works out to peanuts—without quashing the business model.

Another, more holistic solution would be for the government to create a system of prorated fundamental benefits, paid for by deductions from all workers' paychecks, no matter how big or small. Those benefits could include sick leave, maternity and paternity leave, retirement savings, unemployment insurance, and workers' compensation. The entrepreneur Nick Hanauer and the labor organizer David

Rolf have a fleshed-out version of such a plan in the journal *Democracy*, and argue that a "shared security system" would help guarantee a pathway to the middle class without crushing these nascent businesses or precluding the rise of flexible, part-time work.

Improving labor standards would help too. Carrie Gleason directs the Fair Workweek Initiative at the Center for Popular Democracy, an umbrella for local organizing groups. She has led an effort to push companies to stop using on-call workers and "just-in-time" systems and to persuade localities to ban them. "It's not just that we need more sustainable work schedules," she told me. "It's that we need way more control over our workweeks."

But such changes, while helpful, would not ameliorate the catastrophic loss of worker power seen in the twentieth and twenty-first centuries. They would not address the root causes of what young Lefties like to term "late capitalism," an age typified by corporate dominance, social-media ubiquity, miserable work, and a certain postmodern ironic fatalism. They would not solve the problems in the Rust Belt's job market. They would not end poverty wages for home health work, the physically taxing and emotionally wrenching jobs needed to manage the aging of the baby boomers. They would not aid the 46 percent of families who could not come up with $400 in an emergency. They would not push the Ortiz family into the middle class.

Imagine, on the other hand, what would happen if each member of the Ortiz family received $1,000 a month with no strings attached, or even far less. Surely, the members of the family old enough to work would not stop working—not given the family's ambitions to send each girl to college, support their extended family, and build a stable life. But the parents might be able to refuse such terrible working conditions. The teenagers might be able to structure their schedules so the family could see one another for more than a few minutes during the daytime. The younger children might enjoy more time at home with their sisters and parents, and more time for schoolwork and play. The worst of the psychological strain and physical stress of hovering near the poverty line might lift.

· · ·

As I sat with the Pittsburgh drivers and visited the Ortiz family, it became clear to me that they were not just facing the problem of having too little income—and neither were workers across the country. There was more at stake. With money comes power. The fast-food workers and the drivers felt disrespected. They felt used, neglected, and ignored.

Fifty years ago, these workers might have been part of a union that would represent their collective wishes and ensure good pay and good benefits. But most Uber drivers are not part of a union, and the Ortiz family has been harassed and threatened for its relationship with labor organizers. Worker advocacy organizations like Erin Kramer's do what they can, but cannot negotiate contracts or raise union dues, nor can Fight for $15 ensure that a given Burger King treat its workers with respect. "All these jobs might go away," Kramer told me. "And they were never good jobs to begin with, and the company is not treating its workers like it values them."

A UBI would not just drive money and income to these people, I realized. It would act as a kind of twenty-first-century union, returning power to workers and radically redefining them as an investment for businesses, not just a cost to them. With a basic income, workers could refuse to take a job with low pay. With a basic income, workers could demand better benefits. With a basic income, companies would have to compete to win workers over. "It's like making a permanent strike fund for people," Andy Stern of the SEIU told me. "It makes a shift in the power dynamics. Imagine if you're a young person calling in to see if you can get a shift at H&M or Nike for $8 an hour. Now, imagine if you did not need to do that."

Plus, a UBI would be a form of welfare that encourages middle-class wages instead of subsidizing poverty wages, as the current system does. A few years ago, a veteran McDonald's employee named Nancy Salgado, who had worked for minimum wage or close to it for ten years and had two small children, called the company's McResource help line. She hoped that the company would help her get a raise or offer her corporate resources. But the operator instead advised her on how to apply for food stamps and heating assistance, and talked her through the details of the Medicaid program. Rather than tapping into its ample corporate profits to aid its worker, in other words, it sent her to the dole.

This has a tremendous social cost, with taxpayers boosting corporations' bottom lines. One study of frontline fast-food workers found that more than half were enrolled in public assistance programs, double the rate in the population as a whole. The country spends nearly $4 billion on Medicaid and children's health insurance for those workers. It also spends more than a billion dollars on food stamps, and nearly $2 billion on wage supports through the Earned Income Tax Credit, or EITC. Another, broader study on the "high public cost of low wages" found that the government spends roughly $130 billion a year, every year, providing support to working families.

It need not be like this. A UBI would be a way to ensure that workers had a central and vital role in the economy right now. "We are right. We are right morally. We are right economically," said Kramer. "Our ministers know we are right, our teachers know we are right, our doctors know we are right, but it's about power. Do we have the power to disrupt 'progress,' because the progress is progressing into something we don't have value in?"

Don't have value in, and might not always have a role in—even if Silicon Valley's fears about the labor-sapping potential of their innovations are overly pessimistic and even if Silicon Valley's hopes about the transformative potential of their technologies are overly optimistic. Driving around Pittsburgh in the backseat of an Uber, I caught sight of one of the company's driverless cars. A UBI might help support workers with low-wage jobs—but what about workers without jobs? What would it feel like to lose your $60,000-a-year job as a truck driver or $24,000-a-year job as a fast-food worker or $10,000 a year in Uber money picked up in the evenings, and to be told to be happy with a check from the government? What would it feel like to be deemed unproductive by the new economy, your livelihood wrecked by technological marvels and propped up by government policies?

Is our American sense of work compatible with a UBI?

CHAPTER THREE

A Sense of Purpose

COVERING THE LABOR-MARKET CARNAGE LEFT BY THE GREAT RE-cession, I spent years interviewing and writing about the fate of the so-called 99ers. These were workers who had lost their jobs through no fault of their own during the down-turn and had exhausted their unemployment-insurance pay-ments, which the Obama administration had extended for up to ninety-nine weeks in high-unemployment areas. This left them with no safety net as their job searches dragged on.

The 99ers were a subset of a huge pool of Americans who experienced long-term joblessness in the late aughts and early 2010s. The scale of job losses during and after the Great Recession was massive in scope and is shocking to remember from the warm perch of full employment in the early Trump years. Three in four people who responded to one 2010 sur-vey had been laid off or had a close friend or family member who was out of work. Roughly one in three construction workers lost their job, as did one in four manufacturing em-ployees. The number of people on the job declined by nearly 8 million, and it took seven years for the economy to restore all those positions. The *intensity* of the job losses was extraordinary too. The average time spent unemployed soared to forty-one weeks—a record, by far, in the postwar period. The share of people who had been out of a job for more than six months climbed to 45 percent, another record. By the end of 2011, the share of people who had been unemployed for ninety-nine weeks or longer, those "99ers," hit 15 percent, yet another record.

The longer someone was out of work, the harder it became to find work. A study by the San Francisco Fed showed that a newly jobless worker had a roughly one in four chance of finding a new job in any given month for the first six months of looking. Once they were out of work for six months, the chance dropped to one in ten. Those odds in part reflected the fact that the long-term jobless might have been less attractive candidates to hiring managers. Workers' skills tend to atrophy the longer they have been out of work, and they themselves tend to become disconnected and discouraged. Plus, some of the long-term jobless might have had less in-demand and valuable skills to begin with. But economists believe that simple discrimination was a factor too. Businesses just don't like hiring the long-term unemployed. For millions of Americans, joblessness itself became an impediment to finding work, with devastating consequences.

In the eyes of economists, long-term unemployment causes "hysteresis," a word derived from the Greek term for lagging behind. Long spells of joblessness put workers on permanently lower earnings trajectories. If joblessness is widespread, it makes for a less dynamic, less productive, and less employed workforce. Unemployment is not just bad for individual workers. It is bad for an entire country's economy. And not for just the duration of the recession. For years after. The economist Danny Yagan of the University of California, Berkeley, has found that parts of the country that had the worst employment shocks during the recession have still not recovered relative to regions that were sheltered from the blow. The more a local area's unemployment rate climbed in the recession, the less likely it was that a working-age individual from that area would be employed at all nearly a decade later. The economist chalks it up to "general human capital decay and persistently low labor demand."

The dry economic statistics fail to capture the devastating personal consequences felt by millions of Americans. I had met Jenner Barrington-Ward in the fall of 2013, when she was bouncing around between friends' homes in the Boston suburbs. "I've been turned down from McDonald's because I was told I was too articulate," she told me. "I got denied a job scrubbing toilets because I didn't speak Spanish and turned away from a laundromat because I was 'too pretty.' I've also been told point-blank to my face, 'We don't hire the unemployed.' And the two times I got real interest from a prospective employer, the credit check ended it immediately." She described her half decade of joblessness as a "journey through hell," a descent from a self-supported and self-actualized middle-class life into homelessness and abject poverty.

I thought about this experience often as I contemplated the potential robot jobs apocalypse and the supposed salve that a UBI might be. People like Barrington-Ward and other 99ers showed me how deeply Americans love working, and how much they derive a sense of purpose and self-worth from it. While unemployment insurance might have helped to keep their heads above water, and while the resulting financial stress of the insurance payments ending might have proven difficult, it was joblessness itself they hated most. They did not want handouts. They wanted work.

• • •

To paraphrase the essayist William Deresiewicz, every civilization has its virtue. For the Greeks, it was courage. For the Romans, duty. For us, it is industriousness. We Americans see work not just as an economic necessity, but as a social obligation and the foundation of a good life—a part of the American Dream that anyone could start from nothing and end up prosperous and secure. Industriousness is, as Deresiewicz puts it, a "national religion."

It might be worth noting how historically anomalous this is, at least in the West. The Greeks and the Romans valorized a life of leisure and contemplation, with Aristotle seeing it as man's highest calling. The European nobility saw themselves as above mere toil, living off the fruits of their lands and the labor of others. The Spanish conquerors who came to this continent in the 1500s sought a land where the earth would provide, with no need for struggle. But the United States was a country founded in a Protestant work ethic, by Puritans and Quakers who saw idleness as a sin and believed that individuals could demonstrate their love of God and purify themselves through labor. Cotton Mather, the minister and unfortunate enthusiast for the Salem witch trials, inveighed against rest, relaxation, and enjoyment, for instance. "Idleness increases in the town exceedingly," he wrote. "Idleness, of which there never came any goodness! Idleness which is the 'reproach of any people.'"

From the outset, attitudes toward work set the United States apart from European societies. The experience of being a colony, with English nobles and aristocrats benefiting from the labor of continental subjects and hundreds of thousands of slaves, cemented this celebration of toil. "In England a king hath little more to do than to make war and give away places; which in plain terms, is to impoverish the nation and set it together by the ears," Thomas Paine complained in *Common Sense.* "A pretty business indeed for a man to be allowed eight hundred thousand sterling a year for, and worshipped into the bargain!" Americans also felt the need to claim the land by establishing homesteads and conquering the West—expelling or crushing the civilizations that had long thrived there—further deepening the intertwining of industriousness, individualism, and success.

The rich and the poor, the urban and the rural, the elites and the slaves: all worked and worked hard. Here is how Alexis de Tocqueville described American industriousness in *Democracy in America*:

> In America no one is degraded because he works, for everyone about him works also; nor is anyone humiliated by the notion of receiving pay, for the President of the United States also works for pay. He is paid for commanding, other men for obeying orders. In the United States professions are more or less laborious, more or less profitable; but they are never either high or low: every honest calling is honorable.

Or consider the report of a Viennese immigrant living in New England, written around the same time as Tocqueville's account:

> There is, probably, no people on earth with whom business constitutes pleasure, and industry amusement, in an equal degree with the inhabitants of the United States of America. Active occupation is not only the principal source of their happiness, and the foundation of their national greatness, but they are absolutely wretched without it, and instead of the "*dolce far niente,*" know but the *horrors* of idleness. Business

is the very soul of an American: he pursues it, not as a means of procuring for himself and his family the necessary comforts of life, but as the fountain of all human felicity . . . it is as if all America were but one gigantic workshop, over the entrance of which there is the blazing inscription, *"No admission here, except on business."*

Given this love of labor, the myth of the self-made man proves as old as the country too. Benjamin Franklin boasted that he "emerged from the poverty and obscurity in which I was born and bred, to a state of affluence and some degree of reputation in the world," in his autobiography, a wildly bestselling Horatio Alger–type tale. In his enumeration of thirteen virtues, Franklin warned Americans to "lose no time; be always employed in something useful; cut off all unnecessary actions." (Of the thirteen virtues, humility was listed last, by the way.)

Later, Andrew Jackson heralded the "common man" and spoke of his formative penniless background. "The planter, the farmer, the mechanic, and the laborer all know that their success depends upon their own industry and economy," he said in his last presidential address. "These classes of society form the great body of the people of the United States; they are the bone and sinew of the country." Before Richard Nixon, Jimmy Carter, Bill Clinton, and Barack Obama, Abraham Lincoln also extolled his humble roots: "I am not ashamed to confess that twenty-five years ago I was a hired laborer, mauling rails, at work on a flat-boat," he said. "Just what might happen to any poor man's son!"

The virtue of work became a foundational part of the trope of the American Dream, a phrase coined by the popular historian James Truslow Adams in 1931. That dream is of "a land in which life should be better and richer and fuller for everyone, with opportunity for each according to ability or achievement," he wrote. "It is not a dream of motor cars and high wages merely, but a dream of social order in which each man and each woman shall be able to attain to the fullest stature of which they are innately capable, and be recognized by others for what they are, regardless of the fortuitous circumstances of birth or position."

The American faith in hard work and the American cult of self-reliance exist and persist, seen in our veneration of everyone from Franklin to Frederick Douglass to Oprah Winfrey, or in our obsession with antiheroes like Jay Gatsby, Stringer Bell, Al Swearengen, and Tony Soprano. (I would gently note that Donald Trump has persistently promoted the idea that he is mostly a self-made success, turning a $1 million loan into a $10 billion fortune; fact-checkers have disputed this claim.) We believe in hard work, that it will get you ahead and that it is the pathway to righteous prosperity. We believe that we are all responsible for our own success.

Even the Great Recession could not shake this belief. A Pew Economic Mobility Project survey conducted in 2011, one of the worst years of the postwar period in economic terms, found that Americans cited "hard work" and "ambition" as the two most important factors determining whether or not a person succeeded. "Individual attitudes and attributes are considered more important than family background, race, gender or the economy as reasons people get ahead," the study concluded.

Indeed, Americans see individuals as responsible for their own economic fortunes in a way that most people around the world do not. According to the World Values Survey, a significant majority of Americans believe the poor could become rich if they tried hard enough, whereas a significant proportion of Europeans disagree. In a 2014 Pew survey, a majority of Americans disagreed that "success in life is pretty much determined by forces outside our control," whereas a majority of Europeans concurred. "Americans believe that poverty is due to bad choices or lack of effort; Europeans view poverty as a trap from which it is hard to escape," argue the economists Alberto Alesina of Harvard and George-Marios Angeletos of the Massachusetts Institute of Technology. "Americans perceive wealth and success as the outcome of individual talent, effort, and entrepreneurship; Europeans attribute a larger role to luck, corruption, and connections."

If work is virtuous, we Americans are virtuous. We work more than our peers in most other high-income countries: 1,783 hours a year, more than in Japan, Canada, the United Kingdom, and France, and roughly 30 percent more than workers in Germany. We are highly engaged in that work, more so than in any other region of the world and far more than in East or South Asia, Gallup finds. Engaged employees "are involved in, enthusiastic about, and committed to their work," the pollster said, determining those workers across more than 140 countries with a twelve-point questionnaire. "They know the scope of their jobs and look for new and better ways to achieve outcomes." And our work gives us meaning, with more than half of working people saying their "sense of identity" comes from their job.

The loss of a job comes with obvious financial consequences, of course, and long-lasting ones too; losing a job during a recession proves particularly devastating. "These sustained earnings losses stem from the decline in value of certain occupation- or industry-specific skills that become obsolete, from the time-intensive process of finding an appropriate job, in particular for a mature worker, but also from so called 'cyclical downgrading'—when workers take up worse jobs than they otherwise would have had in the absence of a recession," a study by the International Monetary Fund notes.

But it also comes with subtler and further-reaching ones. Work provides social interaction. The long-term jobless, for instance, are much more likely than their employed counterparts to say that they socialize for two hours or less a day, according to a Rutgers study. Work provides emotional benefits too. The jobless are more likely to say that they feel embarrassed about their lives, and are more likely to experience strain and strife among their families. More than that, the unemployed are sicker and more depressed, and they die sooner. These effects hit the next generation. The children of the unemployed have worse grades and a lower chance of completing their college educations than the children of the employed.

Ultimately, the loss of a job acts as a kind of trauma from which many workers never wholly recover. "Most people adapt surprisingly well to changes in their lives. Even after tragic events such as the death of a family member or a chronic disease, they restore their former wellbeing, if not always completely," concluded one study. "There is one event, though, for which this appears not to be true— unemployment. Compared with other negative experiences, the life satisfaction of the unemployed does not restore itself."

Back in the early 1980s, Marie Jahoda, the influential social psychologist, postulated that while people mostly work to make a living, they also benefit from the "latent functions" of employment: a structure for their time, the chance to socialize in the office, the status and identity conferred by stable work, and a feeling of collective purpose. She argued that people "have deep seated needs for structuring their time use and perspective, for enlarging their social horizon, for participating in collective enterprises where they can feel useful, for knowing they have a recognized place in society, and for being active." When a job is lost, so are these functions, and it is a loss that stings. No wonder that older workers who are out of a job become measurably happier when they start to describe themselves as "retired" rather than "unemployed."

• • •

A major and visceral objection to a UBI is that it would allow or even encourage people to stop working. It seems like Economics 101: give people money, require nothing in return, and reduce their incentive to spend long hours at a job. The concern about an economy that provided such a benefit is a practical one: What would happen if fewer people were working? What would happen if everybody got something like a Social Security payment, and many people decided to retire? It is also a moral one. Americans abhor programs they see as letting people freeload, like food stamps, welfare, and even the Social Security disability program. Work is a virtue embedded in our tax code and woven through our safety net and inscribed in our culture. Work is valorized by the rich and the poor alike. A UBI that kept people out of the labor market would likely prove hugely unpopular, both among workers resentful that their tax dollars were going to layabouts and among individuals resentful of having a handout rather than a job.

Yet the research we have on UBI-type programs suggests that even a large unconditional cash transfer might have less of a labor-market effect than that Economics 101 analysis implies, and that the people who choose to work less might do so for socially beneficial reasons, like raising a child or getting a better education. A UBI need not make an economy more sclerotic, need not divide makers and takers, and need not become a pacifier for the fussing, jobless masses, in other words.

One of our best pieces of evidence to this end comes from Iran, of all places. In 2010, the government decided to cut back on subsidies for goods like oil and food, and to start sending money directly to citizens instead. Bread and gas suddenly got more expensive, but households started to receive cash transfers equivalent to 29 percent of the median income to defray or offset the cost. The transfers, all in all, amounted to 6.5 percent of overall economic output.

Iranian politicians worried that the plan would "foster beggars," but two economists in a comprehensive study of tax records and other data found that the program reduced poverty, slashed inequality, and did not encourage Iranians to drop out of the labor market en masse. Indeed, some people actually worked more, probably because they used the cash infusion to expand their small businesses. "With the exception of youth, who have weak ties to the labor market, we find no evidence that cash transfers reduced labor supply, while service sector workers appear to have increased their hours of work," the economists found. "What we have accomplished is at the very least to shift the burden of proof on this issue to those who claim cash transfers make poor people lazy, and to show the need for better data and more research."

There's yet more research showing that a UBI would not lead to a world of layabouts and gadabouts, research from much closer afield. The University of Pennsylvania labor economist Ioana Marinescu conducted a survey of data on unconditional cash-transfer experiments in North America for the left-leaning think tank the Roosevelt Institute. "The evidence does not suggest an average worker will drop out of the labor force when provided with unconditional cash, even when the transfer is large," she found. Marinescu's survey examined studies of the Eastern Band of Cherokee Indians, a Native American tribe with a reservation in the Great Smoky Mountains and ownership of two casinos managed by Harrah's, of Las Vegas fame. The tribe remits the casino profits to members, sending out $4,000 to $6,000 a year. Those sums seem to have little effect on part-time or full-time work. She also looked at data on Alaska residents, who, like the Iranians, receive dividends related to the sale of the state's natural resources. Marinescu again found a muted effect on the whole of the workforce, with the state's dividend checks boosting the number of people working part-time. "Our fear that people will quit their jobs en masse if provided with cash for free is false and misguided," she concluded.

She also looked at the negative-income-tax experiments conducted by the United States government in the late 1960s and 1970s, as the administrations of Lyndon Johnson and Richard Nixon sought more and better ways to tackle the problems of deep poverty, a lack of engagement with the labor force, and the dissolution of the family. (Negative income taxes, or NIT, boost a household's income rather than reducing it.) The government conducted NIT pilots in seven states during the *Brady Bunch* years, the first randomized control trials in the United States. (In a curious historical wrinkle, Donald Rumsfeld and Dick Cheney were involved.) In most cases, there was some reduction in work effort. In a large experiment conducted in Seattle and Denver, for instance, the employment rate fell by a considerable four percentage points. If that were to happen in the United States today, it would mean more than 5 million fewer people working. But, as Marinescu pointed out, these studies were looking at self-reported income, not tax data. With a NIT in place, people would have a strong incentive to hide their earnings in order to get more money—something that would not be an issue with a UBI that would go out regardless of income or employment status. The "misreporting of earnings implies that the hours effect was exaggerated," she concluded.

Of course, there exists some amount of money the government could send out each month that would discourage work. Saudi princes are not known for spending long hours working in elementary schools or performing physical therapy. The Shakopee Mdewakanton Sioux of Minnesota has far fewer tribal members than the Eastern Band of Cherokee Indians and manages some highly lucrative casinos. It distributes profits that reportedly worked out to $84,000 a month as of 2012. "We have 99.2 percent unemployment," a tribal official told the *New York Times,* saying that any paid labor was "entirely voluntary" rather than done for need. Still, for more modest sums, a UBI does not seem to encourage people to drop out in droves.

Plus, in a variety of UBI and NIT experiments, much of the decline in hours worked came from women taking more time to care for children, young people attending school rather than taking a low-paid gig, and unemployed people spending longer looking for a job. People with such benefits might also choose to spend more time taking care of an ailing parent, volunteering, making art, or spending time with their kids. That might lead to a smaller GDP and a lower employment-to-population ratio, but would it really be such a bad thing? Economic statistics only measure what they measure, and fail to capture the fullness of human life.

One basic-income experiment stands out for catching some of that richness. In the mid-1970s, the Canadian government provided a guaranteed income to all of the residents of a small prairie town called Dauphin (the "garden capital of Manitoba"), a tight-knit community of farmers, many of whom were of Ukrainian descent. The pilot ensured that no family's income fell below a certain level, thus eradicating poverty in the community. "It was to bring your income up to where it should be," Amy Richardson, who ran a beauty parlor in the town, later said about the experiment. "It was enough to add some cream to the coffee. Everybody was the same so there was no shame." The experiment had a similar labor-market effect to those performed in the United States, with a modest reduction in work, particularly among mothers and teenage boys. It also had a marked effect on the health and the vitality of the town, the economist Evelyn Forget found, reducing hospitalizations and mental-health diagnoses. It seemed to change community values too, she told me.

As much as it sounds like a UBI would be a policy that would destroy the labor force and turn the United States into a country of retirees, the evidence hardly supports such a radical conclusion. In some cases, a UBI could actually encourage work, or at least replace a system of benefits that discourages it. Finland, for instance, has a very generous unemployment-insurance system. But individuals are discouraged from taking on part-time gigs, since the additional earnings might cause them to lose their government payments. "It always should be worth taking the job rather than staying home and taking the benefits," Pirkko Mattila, the country's minister for social affairs and health, told the *New York Times*. Thus, the country is currently sending €560, or roughly $680, a month to jobless individuals, no strings attached, to see how it affects their interaction with the labor market.

A bigger, broader, scarier question is how a UBI would change our relationship to work—what work even is, and what it might be if people had a fallback so that they did not have to engage in paid labor to survive. In the spring of 2016, in advance of the Swiss referendum on basic income, a group of activists rolled a huge poster out on the Plainpalais Promenade in downtown Geneva. It was Guinness-certified as the world's largest. And it asked a very big question: "What would you do if your income were taken care of?"

Scott Santens has a good answer. He is perhaps the world's foremost basic-income advocate: a participant in the Economic Security Project, the moderator of the basic-income community on Reddit, a tireless cheerleader online, and a "writer focused on the potential for human civilization to get its act together in the 21st century," as he puts it. He is also, I should add, the recipient of a kind of basic income himself. Santens uses the online crowdsourcing artist platform Patreon to fund his basic income of about $1,500 a month, just enough to keep himself over the poverty line. This is not enough to live on comfortably in New Orleans, he is quick to say, but it is enough to give him control over his work life. "When I didn't have a basic income, I'd accept a writing assignment for $50 even if it took me an entire week to research and write, because $50 is better than $0," he argues. "Now that I have a basic income, I know my work has value. I know my time has value. I know *I have value.*"

In Santens's mind, a UBI is not a salve for a world of technological unemployment, or a powerful antipoverty measure, or a form of social dividend, or a way to boost the earnings of the working poor. Rather, it is all those things and more: a paradigmatic shift that would free people from having to do work that they did not want to do at all. A UBI would, in essence, lop off the bottom of the psychologist Abraham Maslow's "hierarchy of needs," where air, food, water, and shelter reside, with self-transcendence up at the other end. A UBI would give people the economic bandwidth to do what they wanted with their lives, he says. Let the robots do the dirty work. Let the people do what they want.

"We are not facing a future without work. We are facing a future without jobs," he argues. "We've got it all backwards thinking that work enables money. Work is not possible without money. As long as we have a monetary system, money comes first. And so we need to make sure everyone starts every month with enough money to be enabled to perform intrinsically motivated work. We don't start Monopoly with zero dollars. Why do we start our economy with zero dollars? Universal basic income then allows a shift towards an entirely new system."

In this paradigm, a UBI would not be a progressive fix for a broken economy, but a bridge right out of the capitalist system of wage labor itself. Society would ensure that every person's basic needs were met, no longer leaving health coverage, housing, and food to the vicissitudes of the markets. With those needs met, individuals would be liberated to do what they wanted, whether it was tackling hard work for low pay, starting a business, caring for a child, or doing something artistic. Of late, thinkers like the British journalist Paul Mason, the digital-economy expert Nick Srnicek, and the futurist Alex Williams have pushed for economies to build that bridge, using automation to eradicate as much human toil as possible and using a UBI, along with policies like universal health care, free access to the Internet, and state-provided housing, to support livelihoods. "The most promising way forward lies in reclaiming modernity and attacking the neoliberal common sense that conditions everything from the most esoteric policy discussions to the most vivid emotional states," Srnicek and Williams write in their engaging, radical book *Inventing the Future: Postcapitalism and a World Without Work*. "This counter-hegemonic project can only be achieved by imagining better worlds—and in moving beyond defensive struggles. We have outlined one possible project, in the form of a post-work politics that frees us to create our own lives and communities." It is worth pausing to note how radical that vision is. Economic growth, household income, and even inequality would become less important metrics than health, longevity, and thriving. GDP might even go down as more qualitative measures of human welfare go up. The world would not be defined by scarcity, but by abundance.

Of course, this kind of utopian vision does not necessarily or immediately address the deep-seated emotional, mental, and financial struggles of someone like Jenner Barrington-Ward, who just wanted a job that would pay. It does not address the fact that millions of low-income Americans want to work and want their children to work, nor the decades of economic, psychological, and medical studies that show how deeply attached people are to their careers. Nor does it take into account that a redistributive system that allowed people not to work would likely be deeply unpopular, and that it might take decades to change society's understanding of value and labor. Before Margaret Thatcher's government, for example, Britain "had an unemployment benefit system that effectively allowed you to decide to live on the dole. There was even a song, 'I'm going down to Liverpool to do nothing, with UB40 in my hand,'" Paul Krugman, the Nobel laureate and liberal economic commentator, noted recently. "That ended up being a very unpopular system, even in Britain, where the politics are much less racially polarized than they are here. It's going to take a long, long time to persuade a significant block of American voters that a system in which you can simply choose not to work is okay."

Someday, our relationship with work might change—

and perhaps that will take the implementation of a UBI. In the meantime, millions of people around the world, in the United States and far more pressingly in low-income and middle-income countries, are still struggling with the needs on the bottom rungs of Maslow's hierarchy. The growing, sprawling conversation about UBI comes not just from the labor and progressive movements and Silicon Valley, and not just from the richest parts of rich, rich countries. It also comes from development economists and poverty experts who see a UBI as an efficient, effective way to alleviate the most grinding forms of deprivation.

I decided to see how and why that might be true first-hand.

CHAPTER FOUR

The Poverty Hack

TO GET TO THE VILLAGE, CLOSE TO THE BANKS OF LAKE VICTORIA and not far from President Obama's ancestral home in western Kenya, you turn off a local highway striped with hand-built earthen speed bumps. You follow a power line along an unmarked series of rutted, red-dirt pathways. Eventually, that power line connects to the primary school in the center of town, the sole building with electricity. Homesteads fan out into the hilly bramble, connected by cow paths.

The village is poor, even by the standards of rural Kenya. (I agreed not to name it, in part to avoid directing robbers to it.) It is poor enough that it is considered rude to eat in public, as it is seen to be boasting that you have food. There is just one working water tap, requiring many of the village's women to walk to a lake or a deep pit to gather water in jerry cans. There is no indoor plumbing and some families still practice open defecation, since they lack the resources to dig a latrine. There are few motorbikes and cars, imperiling anyone with a medical emergency. There is little irrigation and farm equipment—there aren't even oxen strong enough to pull a plow—so most farming is done by hand.

Everybody is working all the time, though only a handful are formally employed. People get by making charcoal by burning wood, raising small livestock, and doing odd jobs. Virtually everybody falls below the World Bank's $2-a-day extreme poverty line, with many subsisting on half or a quarter of that amount, or even less.

On a crisp fall day, I visited Kennedy Aswan Abagi, the village chief, at his home, which was decorated with posters celebrating the death of Osama bin Laden and the life of Barack Obama, known in these parts as JaKogelo, or "the man from Kogelo." Abagi told me about the morning that his town's fate seemed to change. Earlier in the summer, field officers from a nonprofit called GiveDirectly had come to visit him. The organization gave people money with no strings attached, they told him. "I asked, 'Why this village?'" Abagi said. He never did seem to get a clear answer. The visitors just wanted to give them money, some unspecified amount, for some unspecified amount of time.

The village's residents were incredulous. They had seen aid groups come through before. Nearly all of them brought stuff, not money, and many also brought their unique moral impositions as well, turning pregnant teenagers away from scholarship programs, for instance. With little sense of who would get what, how, from whom, and why, rumors blossomed. "We heard that they were child snatchers," said Jenifa Owuor Ogola, a great-grandmother and a co-wife in one of the village's biggest homesteads. Others thought that GiveDirectly was aligned with the Illuminati. That they would blight the village with giant snakes. That they performed blood magic. (More benignly, they also heard the money might be coming from JaKogelo himself.)

But the skepticism regarding the strangers bearing gifts faded on an unseasonably cool morning, when a GiveDirectly team arrived for a special *baraza,* or town hall meeting. Nearly every adult in the village crowded into a blue-and-white tent placed near the school building, right by the power line. They were tense, nervous, expectant, restrained, watching as a group of strangers, a few of them white *mzungus,* sat down on plastic chairs opposite them.

The meeting kicked off in church-revival style, with call-and-response songs, prayers, and the introduction of elders. Then Lydia Tala, a GiveDirectly field officer, got up to address the *baraza* in Dholuo, the villagers' mother tongue. She spoke slowly and sternly, awaiting a hum and a nod from the crowd before she moved on. These visitors are from GiveDirectly. GiveDirectly is a nongovernmental organization (NGO) that is not affiliated with any political party, not here in Kenya and not anywhere. GiveDirectly is based in America. GiveDirectly works with mobile phones. Each person must have his or her own mobile phone, and must not give it away or let anyone else use it. Nobody must get involved in criminal activity or terrorism. This went on for nearly two hours, stares getting more intense, children getting restless. "Can we continue, or are there people falling asleep in class?" Tala said at one point. "Are you snoozing?"

Finally, she passed the microphone to her colleague, Brian Ouma, who got to play Oprah that morning. "People of the village, are you happy?" he asked.

"We are!" they cried in unison.

"Can someone lead us in song?" he said, as the villagers broke into a hymn.

"People of this village, you are really good singers! You love church, right? That's good. I also sing. One day I sang for you here, didn't I?" he said. "Are you happy?"

"We are happy!" the crowd responded.

"That's enough, that's enough," he said, jokingly. "I have just a few things to add to what has been already said." Beaming, Ouma explained that every adult in the village would be receiving money from faceless and nameless donors half-way around the world. "Every registered person will receive 2,280 shillings"—about $22—"at each and every month. You hear me?" he said, to gasps and wild applause. "Every person we register here will receive the money, I said—2,280 shillings! Every month. This money, you will get for the next twelve years. How many years?"

"Twelve years!"

Just like that, the whole village was to be lifted out of poverty. It had become the first beneficiary of an audacious experiment aiming to pull thousands—potentially millions—of people off the bottom rung of the global income ladder. It had also become a test case for a start-up-like non-profit bent on disrupting the humanitarian aid industry, and a radical proof-of-concept for the utopian idea that everybody, everywhere, should get a bit of money every month for doing nothing more than breathing. With the Kenya project, GiveDirectly, which is based in New York and funded in no small part by Silicon Valley, is launching the world's first true test of a universal basic income, providing cash payments that are unconditional, given to an entire community, and guaranteed to come for a long period of time.

GiveDirectly's interest in a UBI had nothing to do with work, and certainly nothing to do with robots or unions or the battle between labor and capital. It was about how to do the most good. Hungry people need food, so give them food, right? Wrong. Give them money. People in need of income need work, so give them job training, yes? No, give them money. Children in impoverished areas need an education, so provide them with preschools and scholarships? Sure, but even better, give their parents money. The argument was about the effectiveness of giving people cash rather than giving them stuff or providing them with services, and burdening them with paternalistic requirements in exchange.

The idea was that a UBI would empower the poor—that cash could empower the poor. Thus, I found myself in Kenya to learn about the costs and benefits of giving money versus giving stuff—and to see if those lessons might apply closer to home.

...

Passing out cash to the poor raises a few obvious questions, relevant everywhere from Kenyan villages to Victorian townhouses in San Francisco, from Swiss cantons to Alaskan oil fields to towns on Native American reservations to farms in rural India.

First, wouldn't it make people lazy, in effect paying them to stop working? Wouldn't a safety net fast become a hammock, as Republicans are so fond of claiming? As we saw, that argument has been disproven conclusively in higher-income countries. Much the same turns out to be true in developing countries and among the world's very poor. A prominent group of economists recently looked at randomized control trials of government cash-transfer programs from Honduras, Indonesia, Morocco, Mexico, Nicaragua, and the Philippines. They found that receiving cash had no effect on the number of hours worked or the propensity to work, for both men and women. Indeed, the cash-transfer programs seemed to boost the amount that men worked, in some cases. Another sweeping review did find that recipients of cash transfers worked less. But those reductions mostly reflected the elderly and those caring for dependents stepping back—outcomes to cheer, in other words.

Okay, so maybe people would continue to work. But wouldn't people waste the money? What if they squandered it all on alcohol, drugs, and cigarettes, thus reducing its intended antipoverty effect? It sounds like something the United States, in the grip of an opioid epidemic, would worry about. The concern turns out to be cross-cultural. In Nicaragua, a senior government official worried that with funds going out from a transfer program, "husbands were waiting for wives to return in order to take the money and spend it on alcohol."

Again, there turns out to be plenty of evidence to the contrary. Two researchers at the World Bank recently looked at nineteen studies of cash-transfer programs from around the world. There was no evidence that people who received cash consumed more vice products. (One study did show that a cash-transfer program in Peru modestly increased the consumption of "candies, chocolates, soft drinks, and meals in restaurants," though who would begrudge the world's poor such small pleasures? That study explicitly found no impact on alcohol consumption, by the way.)

Still, there are many ways to squander cash besides buying booze and cigarettes. What would stop people from frittering it away? This was a prevalent concern in the Kenyan village, as it was among many nonprofit donors, economists, and governments examining the potential of cash aid programs. Quickly following the celebration of the *baraza* came a stern warning: The villagers must use the money on productive investments, like goats and cows and motorbikes and nets, and not on silly things. "Man made money and money made man mad," Richard Olulo, who sits on the school board, warned the assembled crowd.

The evidence here is also strong and reassuring. The Overseas Development Institute conducted a sweeping review of the literature on cash transfers, aggregating data from millions of recipients around the world. The results were clear. Improved school attendance. Greater ownership of productive assets, like cows and farming equipment.

A drop in malnutrition. An increase in savings. Less child labor. Expanded use of fertilizer and seeds. "The evidence reflects how powerful a policy instrument cash transfers can be, and highlights the range of potential benefits for beneficiaries," the review concludes. Perhaps the most important finding, if a tautological one: cash is highly effective at slashing the poverty rate.

Moreover, GiveDirectly argues that cash is more valuable to its recipients than in-kind gifts, such as food or bed nets or sports equipment. If you're hungry, you cannot eat a bed net. If your village is suffering from endemic diarrhea, soccer balls won't be worth much to you. "Once you've been there, it's hard to imagine doing anything but cash," Michael Faye, the group's cofounder, told me. "It's so deeply uncomfortable to ask someone if they want cash or something else. They look at you like it's a trick question."

Of course they want the cash.

. . .

The idea for a nonprofit that would pass out cash to the world's very poorest first came to Faye and his cofounders— Paul Niehaus, Rohit Wanchoo, and Jeremy Shapiro—when they were graduate students at the Massachusetts Institute of Technology and Harvard in the late aughts, just after Mark Zuckerberg and his roommates had founded Facebook. ("We definitely never hung out in a dorm room," Faye said when I asked if they had a Cambridge start-up meet-cute.)

Distributing cash aid in an impoverished country with little to no banking infrastructure outside of major cities seemed impossible at the time, though. Nobody delivers mail to remote villages in rural Kenya. Handing out shillings would require an extraordinary amount of manpower, not to mention raising the prospect of graft and theft. But technology provided a way. Dirt-cheap, mass-produced mobile phones with pay-as-you-go minutes had flooded into sub-Saharan markets in the 2000s. Soon after, enterprising Kenyans and Nigerians and Ghanaians started to use their minutes as a kind of currency, helping out family members, paying off local merchants, and receiving money from abroad. The telecom giant Vodafone and the British Department for International Development decided to make it easier to transfer shillings from cell phone to cell phone, and helped to launch a service called M-Pesa. The country's ubiquitous green Safaricom shacks turned into tiny banks, where Kenyans could add money to their phones and send it to one another.

Over dozens of emails, dinners in student housing, and chats in their Harvard Square offices, Faye and his friends decided to set up a website that would raise money from donors in the United States and send it to very, very poor Kenyans via M-Pesa. The recipient would have the power to spend it on what he or she wanted or needed, rather than accepting whatever handouts that aid groups had on offer. Faye headed to Kenya to test the idea out, walking around camps for people displaced by the country's postelection violence and taking rickety buses from village to village, offering people SIM cards and cash. The four became convinced it could work, and cobbled the project together. A few years later, a chance meeting with a person connected to Google.org, the tech giant's giving arm, led to a $2.4 million donation. Thousands of Kenyans, and later Ugandans and Rwandans, started receiving Silicon Valley's cash.

The nonprofit was always low-overhead and digital-first, working with macro scripts in Excel and Google Earth images. "I remember one of the first things I learned about GiveDirectly was that they used satellite images to see housing changes," Mike Krieger, a founder of Instagram and a GiveDirectly donor, told me, meaning new roofs and other upgrades. "This definitely feels like how a tech company would have approached that problem."

"We view GiveDirectly as a platform connecting donor and individual," Faye said. Uber, but for cash transfers. Airbnb, but for humanitarian aid.

• • •

In Kenya, I was able to see the GiveDirectly process firsthand. To start, the nonprofit would identify a village with a high poverty rate, judging by criteria like the number of homes with thatched roofs rather than metal ones. Fieldworkers—ones who spoke the local language, like Tala and Ouma—would visit the local leaders to talk through what the group wanted to do, later holding a *baraza* with all the town's residents. With a given village on board, GiveDirectly would hire locals to help them perform a census, identifying eligible families, registering them, and collecting basic information, like birthdates and occupations. Then came the hands-on process of preparing individuals for their transfers, one by one.

With the heat of the day upon us, two GiveDirectly fieldworkers, Linda Orwa and Bethwel Onyando, sat with an older "houseboy" named Charles Omari Ager. Wearing a shirt from the El Cortez casino in Las Vegas and a baby-pink digital watch, Ager skeptically examined his brand-new Nokia phone. Up until then, he had been taking his earnings—he helped two widows with their livestock—and sending them back to his wife in another village using someone else's M-Pesa account, he explained. He had no idea how to use a phone himself.

Orwa showed him how to scroll on the phone's small

screen and how to check his text messages. "We're trying to avoid him giving his phone to someone else to help him find his money," she leaned over to tell me. "Because if he does, he will be very vulnerable."

She chatted with him in Dholuo. "The money is going to be coming for a long time, so you should strive to learn to send money and to make withdrawals yourself," she said. "Practice every day until it sticks. Learn every day before the money comes here." He promised to do so.

When the money does come, GiveDirectly follows up via text, phone, local "helpers" hired to aid the charity, and in-person visits to the villages—ensuring that the proper recipients get their money, without ever pressuring them to use it in a given way. It offers them a hotline to call with technical questions or to report graft or theft. Often, people call just to let the charity know that they have gotten their cash, or that they are going to spend it. "The day after the money arrives, people are always flooding the line just because they are excited," Joe Huston, now the group's chief financial officer, told me.

In a GiveDirectly office in Kisumu, a city in western Kenya, Huston walked me through the cloud-based back end that lets the nonprofit follow its thousands of recipients, tracking the dollar sums moving around the world from donors to villagers. "You can actually watch the money getting pushed out to the phones," he said, as hundreds of Kenyan names scrolled by. By the end of 2017, he later told me, GiveDirectly had managed to aid 85,148 people with a staff of 237. More than 90 cents on the dollar went straight to low-income Kenyans, Ugandans, and Rwandans.

"We have built a model meant to scale while keeping costs low," Faye said. "Next year, GiveDirectly could move something like $150 million. The only thing preventing us from getting there, and to $300 million the next year, is capital."

• • •

Before launching its UBI pilot, GiveDirectly provided large lump-sum payments to the poorest people in a given village rather than distributing small payments for a long time to everybody. A randomized control trial, the gold standard for research in academic economics as well as a number of other disciplines, demonstrated that these cash transfers had powerful effects. After receiving payments of $404 or $1,525, household assets increased by 58 percent. Business and agriculture income increased by 38 percent, with an implied annual rate of return of 28 percent. Children were 42 percent less likely to go a whole day without eating. Domestic violence declined. The transfers even reduced the amount of the stress hormone cortisol in recipients' bodies.

One brutally hot Kenyan morning, I went with two of the nonprofit's executives to see the more qualitative effects, driving to a lush town a few hours inland from where the UBI pilot village is located. (In a particularly postmodern moment, a man in a Boy Scout shirt gave us directions when we got lost.)

The recipients' results were not universally positive, to be fair. We visited an elderly woman named Anjelina Akoth Ngalo, her joints painful and swollen with advanced malaria. Sitting in her thatched-roof hut, she told us that she had received only one payment, not the three that she was supposed to get. She had given her phone to a woman in a nearby village who had transferred the money out of it. "She stole it," Ngalo said. She visited the village elder to try to get her money back, but nothing had come of it. She was now destitute, living on about 500 shillings a week. She had not eaten since the day before, she thought, and she had run out of malaria medication. Eight of her nine children were dead. Even so, she added, "It was a good thing GiveDirectly came here." (One of the executives I was with said that Ngalo should have received an in-person follow-up visit from a GiveDirectly fieldworker and should have dispatched a team to figure out what had happened.)

The fact that with GiveDirectly's original lump-sum program there were winners and losers caused significant stress both for GiveDirectly fieldworkers and for residents of the recipient villages. One man we visited, Nicolus Owuor Otin, had acted as a liaison between the community and the GiveDirectly fieldworkers, showing them where different families' houses were. For that reason, the other villagers thought he was determining who would get what. They tried to burn his hut down.

But the results were life-changing for many others, and the risks low. Fredrick Omondi Auma had been in rough shape when GiveDirectly knocked on his door: impoverished, drinking, living in a mud hut with a thatched roof. His wife had left him. But with the manna-from-heaven money, he had patched up his life and, as an economist might put it, made the jump from labor to capital. He had been working giving taxi rides on another man's motorbike, and used the GiveDirectly money to buy his own. He had also started a small business selling soap, salt, and paraffin in a local town center; bought two cows, one of whom had given birth; and opened a barbershop in the coastal city of Mombasa.

His income had gone from 600 shillings a week to 2,500. His wife had come back. He had even stopped drinking so much. "I used to go out drinking with 1,000 shillings, and I'd wake up in the bar with 100 shillings," he said. "Now I go out drinking with 1,000 shillings, and I wake up at home with 900."

"I didn't imagine I would be living in an iron-sheet house," he said, referring to his roof. "I didn't imagine I'd be wearing nice shoes," he said, referring to a pair of pristine hiking boots he had recently bought. "I didn't imagine I would have a business, and earnings from it. I didn't imagine I would be a man who owns cattle."

GiveDirectly anticipates that its long-term UBI might have similar effects to its lump-sum program. But it was hard for some of the shocked recipients to imagine how their lives would change. During my visits to the village, many of the new beneficiaries were just starting to wrap their heads around the idea that for the next twelve years they would never fall into the kind of poverty that they were experiencing that very moment. They had not started to do any kind of long-range thinking. Their impoverishment—the constant grind of worrying where their calories would come from, or whether there would be cooking oil in the house, or whether they felt well enough to fetch water—had trapped their minds in the present.

Economic research shows this effect is common, with poverty acting as a kind of tax on mental bandwidth, along with its many other health, wealth, and wellness effects. "The poor must manage sporadic income, juggle expenses, and make difficult trade-offs," argues one seminal study of the kind of fog and fatigue poverty inculcates. "Even when not actually making a financial decision, these preoccupations can be present and distracting. The human cognitive system has limited capacity. Preoccupations with pressing budgetary concerns leave fewer cognitive resources available to guide choice and action. Just as an air traffic controller focusing on a potential collision course is prone to neglect other planes in the air, the poor, when attending to monetary concerns, lose their capacity to give other problems their full consideration." Pressing financial concerns, it found, have the same cognitive effect as pulling an all-nighter, or losing 13 IQ points.

I asked Olulo, the school board member, and his wife, Mary, what they planned to do with the money. They said their daughter had a thatched roof that they wanted to help her with. I asked them what they thought might be different in five years, given that the GiveDirectly money would still be arriving then. "The roof will be fixed," Mary said, adding no more.

But for others, the potential effect seemed obvious— something to imagine, taste, touch, and feel. In a nearby hut lived a grandmother named Pamela Aooko Odero, who was suffering from a stomach bug when I visited her. She had no refrigerator, no medicine, no means of transportation beyond her own feet, not even a lightbulb. She was working to keep her family of eight afloat on just 500 to 1,000 shillings a week, or a dime or two per person per day. This put them at risk of illness, famine, exploitation, and malnutrition.

Odero described a normal day to me. It started with a meal of porridge and black tea, as her family is too poor to afford milk or sugar. "I prepare my grandson for school, and then I sweep and clean the house," she said. Then, in spite of her age, she went out to the woods to cut firewood to sell. "After chopping the wood, I ferry it here on my back. I tie it in bundles and carry them piggyback from the forest to here. At lunchtime, if there is something to prepare, I do, if not, I take whatever remained from breakfast," she said. This kind of work continued through the afternoon, and in the evening she went to the local school with a jerry can to fetch water and tended to her animals.

"I prepare a little supper for me and the family," she said, explaining that they often ate *nyoyo,* mixed corn and beans, or vegetables with *ugali,* a cornmeal dish similar to polenta. They often went hungry too. "Then, I rest on my bed, listening to what has happened in the world out there on my small transistor radio, then I eventually sleep, after a long, tiresome day." She planned to use her money to boost the number and quality of calories they were eating, first and foremost. "There'll be a lot of change here! There will be no more begging for handouts," she told me.

Others were thinking further into the future. The widowed sister-wives who employ Ager, Margaret and Mary, told me they planned to pool their funds together to start a small bank with some friends—only lending to women, they said, since they were more trustworthy. Another local woman said she wanted to become a hairdresser. Yet others were planning on saving up with their husbands to improve their houses, replant their yards, or buy income-generating assets, like goats.

"I'll deal with three things first urgently: the pit latrine that I need to construct, the part of my house that has been damaged by termites, and the livestock pen that needs reinforcement, so the hyena gets nothing from me on his prowls," Plister Aloo Raudo, a widow, told me, speaking in Dholuo. "One day, a hyena came and took one of my she-goats, dragging her by the legs. She had just given birth to a kid, and it was a pity seeing the kid helpless and so frail. I had to ask my neighbor whose goat had given birth too, to let her goat adopt my new kid so she could suckle and at least have a chance at life."

At 10:43 on the morning of October 24, 2016, the first M-Pesa payments went out to the residents of the village. At the time, Caroline Akinyi Odhiambo was nursing her toddler daughter on a stool in her mud hut as thin chickens wandered in and out, looking for bugs. Her husband, Jack, called from the construction site where he was working to tell her to look at her new mobile phone. A text message had appeared, informing her that she had received 2,280 Kenyan shillings. She had never had so much money in her life, and cracked a tentative smile.

Ager, the houseboy for the two sister-wives, had his phone turned off and wrapped in a plastic bag in his pocket that day. He was driving the widows' goats and cattle from one dried-out, bramble-filled meadow to another when he happened upon an aid worker, who prompted him to pull out his phone, turn it on, and wait. The text was there. So was the money. "I'm happy! I'm happy! I'm happy!" he shouted, jumping up and down and dancing. That very day, he went to purchase a goat.

Erick Odhiambo Madoho was happy too. He walked to the cow-dotted local highway nearest the village and took a *matatu*, a shared minibus overloaded with twenty passengers, down to Lake Victoria. There, he found an M-Pesa stand, and converted his mobile money into shillings. He used the cash to buy the first of the three rounds of filament-thin fishing line that he would need to hand-knot into nets to catch tilapia in the lake.

When the nets were done, in about three months, he told me while we sat in the minibus, he would rent a boat and hire a day laborer to work with him. He anticipated his income, minus costs, to reach as much as 2,000 shillings on a good day. I asked him why he had not saved money for nets before now, given how lucrative the trade was.

"I could not," he said, with a shrug and a smile.

In the village, the idea of waste—as well as the idea of not trusting people with cash—seemed absurd. It was not just that the villagers seemed uninterested in wasting the money, or stopping working, or spending it on frivolous things. It was that their ingenuity with and excitement for the capital far outstripped anything I imagined. They were not charity cases. They were businesses waiting to start, individuals striving to prosper, families searching for a better life. The main thing they lacked was cash.

· · ·

GiveDirectly was not the first charity to visit the UBI pilot village. Walking through its bramble and among its homesteads, I counted a surplus of donated water jugs. "People just keep bringing them," one woman told me. There was a thriving trade in Toms canvas slip-ons, with extra pairs tucked up in the ceiling rafters of a few of the mud homes I visited. An NGO that pays impoverished families' school fees had come through and helped a few of the already better-off residents too. These charities were surely well-intentioned, but their efforts seemed ineffective and even wasteful. Nobody needed more water jugs. Nobody needed Toms shoes. Many people needed help with school fees, the poorest residents of the village most of all. But they were not the ones getting that help.

Of course, cash is not the only effective aid intervention—not by a long shot. Economists have studied and verified the efficacy of microsavings programs, initiatives that let farmers space out their fertilizer payments, facilitate deworming efforts, provide chlorine dispensers for water sanitation, implement remedial education programs, and so on. The huge Bangladesh-based charity BRAC identifies the poorest people in a community and provides them with a grant for a productive asset, like a cow; coaching, training, and support;

a temporary boost of cash; as well as financial products and health services. That program is wildly effective, improving consumption, saving, and food security.

But cash is a proven aid intervention, whereas many of the goods and services provided by charities are not. At times charity aid can even be counterproductive, hurting those it means to help. Take Toms, the popular shoes. Buy a pair and a person living in poverty gets a pair too, a feel-good practice the company calls "buy one, give one." But a glut of Toms shoes disrupts the businesses of local shoe manufacturers and shoe retailers, much as donated clothing from the United States has damaged the local retail trade in many African markets. Toms are also not appropriate in many situations and climates, but Toms shoes are what Toms gives out. And as I saw in Kenya, they tend to make their way into the hands of people who already have shoes, but might not have, say, electricity or clean water.

The same critiques apply to virtually all in-kind donations of food, clothing, schoolbooks, water jugs, and sanitary items, even ones commonly thought of as productive, like the animals given out by those donate-a-cow charities. They also apply to many charities that do things like build schools, supply water pumps, and give out seeds. The intentions are good—so good. But what is the true impact? "The question should always be: 'Would we be better off just giving this money away as cash?'" Faye told me. "There usually is not a way to answer that question." It is just not measured. Toms shoes might help prevent children from getting infected with hookworm, for instance, but taking the value of the shoes and the cost of distributing them and providing the money for vaccinations might be far more cost-effective and life-changing.

Cognizant of these dollars-and-cents effects, aid experts are pushing for donors to give cash, not stuff, to aid groups.

"How can you make the greatest impact in the lives of others this hurricane season?" the United States Agency for International Development advises Americans spurred to give after natural disasters. "The answer is surprisingly simple: Give cash to relief organizations that work directly with people affected by disasters." They are pushing for aid groups to give cash, not stuff, as well. Charities have started handing out cash or prepaid debit cards rather than trying to match wants and needs after calamities like typhoons and floods, for instance. In Houston, hit hard by Hurricane Harvey, the Red Cross gave out $400 to nearly half a million families in thirty-nine counties. GiveDirectly, spurred by its American donors, gave cash in several flooded, lower-income Texas towns too.

Groups that aid refugees have also started providing money, in lieu of trying to guess exactly what displaced people might need. The International Rescue Committee, which works everywhere from Myanmar to Syria, describes cash as one of the most efficient forms of aid. "People escaping from conflict or disaster carry few personal belongings and little money. Cash relief allows them to purchase basic necessities and regain control of their lives. With 60 percent of refugees worldwide living in cities rather than camps, cash has proven to be an effective way to reach them faster and at lower cost," it argues. "The power of choice allows refugee families to decide for themselves what they need most. It also allows them to become active contributors to the local economy." One study performed by the nonprofit, for instance, found that every dollar Syrian refugees spent in Lebanon generated more than $2 in economic output for the local economy. More broadly, the Overseas Development Institute, the World Bank, and the United Nations have pushed for more humanitarian giving to be done with cash.

Still, the vast majority of such aid—an estimated 94

percent—is not provided in cash. I asked a number of aid experts why. Donor resistance is one reason, they said, especially the lingering belief that the poor will misuse the money. It just is not easy to convince American oligarchs, British inheritors, and Japanese industrialists to fork over their money to the extremely poor for them to use as they see fit. "There's the usual worries about welfare dependency, the whole 'Give a man a fish' thing," said Amanda Glassman, a public health and development expert at the Center for Global Development, a Washington-based think tank. "It's so powerful. It's really a basic psychological feature of the landscape."

Cash also seems harder to market. American taxpayers might be perfectly happy to fund education for young women or vaccinations for schoolchildren. Who wouldn't want to help a girl finish primary school, or to prevent an infant from getting measles or diphtheria? But they might balk at the idea of showering helicopter money on poor, unstable countries, or on poor, unstable people. The notion of putting a pill in a kid's mouth is just that much more attractive, Glassman said.

Institutional inertia is another factor. Aid organizations were built the way they were built, with the mandates that they have, and the staffs that they know. "There are a lot of good people working in the system," said Paul Niehaus, a founder of GiveDirectly and an economist at the University of California, San Diego. Many organizations want to do cash transfers but are not structured to do so. They instead have a donor mandate for a specific purpose, whereas cash transfers give the power of choice to the recipients.

Moreover, cash might force aid workers and NGOs to confront the fact that they could be doing better by doing things differently, and often by doing less. "The easy critique for cash-transfer people is, 'Your current input voucher scheme should be cash.' It's easy to muster evidence that you should be giving cash instead of fertilizer," said Justin Sandefur, an economist at the Center for Global Development. "The harder argument is: You should shut down your USAID program, which is bigger than the education budget of Liberia, and give the money to Liberians."

Giving cash is often proffered as the efficient option, if not an intuitive or emotionally resonant one. But in circumstances where children go hungry, where adults die young, where there is not enough food, where disease is omnipresent, where kids drop out of school because of too-high fees, that question of efficiency takes on a profound moral quality. Inefficient aid is not just inefficient, but wasted. And that wasted aid could go a far way to ending poverty. Right now, the poverty gap—the amount of money it would take to lift every man, woman, and child across the World Bank's extreme poverty line—is about $66 billion, as estimated by Laurence Chandy and Brina Seidel of the Brookings Institution. That's about what Americans spend on lottery tickets every year. It is half of what the world spends on humanitarian aid.

Leaving Kenya, I wondered what kind of carryover GiveDirectly's UBI experiment might have for the broader debate over cash transfers. Kenyan villagers are far different from unemployed Finns or American bus drivers. But in order for a UBI to go mainstream, there needs to be more evidence on it, full stop—a common feeling among GiveDirectly's Silicon Valley backers. "There's tons of discussion and tons of opinion, but almost no factual basis for that discussion," Mike Kubzansky of the Omidyar Network said. "From our point of view, we need two fact bases: one for wealthy OECD countries like the United States and another for emerging-market countries."

Boosters also said they needed functioning examples to

show the world that UBI is possible, so that when the time comes to implement it here in the States, it's been thoroughly vetted. There might be something of a UBI "demonstration effect," Chris Hughes of the Economic Security Project told me. "You might need stories to make the idea approachable." I thought back to people like Erick Odhiambo Madoho and Charles Omari Ager, putting their cash transfers to good use in Kenya.

Ultimately, there might be a deeper lesson too, in the power and ease of unconditional transfers and the discomfort we have with the decision-making prowess of the poor. GiveDirectly trusts the world's most destitute to use their money in the best way they see fit, something we Americans so often refuse to do.

CHAPTER FIVE

The Kludgeocracy

WITHIN DAYS, THE MONSOONS WERE DUE TO START IN THIS RURAL corner of eastern India—or over and on top of and through it, soaking everything and breaking the stifling heat. Children were working the fields to prepare crops for the coming rains. Roadsides were dotted with tents and diesel generators for wedding parties. Animals were huddled under what shade they could find.

The six members of the Mahato family were cramped by the doorway of their mud-and-concrete home—one room for living and sleeping, one for cooking, plus housing for their buffalo—just off the main road running through the village of Bamni. This community of roughly three thousand people lies in Jharkhand, one of India's more destitute states. Despite being rich in minerals extracted by the country's industrial conglomerates, it is poor in terms of agricultural development, earnings, and infrastructure. Roughly three-quarters of the state's workforce is still involved in farming, yet that farming makes up less than one-fifth of its overall economic output.

In contrast to Kenya, there were a considerable number of government programs meant to help lift families like the Mahatos up above the poverty line, and some were indeed helping them, as a man who gave his name only as R. Mahato explained to me. His children old enough to attend school were benefiting from the country's free midday meal program, which bolsters the caloric intake and encourages the continuing school enrollment of some 120 million kids every year. The family also received rations of reduced-price staples—rice, wheat, salt, sugar—from the country's sprawling Public Distribution System (PDS).

But they were supposed to be getting six rations, one for each member of the family, and were only receiving two. "We have only been getting ten kilos of rice," Mahato, a farmer and laborer, complained, explaining that it sometimes left the family hungry. "We have been ten times to try to correct it." Neither parent was receiving any income from the massive Mahatma Gandhi National Rural Employment Guarantee Scheme, meant to ensure wages to poor individuals willing to aid in local public-works projects. Moreover, though she was nursing an infant as she spoke with me, Mahato's wife had never even heard of a cash benefit meant to go to impoverished women who were pregnant or breastfeeding.

There seemed to be little question that in principle cash benefits would be better for poor families like the Mahatos, and better for the Indian government. Many of the country's antipoverty programs are ill targeted, missing millions of their intended recipients. Many are regressive, helping middle-class families rather than the poorest of the poor. Others are subject to tremendous amounts of waste, fraud, abuse, and corruption, with grains going missing on the way to the PDS fair-price shops, wages never making it to workers, local officials charging inappropriate fees to program participants, and work getting recorded as finished without ever being done. Yet others have considerable overhead costs, benefiting bureaucrats at the expense of the destitute. The Indian government runs not a slender, bureaucratically nimble set of antipoverty efforts, but a kludgeocracy, in the memorable neologism of the political scientist Steven Teles of Johns Hopkins University.

For that reason, economists, politicians, and public officials in India have for decades called for the country to shift away from subsidy programs toward cash transfers or other simpler benefit programs. In the past half decade, Delhi has signed up nearly every man, woman, and child in the country for a cloud-backed biometric ID system called Aadhaar, the Hindi word for "foundation." It has started to link its antipoverty programs to that system, in an effort to stamp out abuse and fraud and to better identify and reach the poor. And it has started to provide cash to some poor individuals via Aadhaar, rather than selling them subsidized goods.

A UBI stands as a natural end point and an overarching ideal for these efforts, Arvind Subramanian, the government's chief economic adviser, told me. If the government were to implement one at 7,620 rupees a year, roughly $100, he added, the country's absolute poverty rate could fall from 22 percent to less than 1 percent. That is worth restating: A country home to one in every three of the world's extreme poor, a country infamous for its slums and subsistence farms, a country notorious for inefficiency and corruption, is contemplating stamping out deprivation with a UBI as its north star. Its kludgeocracy might become a technocracy, its poverty eliminated in turn. For all the excitement about UBI coming from Silicon Valley, progressives in Washington, and green parties in Europe, this, to me, seemed to be the most transformative application of the idea. It would not be a charity stamping out poverty with an efficient, effective, empowering, and judgment-free cash transfer. It would be a whole country stamping out poverty with an efficient, effective, empowering, and judgment-free cash transfer.

The brute power of global growth has proven remarkably effective at eradicating poverty already, both in India and around the world. According to the World Bank, roughly one in ten people lived in extreme poverty as of 2016, down from one in three in 1990, with more than one billion people rising above the extreme poverty line. The world met the ambitious Millennium Development Goal to cut such poverty in half five years early, and the World Bank expects extreme poverty to be functionally eradicated by 2030. Globalization, industrialization, trade, peace, foreign investment, technological change, international cooperation, and government policies aimed at bolstering growth are primarily to thank.

Still, the end of extreme poverty as measured by the World Bank would not mean the end of deprivation and its attending lack of options, freedom, self-determination, health, and inclusion. The extreme poverty line is very, very low. A person living below it might be able to afford, on a given day, some cornmeal porridge or rice, some fruit and vegetables, a few tablespoons of oil and sugar, a bit of protein, and perhaps a handful of nuts, researchers point out, with just pennies to spend on transportation, housing, education, health care, and everything else that life requires. The extreme poor are unlikely to own assets like bicycles that might help bolster their incomes, and it is not uncommon for them to spend half or three-quarters of their income on food. Getting across the $2-a-day line—different development groups have used different measures at different times, and governments often have their own measures too—means little in and of itself, and living near $2-a-day poverty is not radically different from living in $2-a-day poverty.

Moreover, strong growth and falling extreme poverty rates do not guarantee better living conditions for all, as India itself shows. The development economists Jean Drèze and Amartya Sen, in their book *An Uncertain Glory: India and Its Contradictions,* offer a comparison between India and Bangladesh to prove the point. India's per capita income was 60 percent higher than Bangladesh's in 1990 and twice that of Bangladesh in 2011, they write. Yet, over the same time period, Bangladesh overtook India in terms of a wide range of development indicators, including fertility rates, educational achievement, child mortality, and life expectancy. "One indication that there is something defective in India's 'path to development' arises from the fact that India is falling behind every other South Asian country (with the exception of Pakistan) in terms of many social indicators, even as it is doing spectacularly better than these countries in terms of the growth of per capita income," they argue. GDP and median income aren't everything, in other words.

Might a UBI be part of a broader arsenal to end deprivation and make development work—to ensure that the benefits of growth reach the poorest people across the world? India offered, if not an answer to that question, an extraordinary place to explore it and in particular, a place to explore the contention that a UBI would be a simpler, and therefore naturally more effective, antipoverty solution. In far western Gujarat, I journeyed with local officials to see how their efforts to make benefits simpler and more effective were working, and to find out if Aadhaar and cash payments were functioning like a UBI. In far eastern Jharkhand, I embedded with Drèze and his researchers as they performed fieldwork, skeptical of the government's extraordinary claims and the glossy promise of this newfangled and yet very old idea.

...

Though aid groups and NGOs have been slow to expand or implement cash-transfer programs, the world's low- and middle-income countries have not been. An estimated 130 of them now provide some form of cash aid to their citizens, through a dizzying variety of conditional and unconditional transfer programs, pensions, and other schemes.

This is no less than a "revolution from the global south." It started in the 1990s, with pilot schemes launched in Brazil and Mexico that gave cash to low-income families with a few conditions attached. Seeing promising results, the two countries quickly expanded their pilots into massive and massively popular programs, the model picked up by countries across Latin America, Asia, and Africa. Brazil's Bolsa Família now grants millions of people transfers in exchange for keeping their children in school and making visits to local health clinics. In Mexico, Prospera benefits one in four families, asking for similar commitments to education and public health.

Of course, cash is not a panacea—not for charities and not for governments either. It is no substitute for the development of public goods, like schools, courts, highways, electrical grids, clean water, and health facilities. It is also not a substitute for development priorities like widespread immunization or ending violence against women. Moreover, it is not yet clear whether cash transfers have long-range benefits after families stop receiving them, though the study of some programs suggests that they might. It also remains to be seen how much such antipoverty transfers might aid in the broader goal of development—not just ending deprivation, but improving a country's human capital and bolstering its economic growth. It is clear that dollar for dollar it is better to give a family money rather than to send in volunteers to improve their house, or to give a family cash rather than to supply them with clothes and books. It is not always clear whether and when a government would be better off spending a dollar on an electricity-generating dam.

Still, cash-transfer programs have proven fantastically effective antipoverty tools for middle-income governments, and have fueled the current UBI conversation. Prospera has slashed Mexico's rate of anemia among toddlers, improved educational achievement for poor kids, and lifted millions of families above the poverty line. As for Bolsa Família, economists at the World Bank credit it with helping Brazil cut its extreme poverty rate in half and reduce its sky-high measures of income inequality. Done right, cash works.

Right now, India spends a considerable amount of its GDP on antipoverty efforts, but with few programs based in cash and with less than stellar results. The PDS, for instance, costs about 1 percent of India's GDP each year. But a sweeping economic survey conducted by the government in Delhi found that just 28 percent of the program's spending ends up benefiting the neediest 40 percent of people. In any given year, up to half of the grains that the government purchases for the poor go missing. And despite billions of dollars in spending, the program has failed to ensure that impoverished rural Indians meet the government's calorie targets.

Measures of inefficiency in the sprawling rural employment guarantee scheme were similar in scope by some counts. The decade-old program, Drèze one of its intellectual forefathers, aims to provide at least one hundred days of work a year to poor individuals willing to do unskilled labor. In recent years, it has helped something like 50 million households. Yet an estimated 40 percent of the program's benefits accrue to families who do not need it most, and 20 percent of its money "leaks" out of the system, skimmed off the top. One recent study surveyed 1,499 households using the jobs scheme, and found that only half of them really existed and had members who had done the work described. And most people who had done some work received less money than they were supposed to. "To benefit, you need to be in a village where the *sarpanch* has arranged for the program," the development economist Abhijit Banerjee of the Massachusetts Institute of Technology told me, using a term for a village leader. "Sometimes the work is intermittent. Sometimes you do not get paid. Either way, you are at the mercy of the *sarpanch*."

More broadly, the Indian government struggles to determine who is poor and who is not—thus diminishing its capacity to aid the poor. "In countries where you know who the poor are through tax returns or another mechanism, then you can question whether it is better for transfers to be conditional or unconditional," said Pranab Bardhan, an economist at the University of California, Berkeley. "But in India, even identifying the poor has been characterized by controversy, corruption, and complications." One survey failed to identify half of the poor, and classified one-third of the nonpoor as poor, he said. "In a country of 1.3 billion, that is quite the discrepancy," he said. "The process is riddled with corruption."

To my surprise, Subramanian agreed with much of this assessment, describing the welfare system as well-intentioned but in many ways inefficient. A UBI or something like it, he thought, would solve any number of problems. It would reach more of the poor. It would standardize distribution, leveling out the capacity and corruption differences among the three dozen Indian states and territories. It would reduce fraud. It would be cheaper and easier to run. It would eliminate middlemen. It would be more progressive. "Take a state like Bihar, which is probably the second-poorest state in India. The employment guarantee scheme virtually doesn't function there," he said. "The advantage of a universally based income is that someone just sends a check to a bank account and you bypass all the intervening stages of the bureaucracy, which is where all the leakages and the corruption take place."

Plus, given how much the country already spends on its antipoverty programs—and given how poor its poor citizens are—paying for a UBI might not be an impossible barrier to overcome. The government could end or reduce current subsidies for food, fertilizer, fuels, train travel, air travel, cooking gas, and loans, and could shutter the rural employment guarantee scheme as well, freeing up billions of dollars a year. Excluding the owners of cars, air conditioners, and large bank balances could help bring the cost down too. The rest might be made up with increased taxes and better tax compliance. "Our tax-to-GDP ratio has been more or less constant," said Bardhan. "The United States has capital gains tax. India has zero tax on long-term capital gains. The United States has taxes on agricultural profits. We have no taxes on agricultural profits. We could mobilize 10 percent of GDP if we wanted to!"

• • •

The way that Subramanian sees it, moving the country toward a UBI or a UBI-inspired system of cash benefits comes with the "first-mile" challenge of identifying the poor and the "last-mile" challenge of connecting them to the government. A system that he calls the "JAM trinity" might help Delhi do that.

The *A* in that system stands for Aadhaar. Started under Manmohan Singh's government and embraced fulsomely by Narendra Modi's, this system provides each Indian with something like a Social Security number, thus tying every ragpicker in Kolkata and billionaire in Mumbai to the federal bureaucracy in Delhi. "What we are creating is as important as a road," Nandan Nilekani, the tech billionaire who helped shepherd the project into existence, told the *New York Times.* "It is a road that in some sense connects every individual to the state." The government really means every individual: as of mid-2017, more than 99 percent of adults were signed up for Aadhaar, with well more than a billion numbers issued.

To receive an Aadhaar number, individuals have their irises and fingerprints scanned at a government office or a public facility. They provide information on their caste, marital status, age, and so on to the government. Then they use their iris or their fingerprint to access their benefits. "The system in India is the most sophisticated that I've seen," Paul Romer, the former chief economist at the World Bank, told Bloomberg. "It's the basis for all kinds of connections that involve things like financial transactions."

The *J* in the trinity stands for Jan Dhan, an effort by the Modi government to provide formal banking services to the poor. To end poverty, "we will have to lift the poor out of financial untouchability," Modi said, kicking off the program in 2014. (Its tagline in Hindi is *mera khata, bhagya vidhata,* meaning something like "my account, making my destiny.") The effort has signed millions of people up for low-cost bank accounts linked to Aadhaar, encouraging in-dividuals to use them for savings, remittances, pensions, lines of credit, and so on. Still, hundreds of millions of Indians re-main unbanked, and cash still accounts for nearly 80 percent of consumer and business payments, including high-ticket items like houses and cars.

Finally, *M* is for mobile. The World Bank estimates that there are just 20 ATMs for every one hundred thousand adults in India, versus 165 ATMs in the United States. Tens of millions of adults live a prohibitively long walk from a bank. Tens of millions more have never had any formal relationship with the banking sector. "Extending financial inclusion to reach the remotest and poorest will require nurturing banks that facilitate payments via mobile networks," Subramanian has argued. "India can then leapfrog from a bankless society to a cashless one just as it went from being phoneless to cellphone-saturated." Still, nothing like a Kenya-style M-Pesa system exists in India.

The expansion of Aadhaar and the tying of major anti-poverty programs to it have started to address those first-mile and last-mile problems. Now, to receive subsidized rice or wheat in a government-run shop, an individual must be signed up for Aadhaar and present his or her fingers for a scan. To receive payments from the employment guarantee scheme, he must do the same, and he must send the wages to an Aadhaar-linked bank account. Plus, Delhi has started to send rupees to families eligible for a cooking-gas subsidy rather than subsidizing the cost of the cooking gas—what Subramanian hopes is the first of many conversions of subsidies to direct-benefit transfers. "That's the infrastructure that we want to build on, which gives us confidence that we can actually overcome the last-mile problem," he told me. "If you scale up cash transfers, it kind of approaches a UBI."

• • •

From Washington, the promise of a UBI to tackle these problems seemed thrilling: With such an inefficient system, wouldn't it clearly be better for a country like India to just give people cash? Wouldn't Aadhaar pave the way for such payments? If a country like India could do it, why couldn't a country like the United States? But spending time with Indian officials and economists and villagers and politicians complicated my understanding of both the potential of UBI and the difficulty of implementing it on the ground. The principles of simplicity and universality were good ones. But a UBI need not be the best or only way to honor and implement them.

In Gujarat, a well-to-do province in India's western corner, I visited the village of Ranjitnagar. There, in the local shop distributing PDS-subsidized goods, a wordless fifty-year-old woman named Baria Dhuliben, dressed in a white sari brocaded with red flowers, pushed her finger down onto the Aadhaar thumb-reader in order to verify her identity and to obtain her allotments of rice, sugar, and salt. The system malfunctioned. She tried again, as a shopkeeper fussed with the computer screen. After two server errors, the shopkeeper determined that the bank was the problem, clearly annoyed that such an issue would arise with a white journalist sitting in the shop. He asked her to return later. She left without a sound.

Preliminary surveys done by social scientists in India have found that such problems are common. The prior PDS system involved paper cards, paper records, personal connections, and a not inconsiderable amount of paper fudging. Now, the shops require reliable Internet and electricity to make a transaction, rarities in swaths of rural India, particularly in its very poorest and most remote parts. Even when such online transactions do work, surveys show that many identifications come back as false negatives, denying needed calories to some of the poorest families on earth.

Other issues were more profound. In Jharkhand, all the way over near Bangladesh, I embedded with Drèze and his colleagues, who were doing a field survey on Aadhaar, poverty, and the safety net in the region. In Bamni, sleeping on the porch of the town primary school and attending an arranged marriage ceremony at the joyful insistence of the bride's father, I spoke with residents about how the government was and was not helping them. A subsistence farmer named Abhay Kumar Nag told me about his problems using the Aadhaar-linked systems. "You must put your thumb again, and again, and again," he said, holding out his hands to show me. The issue was that his hands and fingers were so swollen and gnarled that the reader failed to identify his prints—a common issue among hard laborers. He also complained that he used to be able to send a friend or a family member to get his rations with his card. Now he had to go himself, even if the local shopkeeper knew everyone in the village by name.

Indeed, having to go to a PDS shop yourself because of Aadhaar also proved to be a common complaint. Millions of individuals in India practice something called "circular migration," the seasonal movement of farmers from cropland to cropland, the rhythmic travel of workers to towns and cities and then back home to their families in the fields. The Aadhaar changes had tied individuals to a single fair-price shop, with nobody else allowed to pick up their grains. If they were not there, they received no rations. And circular migration was not the only lifestyle change that could disrupt grain receipt. "There is a problem when a woman leaves the village to get married," a fifty-two-year-old named Ram Shankar Haldar told me, standing on the outskirts of Bamni village. "The rations stay with her card," and the card is tied to one shop, he said.

A Gujarati official responsible for the connection of Aadhaar to the PDS acknowledged that problem and said that the government would hopefully solve it quickly. Aadhaar "does make it much easier to dovetail them, and this will be the next logical step," said Sangeeta Singh, spending Saturday in her office in the regional capital of Gandhinagar. "We must improve portability." But in Jharkhand, there was little talk of such changes being made.

Registering for Aadhaar and linking Aadhaar to the PDS in addition seemed to have left many families without their subsidies, whether for grains, fuel, or other substances. That was true of the Mahato family. Close to their homestead, another woman showed us her empty cooking-gas canister. She had gotten fed up waiting for her cash and bought one at full price. "They keep on saying that it will come, it will come," she said. "It never comes."

Some Indians did say they appreciated the changes. "It's all cashless here," said Amrutbhai Prajapati, the proprietor of a ration shop in the small Gujarati hamlet of Jaspur, showing off the printed records of all the transactions made in the past month. "I no longer have to give credit," he said. A small line of customers waited around his store to purchase their provisions, as well as to pay their electricity bills and insurance premiums, to book bus tickets, to top up their mobile phones, and to recharge their satellite television packages—all using bank accounts linked to Aadhaar.

Babubhai Patel, a sixty-two-year-old farmer, was sitting in a plastic chair outside. He showed off his passbook, with his stamp for his government gas subsidy in it. "In the past, it would take us about forty-five days to get a gas cylinder and sometimes it wouldn't come at all," he said. The local agency would dispatch the cylinder, but the delivery person would sometimes sell it to the highest bidder along the way. To register a formal complaint, he had to go to a nearby town, meaning that his family had to cook on firewood or dry cow dung until the issue got sorted out. "It's suffocating," Patel said of cooking with those fuels. "Lungs, eyes, and the house are full of smoke." A layer of soot would cover the house, which would have to be whitewashed each year. The family would eat less, he said. Now, he said, he received his cylinder quickly and received his money quickly too. He no longer had to huff and puff for his chapati.

Plus, at least one fair-price shop proprietor told me that the transition to Aadhaar had led him to stop skimming grains off the government allotments, since the new system required evidence of precise bookkeeping. "No, I never was skimming grain for sale on the black market," said Prajibhai Ghanshyambhai Patel, proceeding to describe how he had indeed made a practice of taking grains for gifting to customers or for keeping himself. The new system meant heavier bags of grains—properly weighted bags—for the people in his village.

Still others reported that not much had changed: Aadhaar was a distribution mechanism that had not shifted what was being distributed to whom or much else about their lives. In the remote village of Ghadi, a farmer named Ranjanben Parmar, dressed in a hot pink sari and seated on her front porch, showed me her bank statement. She had 544 rupees in her account, or roughly $8.50. The government had helped her to build a latrine and had given her a bicycle, she said. But she could not tell me what benefits she was entitled to, and many of the ones I listed she had never heard of. Aadhaar made little difference, she added.

Seeing us talk, her neighbor welcomed me into her two-room home, showing off her refrigerator and talking about how she had met with two potential brides for her son, her only child. Her husband had died fifteen years prior, but she had never received a widow's benefit. "I have no idea what happened to it," she explained, throwing her hands up.

In Jharkhand, a farmer named Subhash Gorai stopped to speak with me. The year before the Aadhaar changes, the shop had provided him with salt that was blue, so tainted that even his livestock refused to touch it, he said. How would Aadhaar help with such problems? There were issues with the rural employment guarantee scheme in the town too, he said. Technology had reduced the demand for human labor for public-works projects, since it was much faster to dig irrigation holes now with the help of machines. While that had improved the outcomes for some farmers, it had also taken away a ready supply of income.

At the same time, some noncash programs were working well. The midday meal scheme in both Gujarat and Jharkhand was in full effect, feeding children nutritious, calorie-controlled lunches. Moreover, people said that they liked the PDS and the rural employment guarantee scheme, and did not want to see them converted into a cash program. Why change something that they knew and knew worked, if imperfectly?

• • •

India's reforms are still so preliminary and new that their impact is unclear, a problem compounded by the relative lack of information on the receipt of benefits and the extent of household deprivation in India. "You have people on two ends of the spectrum arguing back and forth with very little data," said C. V. Madhukar, a Bangalore-based investment partner in the Omidyar Network. "Journalists find particular anecdotes that make powerful stories, so, one old woman in Rajasthan not getting a benefit. Then the government finds particular anecdotes that make powerful stories, this or that woman receiving the money. I'm not saying any of that is false. But there is little hard data."

Whatever the promise and whatever the short-term effects of Aadhaar, it became clear to me that linking anti-poverty programs to it alone would do little. "When it came around, it was being projected as something welfare-enhancing and enabling, because it would include people in government programs," Reetika Khera, an economist, a collaborator of Drèze's, and a vocal critic of Aadhaar on privacy grounds, told me. "It has no role in that. Even in principle, the possession of the number does not guarantee benefits, unless you qualify for the criteria of the programs and can prove it."

More than that, the process of converting existing welfare programs into cash transfers would inevitably leave people out, leave people behind, and hurt many of the people who need help the most, it seemed to me. Farmers with damaged thumbs. Women unsure of what they were eligible for. Grandparents unable to find an ATM, let alone use one. It would mean moving money away from bureaucrats, middle-income families, and even some low-income households—something that might prove politically impossible, if the government were to try to do it in time. Banerjee, who is enthusiastic about a UBI in India in principle, told me: "Think of water subsidies and power subsidies—getting rid of those is a political minefield, because the people who benefit are middle-class people who are politically savvy." It would also mean disrupting the lives of some of the world's poorest, taking away programs they understand and trust and replacing them with uncertain initiatives that might be subject to different forms of graft and failure. Drèze and Khera's study described the imposition of Aadhaar, verifying transactions as "pain without gain" and finding that it excluded families without solving the issues of graft, inadequate outreach, connectivity problems, and so on.

Drèze noted that streamlining systems might very well be

a sneaky way to cut them too—plus, the government would now have ample information on and a financial tie to sever with minority groups, political activists, and individual citizens. "I don't see how Aadhaar is supposed to help," he told me while driving in a car out to Bamni village. "If you want to increase cash programs, then increase cash programs." A good first step, Drèze said, would be for India to expand and fully fund its high-quality existing cash-transfer programs, like that little-known one for nursing mothers.

The principles of universality, simplicity, and unconditionality were powerful, India and Kenya showed. But a UBI need not be the best or only way to achieve them. Making the rural employee guarantee scheme work better and work everywhere, publicizing and signing people up for old-age pensions and mother's benefits, and converting subsidies to cash—these would be simpler and more immediately effective solutions for the residents of Bamni. Granting more resources to the profoundly poor people there seemed a vital and urgent priority too, however the government chose to do it.

The same seemed true for the United States.

CHAPTER SIX

The Ragged Edge

I MET SANDY J. BISHOP ON A COLD, DAMP MORNING, AS MAINE'S long winter was just giving way to spring. At that point, she had been living in the Oxford Street Shelter in downtown Portland for 247 days.

Her slide into poverty and homelessness had in some sense started in 2006, she told me, sitting in a soup kitchen, a yogurt cup and piece of fruit saved for later in the day on the metal table in front of her. She got divorced that year and found herself without a job or much social support in the tiny coastal hamlet of Waterville. The closure of the local paper mills had had brutal knock-on effects, draining money from restaurants and apartment buildings and gas stations, depressing the economy across the region. "There were no jobs," Bishop told me. "Downtown was like a ghost town." With no car, she had no way to get to Augusta or another city for work. Plus, she had a daughter to take care of, getting by with the help of food stamps and welfare. That social support ended when her daughter moved out and went to college in 2012.

Bishop decided the best thing would be for her to go to

college too, to study liberal arts and to put herself on a better earnings trajectory. She enrolled in community college with support from a popular state program for welfare recipients called ASPIRE. But her health problems flared up, making attending difficult. She lost her housing, and continued to struggle to figure out transport in the vast rural state, lacking the money to buy and maintain a car.

She received a small inheritance from her father and lived on that money for a while as she took night classes. "I should have continued trying to go to college at night—that would have been a support group," she said. "But again, transportation was a problem and getting around was a problem. Big time."

With the economy now suffering in the wake of the Great Recession and Maine's Tea Party–backed governor slashing social spending, Bishop fell through the holes in the safety net and into the abyss beneath. Her story twisted and turned and looped back on itself: She got SNAP, lost it, found housing, lost it, got health coverage, lost it, got case-workers, lost them. All the while she struggled with major health issues—arthritis, fibromyalgia, asthma, diabetes, attention deficit disorder. Without the disability certification that would make her eligible for Maine's Medicaid program, MaineCare, she struggled to get prescription medication. Constant pain constrained her.

The process of trying to sign up for social support sounded Kafkaesque, even with her computer skills, her tenacity, and the support of a caseworker. "I spent a lot of time going to Augusta, traveling back and forth," she told me. "It was too complicated!" She went on: "I lost food stamps three or four times because I couldn't get the paperwork, or couldn't call the right number. I did everything I was supposed to do."

By the spring of 2016, things were looking up. Bishop

had a job offer, and a caseworker was trying to help her get disability and health coverage. "I just needed someone to stay with, or if I had just the income for another month or so I would have been able to get housing," Bishop told me. "I would have gotten a job. And I would have gotten medical care. I got that close."

It all fell apart. She was supposed to get a small lump-sum inheritance from an aunt in May. She ran out of money to pay her rent in June. She got evicted from the extended-stay hotel where she was living on July 24. She received the inheritance on August 12.

Given her recent eviction and her lack of a down payment or credit, no landlords would take her in. She became homeless, and ended up in the Portland shelter. That meant she lost her job offer in Augusta. She sank into the kind of deep poverty that so often becomes its own trap. "Once you become homeless, then you lose everything," she told me. "You can't apply for a job. You can't apply for an apartment. There are all these little glitches."

Every morning, she took all her belongings with her when she left the shelter, as there was no storage space available and clients were not allowed to stay in the dorms during the day. She piled her bags onto her walker and tossed her handbags over her shoulder, wrapping three scarves around her neck and carting her two canes. Most days, she ate at the soup kitchen and then went to the public library or a day shelter with tables and restrooms. (Due to the state's heroin and prescription-painkiller epidemic, workers had cut a few inches off of the bottoms of the bathroom doors, so they could see inside to make sure that nobody had overdosed. Nevertheless, it happened every other day or so.) Bishop's wallet had gotten stolen, so she lacked identification. She had a cell phone, but no money for service. She had needed to get her birth certificate replaced twice since becoming homeless.

By this point, Bishop's income was nil, none from earnings and none from government programs, whether welfare, the EITC, or Medicaid. It was so low that the World Bank would classify her as living in poverty in any country on earth. But Bishop was poor here, in the United States, where about 40 million people live in poverty and more than one million households with children subsist on less than $2 a person a day. A "crude" assessment of extreme poverty done by researchers at the Brookings Institution showed as large or larger a proportion of Americans living in extreme poverty as people in Russia, the West Bank, Albania, even Thailand. "Many of these countries are recipients of American foreign aid," the authors noted dryly.

Of course, in many vitally important ways poverty in the United States is less dire than it is in those countries. Hospitals have to treat people who come to them with medical emergencies. There are caseworkers. There is disability, Medicare, Medicaid, Social Security, welfare, food stamps, and the EITC. There are charities and nonprofits. There are public schools that kids can attend tuition-free. Even so, the social stigma of poverty and the high cost of basic goods and services, like health care and housing, might make extreme poverty feel worse here than in the developing world, Angus Deaton, the Nobel laureate in economics, told me. "If you had to choose between living in a poor village in India and living in the Mississippi Delta or in a suburb of Milwaukee in a trailer park, I'm not sure who would have the better life," he said.

This situation is due entirely to the design of the American safety net, woven as it is with deliberate and large holes for people like Bishop to fall through. It exists to aid certain kinds of people living through certain life circumstances, and to help them with certain wants and needs. Unemployment insurance for people who lose their jobs through no fault of their own. The Women, Infants, and Children program, or WIC, for young mothers struggling to feed their babies. Section 8 for low-income individuals who cannot afford their rent. Medicaid for low-income and disabled people. The EITC for parents working for poverty wages.

In many states, able-bodied adults without dependent children are ineligible for any kind of benefit. If trapped in extreme poverty due to homelessness, theft, addiction, a local economic calamity, an abusive partner, or simple bad luck, there is often scant or no support to aid them. In Kenya and India, such poverty seems a regrettable, but perhaps unavoidable, function of a lack of development. But in the United States, it is not. It is a policy choice, given the capacity of the government, the wealth of the citizenry, and the example of other high-income countries that have ended deprivation within their borders. The issue is not that the United States cannot pull its people above the poverty line, but that it does not *want* to. A UBI puts this choice in stark relief, does it not? It also casts the old argument about whether universal or means-tested benefits are better. Means-testing allows the government to better target the poor. But means-testing also allows the government to exclude many of the poor. I went to Maine to study this trade-off. Who would a UBI reach that the existing safety net lets fall through?

• • •

The modern American welfare system has its roots in Elizabethan England. In the latter half of the sixteenth century, that country faced any number of economic calamities, chief among them famine caused by poor harvests, unemployment caused by the conversion of feudal public lands to private farms, and deprivation rooted in war. Thousands were indigent or starving, and young men and women were accumulating in town centers looking for work. Given the risk of social unrest, Parliament and the Crown decided to make antipoverty efforts a function of the state, not just the church. A series of "Poor Laws" empowered parishes to raise taxes and provide aid, but only to those deemed worthy. The "deserving poor" (the elderly, children, and the infirm) were to be given "outdoor relief" in the form of a cash dole or food. The "deserving unemployed" (jobless but seeking work) were provided "indoor relief" at orphanages and workhouses. The "undeserving poor" were punished. Beggars were whipped and jailed, even in some cases executed, and vagabonds were burned through the ear.

This Puritanical obsession with differentiating the deserving from the undeserving crossed over to this former British colony, where it married with our country's deep sense of individualism and our cult of self-reliance. In the 1800s, many local governments provided things like fuel, food, or cash to the indigent, but often only to widows, impoverished mothers, and other excused groups. But starting with the Great Depression, the United States built a huge federal apparatus providing social insurance and assistance, funded with new taxes. With the disastrous Herbert Hoover swept out in a landslide election, Franklin D. Roosevelt enacted the New Deal, boosting infrastructure investment, launching public-works programs, reforming the banking sector, and so on. The Social Security Act of 1935 provided "old age payments," and the government set up the Aid to Dependent Children program that later became welfare.

Three decades later, Lyndon Johnson led another dramatic expansion of this safety net as part of his civil rights–era "unconditional war" on poverty. "Many Americans live on the outskirts of hope—some because of their poverty, and some because of their color, and all too many because of both," he told a joint session of Congress at his 1964 State of the Union. "One thousand dollars invested in salvaging an unemployable youth today can return $40,000 or more in his lifetime." With bipartisan support, his administration expanded Social Security, and also created the food stamp program, Medicare, and Medicaid.

Later advances sought to boost the earnings of the working poor, with Gerald Ford passing the EITC and Ronald Reagan expanding it. Bill Clinton reformed the New Deal–era welfare program, once aimed at widows and their children, but by the 1990s primarily used by unmarried mothers. He campaigned on "ending welfare as we know it," twice vetoing Republican reform proposals for being too punitive but eventually signing a 1996 law that put a lifetime cap on benefits and required recipients to find a job. Finally, Barack Obama attempted to pass a rare universal program, if a means-tested one, with his health care law.

This system has dramatically reduced deprivation. As of 2015, Social Security lifted 26.6 million people out of poverty; refundable tax credits, 9.2 million; SNAP, 4.6 million; Supplemental Security Income, or SSI, a program for the indigent elderly, blind, and disabled, 3.3 million; and housing subsidies, 2.5 million. The impacts are profound, long-ranging, life-changing. SNAP and the EITC reduce the incidence of low birth weights. Tax credits to parents increase elementary- and middle-school test scores among kids.

Yet the system privileges some people over others. The elderly, the disabled, the working poor, and some children— these folks "deserve" help. But since the 1970s, spending has drifted away from the jobless, leaving many of the most vulnerable families adrift. Indeed, the United States spends vastly more on safety-net programs today than it did in 1975, but for the single-parent families with the lowest levels of earnings, spending has dropped by a third. "You would think that the government would offer the most support to those who have the lowest incomes and provide less help to those with higher incomes," the Johns Hopkins economist Robert Moffitt, who calculated these figures, said. "But that is not the case." No program addresses the needs of adults in deep poverty. No program tackles the issue of deep poverty directly and unconditionally.

The safety net's holes are not design flaws, but intentional features.

• • •

The people I met traveling in Maine—from gentrifying Portland to the rural eastern coast, at blueberry farms and by lobster traps, in food pantries, shelters, group homes, and nonprofit offices—demonstrated the perniciousness of the poverty trap.

In some cases, payments from antipoverty programs seemed far too parsimonious, failing to provide any real boost to the living standards of their recipients. Deborah Marvit, an elfin woman dressed in bright purple, was in her mideighties when I met her at a meeting of members of Homeless Voices for Justice, a Portland-based advocacy group. She was nursing an eye infection at the time. She had been homeless and living in a women's shelter since July. "I receive $104 a month in Social Security," she told me, explaining that she had been self-employed for much of her life and therefore did not qualify for a standard benefit payment.

Then there were the programs too confusing for the very poor to access. I went with Jan Bindas-Tenney, the advocacy director at the antipoverty nonprofit Preble Street, to visit an older woman named Carolyn Silvius. She had become homeless after getting evicted by a landlord who insisted she had been smoking indoors. (She had not, she told me.) She lived with her children for some time after that, but it became too burdensome for them and her kids thought she might get better social support if she were in a shelter. "We talked it over, the three of us," Silvius told me. "They said, 'You're not going to get any services unless you're actually homeless.' And that Maine wouldn't let a disabled little old lady stay in a shelter for long."

It ended up being months as she struggled to find housing and navigate the maddeningly dense bureaucracy, much like Bishop had. " 'You're going to get $17 a month worth of food stamps,' they told me," Silvius said. She asked why, and was told it was because she had not applied for heating assistance. But she had not applied for heating assistance because she was living in a shelter. "I wasn't paying rent. I had no heating bills," Silvius said. She added, as did several other individuals I spoke with, that a Portland Social Security office had moved from downtown out to an area near the airport, making it inaccessible for many of the indigent.

Others talked about their difficulty meeting the paperwork standards of programs they clearly qualified for. I met Laurie Kane and her partner of seventeen years, Edmund Osborne, in the rural town of Orland. Kane has a crippling anxiety condition, along with several other health problems. The couple is penniless. No health clinic is in walking distance. She has not managed to get MaineCare because she cannot get a doctor to certify her as disabled, because she lacks the funds to go to the doctor. "I was denied MaineCare because I'm considered an able-bodied person, able to work," she told me. "A lot of people say, 'Well, you can just get free care. They say, you can go to a clinic with a sliding-fee scale, which would be $20 a visit. But what if I can't come up with $20?"

Kane said she also struggled to meet the Maine SNAP program's work or volunteering requirements, because of her health condition and unrecognized disability. Just filling out the paperwork and sending it in seemed like a lot, she said. "I'm very worried about losing it."

Over and over again, these people, barely hanging on, stressed how poverty itself prevented them from getting out of poverty. How a lack of support made helping themselves impossible. How being that poor led to a loss of dignity. How nobody would hire a homeless person. How health care needed to come first. How worried they were for their children and grandchildren. How life in a shelter made them sick, tired, depressed.

At Preble Street, I met with Thomas Ptacek, a veteran who became homeless after he lost a job as a manager at a pizza restaurant. He sold his CDs and his other belongings, but could not find a position fast enough to avoid losing his apartment. With no experience of poverty, he found himself living in a homeless shelter. He ended up staying there for a year, feeling more and more out of touch with his family, his friends, the workforce, society.

"To me, SNAP is about bringing normalcy to people's lives," he said. "That normalcy is what they parlay into other successes and other advances." He talked about getting benefits and being able to buy a pint of ice cream. "It had been over a year since I could make any kinds of choices" about what he could eat, he said. "People see people using their SNAP at the store and they judge what they're buying. But you don't know what that means to them."

• • •

Maine governor Paul LePage was elected mostly by accident in 2010, winning when the Democrat and Independent who were running split the vote. Despite having no clear mandate from Maine's purple voters, the Tea Party–supported politician nevertheless set about reforming—slashing—the state safety net. He used executive power to attach work require- ments, an asset test, and time limits to SNAP, making re- cipients work twenty hours a week or volunteer twenty-four hours a month. He rolled back MaineCare for nondisabled but very low-income adults. He slashed the TANF case rolls, spending less and less of the state's federal grant on cash as- sistance.

In his bluster and bluntness and his occasional outbursts of racism, LePage sounded a lot like Trump, and he had described himself as "Donald Trump before Donald Trump became popular." (He hates Trump, for the record.) But his policies have won plaudits from conservatives intent on shrinking the size of the welfare state and concerned with welfare depen- dency. "The Maine food stamp work requirement is sound public policy," scholars at the Heritage Foundation, a think tank that tends to feed policy thinkers into Republican ad- ministrations, wrote in 2016. "Government should aid those in need, but welfare should not be a one-way handout. Able- bodied, nonelderly adults who receive cash, food, or housing assistance from the government should be required to work or prepare for work as a condition of receiving aid."

As I worked on this book, a number of red states were following the path LePage had carved out in Maine, seek- ing to attach work requirements to SNAP, expand drug test- ing, increase the paperwork burden on low-income families, shorten eligibility periods, and so on. (Some politicians have started to use the New Testament as justification for the SNAP changes, citing a passage in Thessalonians that reads: "If a man will not work, he shall not eat.") Speaker Paul Ryan himself has indicated a willingness to attach work re- quirements to Medicaid and housing programs at the federal level. And the Trump White House was gearing up for a welfare-reform effort to do the same.

Ostensibly, the motivation would be to encourage people on these programs to work and to reduce so-called welfare dependency. "The important part here is defining what constitutes success, and our approach in reforming and transforming our welfare programs in Maine was because we refused to define success by ever-increasing caseloads on welfare programs that have been trapping people in poverty," Mary Mayhew, the director of Maine's Department of Health and Human Services at the time, told me. "We talk about the American Dream, but have designed welfare programs that have trapped people in a nightmare of poverty. Our focus was to not evaluate individuals through the lens of their poverty or their current circumstance, but through the lens of their potential, and to restructure these programs to be pathways out of poverty through employment."

But antipoverty advocates said it was unlikely that such changes would reduce poverty or boost employment rates. Work requirements do little to aid individuals who would have found a job anyway, and nothing to aid individuals unfit for the workforce, said LaDonna Pavetti of the Center on Budget and Policy Priorities, a think tank based in Washington. "Too many disadvantaged individuals want to work but can't find jobs for reasons that work requirements don't solve: they lack the skills or work experience that employers want, they lack child care assistance, they lack the social connections that would help them identify job openings and get hired, or they have criminal records or have other personal challenges that keep employers from hiring them," she wrote. "In addition, when parents can't meet work requirements, their children can end up in highly stressful, unstable situations that can negatively affect their health and their prospects for upward mobility and long-term success."

For proof, look at what happened with welfare in 1996.

Immediately following the reform, the initiative looked like a success. But it was the booming economy and tax incentives to make work pay, like the EITC, that were primarily responsible for moving mothers into the workforce. Later, when the economy cooled, it became clear that the program's rolls were shrinking due to a lack of funding and access restrictions, with states tightening eligibility standards or simply choosing not to dole out benefits. In 2015, for instance, Wyoming's welfare program covered just 5 percent of its impoverished children. Georgia's welfare program scarcely existed, despite the deep poverty prevalent in the state.

The country's most vulnerable families have ended up more vulnerable. That includes parents without the time and resources to sign up for programs, individuals scared off by the stigma attached to welfare, and people turned away by administrators. In their book *$2.00 a Day,* Kathryn Edin and H. Luke Shaefer, poverty researchers who have studied the lives and coping mechanisms of America's extreme poor, describe a woman told that there was not enough TANF money for her in the state program. "Honey, I'm sorry," the administrator said. "There are just so many needy people, we just don't have enough to go around."

In Maine, the results are similar, with access restrictions and programmatic reforms coinciding with a decline in the number of people on assistance without necessarily causing the decline—and punishing the most unstable and the poorest families in turn. Indeed, the state's assistance programs have gotten smaller, but during a time that the employment rate has fallen by half. People booted off programs, on the other hand, have fared miserably, studies show. A University of Maine survey of families hit by the time limit on SNAP benefits found high rates of hunger and homelessness, with the median income of affected families just $3,120 a year. No wonder LePage's changes seem to have intensified poverty: the deep poverty rate among children in Maine has grown at eight times the national average, increasing more than in any other state between 2011 and 2015.

With LePage's policies coming into full effect, nonprofit workers said they were struggling to meet demand. Soup kitchens were overfull, and food pantries were having trouble. "We are not able to keep up," Bindas-Tenney told me. "Not close." Up north in the remote, rural town of Cherryfield, "the blueberry capital of the world," I stopped by a food pantry. It had started stocking a closet at the local elementary school, because so many kids were coming in hungry.

. . .

Much of the Republican rhetoric on the safety net focuses on "dependency" and "pathways to work." Granted, there are some situations where the safety net sharply reduces the incentive to get a job or earn more, due to the benefit losses that making any more income would entail. Granted, building pathways to work seems like a good use of money for people who need training, or help accessing a first job, or a hand in getting their life in order. And granted, more and more Americans have become reliant on and intertwined with federal programs as they have expanded in both Republican and Democratic administrations.

Yet the talk of "dependency" and "pathways to work" seems strange in the context of homelessness and abject deprivation. Living in deep poverty in the United States, as determined by the federal government's income thresholds, means earning just $6,000 a year if you are a household of one, or raising a kid on just $8,000. The people I met described it as traumatic. Silvius hated waiting for the communal bathroom at the shelter, and once wet herself standing in line. Bishop despised that she had no private place to put her personal items, which were often stolen. "You're in the shelter sleeping on a mat," she told me. "It's very difficult, and a lot of people need a different setup to actually be able to sleep. The shelters are too small, too overcrowded, and there's not enough space. They're old and falling down. What you really need is a situation where people get placed in a home first and then you get the services."

For Kane, the primary needs she was struggling to meet were shelter and medical care. "My caseworker said, 'We're going to get you some kind of insurance,'" she said. "I just need that disability." Others said that they required support kicking alcohol or opiates, or money for transportation, or intensive counseling and medication for mental-health issues. In such cases, a job or a work requirement cannot be the first or primary pathway out of poverty, and something like food stamps or a housing voucher might not be nearly enough either. "I often say that [from here] to there were thirty first steps," Ptacek, the vet who lost his job managing a pizza shop, told me, describing how much had to go right for him to get back on track. "And I couldn't take all thirty first steps."

But providing the poor with those steps might mean seeing them as deserving for no other reason than their poverty—something that is not and has never been part of this country's social contract. We believe that there is a moral difference between taking a home mortgage interest deduction and receiving a Section 8 voucher. We judge, marginalize, and shame the poor for their poverty—to the point that we make them provide urine samples, and want to force them to volunteer for health benefits. As such, we tolerate levels of poverty that are grotesque and entirely unique among developed nations.

This poverty comes at an extraordinary cost—not just

to the people experiencing it, but to us all. In 2007, Harry Holzer, a labor economist at Georgetown University, calculated that child poverty alone costs the United States about 4 percent of GDP a year, every year, by reducing productivity and work output, increasing the incidence of crime, and pushing up public health expenditures of children when they become adults. That adds up to roughly $700 billion a year, a little more than the United States spends on the military and a little less than it spends on Social Security. Even that is probably an underestimate, he has said. "They ignore all other costs that poverty might impose on the nation besides those associated with low productivity, crime, and health— such as environmental costs and much of the suffering of the poor themselves."

Providing everyone with the dignity of a stable life away from the poverty line need not be just an act of charity, in other words. It would also be a simple investment in the lives of people with creativity, ingenuity, and work to give to the greater good.

· · ·

The problem with the welfare state, the libertarian Charles Murray told me, is twofold: that the United States manages to leave millions of people in poverty, and that it manages to spend significant amounts of money doing so. His is the libertarian case for a UBI, one also made by Friedrich Hayek and Milton Friedman. Indeed, Hayek pushed for a "certain minimum income for everyone," as a "floor below which nobody need fall even when he is unable to provide for himself." Friedman advocated for a negative income tax, the proposal later taken up by Nixon. "Let us place a floor under the income of every family with children in America," Nixon said in his 1971 State of the Union address, "and without those demeaning, soul-stifling affronts to human dignity that so blight the lives of welfare children today."

For more than two decades, Murray has called for eliminating the existing welfare state—Medicare, Medicaid, Social Security, welfare, Section 8, all of it, as well as corporate giveaways and subsidies for agriculture—and replacing it with an $833-a-month credit. It is "our only hope to deal with a coming labor market unlike any in human history," he argues. "It represents our best hope to revitalize American civil society," by making people more responsible for their own thriving, without government interference. And it would push people to rely more on one another and less on the government teat. "Government agencies are the worst of all mechanisms for dealing with human needs. They are necessarily bound by rules applied uniformly to people who have the same problems on paper but who will respond differently to different forms of help," he has written.

There are, however, a few problems with Murray's approach. He is right that there are a considerable number of antipoverty programs in the United States, and that they can be confusing to use and in some cases difficult to administer. But their overhead costs are generally quite low. All of the major antipoverty programs—SNAP, Medicaid, housing vouchers, Supplemental Security Income, the EITC, and the school-lunch program, among others—spend a minimum of 90 cents on the dollar directly on benefits. Most spend far more than that. The Social Security system spends more than 99 cents of every dollar on benefits. There just is not that much money to be saved by streamlining overhead.

Second, eliminating the country's existing antipoverty programs and converting them to a UBI without making other changes to the safety net would likely result in an increase in poverty. The math is straightforward. Getting rid of all means-tested initiatives, save for those that provide or subsidize health insurance, would raise about $1,582 per person per year, the economist Ed Dolan has estimated. That, by itself, would not lift anyone above the poverty line. Murray himself suggests giving each American $13,000 a year and requiring that $3,000 of it be spent on health insurance. He also envisions reducing the grant to $6,500 a year for people earning more than $60,000 a year. Still, under that system, millions of lower-income families might end up worse off. Poverty and inequality might increase.

Even some progressive proposals for a UBI might end up doing little for poverty and nothing for inequality. Take Andy Stern's suggestion to give $1,000 a month to all adults, plus a bonus for seniors. He specifies that he would end "many of the current 126 welfare programs" and cut Social Security to pay for such an initiative, along with hiking some unnamed taxes. This might be less radical than Murray's plan, but it could still fail to depress the poverty rate. "A single parent would have to work at least 32 hours a week at the federal minimum wage of $7.25 to clear the poverty line with Stern's UBI," writes the legal scholar Daniel Hemel. "That's not so easy if the parent is the sole caregiver—especially if Stern is paying for his UBI by cashing out federal funding for child care."

The point is that UBI is hardly a silver bullet, and that policy design matters. And a UBI, despite its reputation, is not really a bipartisan policy solution. Right now, there is a pernicious and nonsensical idea that a UBI would appeal to both sides, acting as a bipartisan means that could be used for bipartisan ends. The *idea* of a UBI might be bipartisan, but the ends and means would never end up pleasing both sides of the aisle. A UBI could be used to shrink the safety net or to expand it massively. It could lead to lower taxes, or to soaking the rich. It could, of course, not do all those things at once.

What I saw in Maine, as well as in Kenya and India, confirmed for me one thing: that poverty, as economists have long held, is about social exclusion as much as it is about deprivation. Implementing a UBI or another universal, unconditional cash program might help us to tackle other forms of exclusion, whether the racial hegemony that stifles the potential of young children of color or the gender inequality that hurts the earnings of women or a thousand other inequities and differences and disparities.

Back in the bleak winter of 1944, with American soldiers fighting and dying everywhere from Burma to France to Egypt and the ravages of the Great Depression still present in American minds, Franklin D. Roosevelt made a case for a second bill of rights in a speech before Congress. Since its founding, the United States had committed to the protection of "certain inalienable political rights," such as free speech and a trial by jury, he said. But those political rights had proven inadequate to give everyone "equality in the pursuit of happiness." Americans needed more security and more interdependence, with each individual given the opportunity to make their name and pursue their dreams. The United States would ultimately be judged by its ability to provide that security, opportunity, and interdependence, he said. To that end, Roosevelt called for Congress to create programs to ensure all citizens income and employment, housing, medical care, social security, an education, and freedom from unfair competition and monopolies.

That kind of radical vision mostly disappeared during the technocratic and neoliberal Clinton, Bush, and Obama years. But the UBI conversation has started to bring it back. Do we want a society without poverty? Do we want the guarantee of opportunity? What would we be willing to give up to get those things?

CHAPTER SEVEN

The Same Bad Treatment

ONE MORNING IN THE FALL OF 2015, ARETHA JACKSON, A DISABLED African-American veteran and single mother who lives in Washington, put on a bright red top and a pearl necklace. Along with her mother, son, and daughter, she made her way to the Senate side of Capitol Hill and sat down at a briefing table. Facing a predominantly white, predominantly male, and predominantly gray-haired ring of legislators on the Finance Committee, she testified about her experiences with the safety net, detailing her childhood in the projects, her two decades of military service, and her treatment in what might be the United States' most punitive aid program.

Her experiences with welfare were not universally negative. She had first sought help from the program before its Clinton-era reforms, back in 1991. "It was not difficult to get food stamps and cash assistance" then, she said. "The housing assistance program in D.C. helped me with my security deposit and furniture for my first apartment. The program focused on getting my basic needs met, which allowed me to focus on my child and getting back into the workforce." And during her most recent time on welfare, she had gotten help

from a Washington-based workfare program called America
Works, leading to a full-time job at the Veterans Administration. "They had very realistic guidelines for someone who
had to go back to work," she recently told me. "You got a
stipend for your hours, and got docked if you didn't do what
you were supposed to do. It was realistic, in comparison to
a real job." She added that she always felt respected and empowered by the employees there too.

But at other points in her life—struggling with homelessness, trying to raise her children alone, suffering from
post-traumatic stress disorder related to a wartime deploy-
ment in Iraq—she found the program hard to use and its
employees judgmental and uncaring. "It's a lack of profes-
sionalism," she told me. "With me being a disabled veteran,
that put a whole different twist on it for me. I had worked,
I just had different situations that occurred that had me back
needing welfare. My comparison is: I *know* what profession-
alism is like. But with welfare, it is like I'm talking with you
and you treat me as if I'm asking for some of *your* money out
of *your* bank account. It's unexplainable. It's a demeaning at-
titude toward folks on welfare. It's really belittling."

On top of that, many of the safety-net programs she
worked with never did help her gain new workforce skills,
find housing, care for her children, or just keep the family's
heads above water, even after she earned a bachelor's degree.
Jackson found the various programs she qualified for—food
stamps, welfare, and aid from the military and the Veterans
Administration—confusing, contradictory, and at odds, especially given welfare's stringent and arbitrary rules.

"Were the benefits enough?" she said. "No, no, no, no.
So, no. No way." Worse, the complicated process seemed
designed to bamboozle and punish. Jackson was afraid if she
made a misstep she would be locked up for fraud. "They'd
highlight all the bad things that could happen. And they

wouldn't tell you how to best work the system. If you're disabled, like me, things are coming from different places. They'll say, 'Okay, if you're on this, you can't get that.' But it's not enough. It's very intimidating, more than confusing." At one point, she got a letter telling her that she owed the government thousands of dollars. She protested in writing, and simply never heard back.

From her apartment complex in Washington, she could see the gleaming white Capitol building, she told me. As the head of her tenants' association, she had fought to make sure that the developers buying her building and gentrifying the area were aiding the longtime residents. "The previous owners had not increased the rent in years," she said. "But the new owners came in, and apartments that were in the seven hundreds were up to nine hundred and seventy-five dollars." The agreement the tenants struck ensured that the new owner would renovate all 549 units, redo the ductwork and the windows, and fix up the roof. "They just finished tearing down the clubhouse last week, and are building a brand-new, state-of-the-art facility. It's going to include a child care facility and an education center," she told me. But the tenants were still tenants—renters, not owners—and thus shut out from the spoils of Washington's rapid gentrification, itself fueled by government contracts, subsidized loan programs, and initiatives for property developers.

That families like Jackson's still live in or near poverty was a choice and a failure of government policy—something the politicians at the hearing on the Hill acknowledged. "To have a single mother of two kids working for $7.25 still be below the poverty line," Senator Michael Bennet of Colorado said, "I think is a disgrace." That a large share of American children live in poverty and that millions of kids live in households with no cash income, he added, "should be unacceptable to everybody in this building, and the politics

that are so corrosive in this place should be utterly unaccept-
able when we are facing that kind of challenge as a country."

Yet the everybodies in that building were largely responsible for those policy outcomes, ones deeply tied to America's legacy of racism. Government policy explains why black
families are more likely than white families to be impoverished. It has nudged black families into stingy and judgmental
welfare programs rather than generous and invisible wealth-
building programs. It has driven a wedge between tenants
and owners. Government policy treated Aretha Jackson as a
burden rather than a client, a participant, a citizen, an opportunity for investment. "It is that abnormal norm," Jackson
told me, talking about experiencing the safety net through
the lens of gender and race. "It is abnormal and it shouldn't
be accepted. But it is accepted. Wherever I go, whatever I
do, the fact that you're a minority woman, a single parent, a
disabled veteran, receiving welfare, and just continue to pile
the other stuff on . . ." she trailed off. "It doesn't matter what
office I go to. I'm still getting the same bad treatment."

Jackson's story emphasized the inextricability of race
from any discussion of poverty, work, and welfare in the
United States. Having already considered UBI in relation to
work and in relation to income, I wanted to consider UBI in
the context of social justice and inclusion. Could a UBI not
just eradicate poverty, but also make government more fair?

· · ·

Europe and the United States have a lot in common. Big, di-
versified economies. Representative systems of government.
Roughly equivalent systems of law. An aging workforce and
falling measures of fertility among native-born families. Median incomes around the $50,000 mark. Growing measures
of wealth and income inequality. But in one crucial way,

they are different. Europe has a safety net that eliminates poverty for nearly all of its native-born citizens, doing far more to blunt the effects of income inequality as well. To accomplish this, the governments of the European Union tax and spend an amount equivalent to half of their economic output each and every year, versus about a third here in the United States.

In 2001, three top economists—Alberto Alesina and Edward Glaeser of Harvard and Bruce Sacerdote of Dartmouth—asked why the two economies on either side of the Atlantic were so different in that way, given how similar they were in so many others. They looked at a few economic explanations: the shape of income distribution before taxes and transfers, the volatility of earnings for individual workers, and expected growth in earnings among them. They came away unconvinced that those factors played much of a role. No, their blunt conclusion was this: "Within the United States, race is the single most important predictor of support for welfare. America's troubled race relations are clearly a major reason for the absence of an American welfare state" and thus its smaller government.

Sociologists, psychologists, and political scientists were presumably not surprised by the economists' findings. Any of the thousand ways that those researchers test it, studies show that relatedness intensifies reciprocity, that closeness inculcates altruism. We humans do not trust faces that do not look like ours. We do not vote for programs that serve to help those we have "othered." We become less trusting and less giving when new faces show up in our communities. A famed study by Robert Putnam, the author of *Bowling Alone* and a professor at Harvard, found that "in ethnically diverse neighborhoods residents of all races tend to 'hunker down.' Trust (even of one's own race) is lower, altruism and community cooperation rarer, friends fewer." Another study holds that "heterogeneity hampers all forms of cooperation" among different groups of people, particularly if there is a commonly known negative history between groups—as the chattel enslavement of people of African descent surely is.

Here in the United States, just thinking about race tends to make people more conservative and more anti-redistribution. Consider one study by the social psychologists Maureen Craig of New York University and Jennifer Richeson of Yale University. They took two groups of white political independents. They asked half if they knew that "Hispanics had become roughly equal in number to Blacks nationally." They asked half if they knew that "California had become a majority-minority state." They then asked about their political leanings. People in the first group, asked a question that did not threaten their racial status, were roughly twice as likely to lean to the left as to the right. People in the second group, asked a question that did threaten their racial status, were roughly twice as likely to lean to the right as to the left.

It seems unsurprising, then, that it is small, homogeneous countries that have tended to build strong welfare states, not big, diverse ones. Finland, for instance, has about as close to a UBI as might be achieved with means-tested policies, and it has just 6 million people, nine out of ten of whom speak Finnish at home. Norway has just 5 million, all of whom save for a rounding error have roots in Norway or a nearby country. These small, white nations tend to have strong, centralized governments that are proportionally representative and consensus based. The United States, on the other hand, has a polarizing two-party system and an upper chamber where low-population rural states get equal footing with high-population urban ones. It also has a powerful states' rights tradition that has repeatedly suppressed the development of universal benefit programs.

Polities build political systems, political systems build redistributive mechanisms, homogeneity affects how much countries spend on social programs. Countries with greater racial diversity tend to put only a small fraction of their GDP to social spending, while nations with a more uniform population spend much more. Belgium, Luxembourg, Sweden, the Netherlands, and France—all fairly to highly homogeneous in terms of race and language—spend close to or more than 20 percent, Alesina, Glaeser, and Sacerdote found. The United States, on the other hand, spends half of that amount.

Historians would not have been surprised by the conclusions of Alesina, Glaeser, and Sacerdote either. Large swaths of the American safety net and wealth-building programs were designed to exclude, punish, and discipline the descendants of the country's slaves. In the wake of the Great Depression, Washington built that comprehensive federal insurance system to keep seniors, children, and the disabled out of poverty and to support the unemployed. But the Social Security Act of 1935 excluded farm and domestic workers from coverage, with Senator Harry F. Byrd of Virginia arguing that to include them would "serve as an entering wedge for federal interference with the handling of the Negro question" in the South. The history is complicated and contested, but the policy consequences are clear. When the act passed, it exempted two-thirds of black workers in the South from its pension and insurance programs.

Moreover, southern states insisted that a number of benefits outside of Social Security be managed by the states, not the federal government, thus giving them a chance to exclude black families. Take the Aid to Dependent Families program that became welfare, the program that Jackson testified about. Jim Crow–era legislation ensured that black women had access to a far different system than white women, with states and localities enacting a convoluted set of policies to bar, stigmatize, and punish black mothers. Residency requirements kept black Americans from migrating from state to state within the South for a better job, or from moving north to qualify for aid at all. Numerous states had a "man in the house rule," meaning workers could drop by unannounced to see if any man had been there. If a male presence was detected—a hat on the coatrack, say—cases were closed. One effect: encouraging fathers to leave the family home.

Similarly, racism was instrumental in derailing plans for a universal health program in the United States, even though most European countries created one in the nineteenth or twentieth century. Rather than move toward nationally financed and provisioned care, we doubled down on the existing segregated system, which relied heavily on private providers. "In essence, the United States' peculiar private-based health-care system exists at least in part *because* of the country's commitment to maintaining racial hierarchies," explains the *Atlantic* writer Vann R. Newkirk II. "The results were deep racial disparities in almost every major disease, an enduring gap in lifespans and mortality, and the creation of entirely separate medical and public-health infrastructures."

Such discrimination persists, even after the passage of the Affordable Care Act. Consider the Obama-era expansion of the Medicaid program to nondisabled, childless adults below or near the poverty line. In a 2012 Supreme Court ruling, states were granted the right to opt out of the federally financed expansion effort. As of mid-2017, just two of the eleven states that made up the Confederacy had taken the expansion, Louisiana and Arkansas. Of the twenty free states in the Union, all had save for three: Maine, Wisconsin, and Kansas. Whether or not a state adopted the expansion seemed to depend exclusively on white opinion, not minority opinion, researchers found. Plus, if the black population in a state was increasing, it became "significantly less likely to expand the Medicaid program."

The United States' abject racism is perhaps clearest in the design of its cash welfare program, the stingiest, most contingent, and most judgmental of its major aid intiatives aimed at the very poor. By the 1970s, a program initially conceived to help white widows was helping more and more black single mothers. Republicans, in particular, became obsessed with the notion that these women were gaming the system. There was a woman in Chicago with "80 names, 30 addresses, 15 telephone numbers" used "to collect food stamps, Social Security, veterans' benefits for four nonexistent deceased veteran husbands, as well as welfare," Ronald Reagan famously warned about a mythical Welfare Queen, who ended up being a highly charismatic criminal not particularly representative of any social trends. "Her tax-free cash income alone has been running $150,000 a year."

Such stigmatization paved the way for the Clinton-era reform that capped the program's overall spending at a sum where it has remained since 1996, helping fewer and fewer and fewer children escape extreme poverty—and disproportionately penalizing black babies and black mothers, though the program remains majority-white to this day. It was Clinton who made benefits contingent on work, amplifying the racism that black women experience in the labor force. "Work requirements and time limits that coerce women into the paid labor force are not implemented in a gender- or race-neutral environment," argues Linda Burnham, the cofounder of the Women of Color Resource Center. In other words, work requirements hit people discriminated against in hiring harder than people preferred in hiring, and anti-black discrimination is a cemented feature of American life.

The Clinton reform also gave states wide latitude in what kind of aid to offer to families in need. Inevitably, states with large black populations became more penny-pinching and more restrictive. Lily-white Vermont covers 78 percent of families in poverty with welfare, whereas former slave state Louisiana covers just 4 percent. The maximum monthly benefit for a family of three ranges from just $170 in Mississippi, 37 percent of whose residents are black, to $923 in Alaska, which is 4 percent black. "When we look at some of these individual policies, we can see how having a higher share of African Americans in the population translate to a lower maximum benefit level, and harsher initial sanctions," Heather Hahn, the author of an Urban Institute paper on the subject, told the *Atlantic*. "When we put them all together and look across the board, we see this consistent pattern."

More broadly, black Americans find themselves over-represented in means-tested benefit programs that carry a heavy social stigma, with white Americans overrepresented in invisible, automatic, and nonstigmatized tax breaks. In any given month in 2012, for instance, white families were much more likely than black families to benefit from neutral, invisible policies like the mortgage interest deduction—60 percent of whose recipients say that they have "never used a government social program." About 40 percent of black Americans received a means-tested benefit in that year, versus 13 percent of white Americans. "American social programs, created and shaped over time in large part by interest group influence and electoral pressure, reflect those institutionalized political inequalities," wrote the famed sociologist and longtime UBI advocate Frances Fox Piven.

• • •

Of course, as the United States built a safety net that excluded and punished black families, it created a wealth-building apparatus to buoy and enrich white ones. It is not market forces and individual effort alone that determine who succeeds and prospers and who remains impoverished and excluded in the United States, but government policy and deep-seated cultural and societal mores.

The history is as long and complicated as the country itself, but even in capsule form it is damning. In the midst of the Great Depression and Jim Crow, Congress passed the National Housing Act, designed to stabilize home prices and make mortgages more affordable. From the outset, the Federal Housing Administration declined to insure mortgages in black neighborhoods, meaning that even wealthy black individuals could not get loans to buy homes. Builders creating housing developments "received federal loan guarantees *on explicit condition* that no sales be made to blacks." Moreover, black veterans were largely unable to take advantage of the home loans guaranteed by provisions in the GI Bill. (*Ebony* magazine examined 3,229 loans guaranteed by the Veteran Administration in 1947 in Mississippi. Just two went to black mortgage recipients.) By the mid-1980s, the median white household had a net worth of nearly $40,000, more than eleven times that of the black household. Most of this disparity stems from black families' lack of home ownership, the historian Ira Katznelson argues.

The Greatest Generation of white families started building wealth that transferred to the baby boomers, the gen Xers, and the millennials. They occupied neighborhoods that won government investment, and took advantage of generous tax subsidies. The Greatest Generation of black families remained renters or bought properties in undesirable neighborhoods. They occupied parts of town cut off by highways and neglected by investment. These policies still affect home values and the distribution of American wealth today. Most high-poverty neighborhoods are now majority-minority, with black and Hispanic individuals making up four out of every five people living in neighborhoods in concentrated poverty. The average rich black worker lives in a neighborhood with a higher poverty rate than the average poor white worker. That has a profound effect on the mobility of black children. About 20 percent of the black-white earnings gap comes down to the resources and wealth of a person's childhood community, economists have estimated.

Black families and workers suffered other racist implementations of the GI Bill as well. When the war ended, black men who wanted to go to college in southern states got to choose from just one hundred institutions, mostly schools that tended to be small and underfunded. These black colleges turned down an estimated 55 percent of applicants, at a time higher education was booming across the country. Thanks to the GI Bill, white veterans added an average of four months of schooling. Black veterans from nonsouthern states added five months. Black veterans from southern states added nothing.

Institutional segregation damaged the educational prospects and the human capital of millions of black children and black workers as well. By 1950, about one in five white adults had attended college, versus one in twenty black adults. Researchers estimate that a "truly 'separate but equal'" education system would have cut black-white wage inequality by as much as half. Again, such inequalities persist. Sixty years after *Brown v. the Board of Education*—the landmark case that desegregated the public school system—schools with predominantly white students spend $733 more per pupil than schools with predominantly minority students, a report by the Center for American Progress has found. And in some ways, educational segregation has gotten worse in recent years, the writer Nikole Hannah-Jones has shown.

The force of government policy, along with the force of racism, has helped to ensure that black families have fallen behind white families. The unemployment rates of black workers in any given age range and for any level of educational achievement are roughly twice as high as they are for white workers—a gulf that has proven remarkably persistent and consistent since the 1940s. That employment gap helps to fuel the racial income gap. There are many ways to measure it. The hourly wage for black men was $15 as of 2015, compared with $21 for white men. The median income of black households is about $36,000, versus $61,000 for white households. Worse, the black-white wage gap has increased since 1979, as income inequality has intensified.

The most pernicious of all of these disparities and the one most clearly constructed by American economic policy is the racial wealth gap. Data compiled by the Economic Policy Institute finds that the median net worth of white families is twelve times higher than the median net worth of black families. A quarter of black families have no or negative net worth, versus just one in ten white families. This holds true even when taking things like age, income, and occupation into account. Blacks and Latinos make up nearly a third of the American population, yet own just 5 percent of its wealth. In terms of liquid assets, "blacks and Latinos are virtually penniless," the economist Darrick Hamilton of the New School writes. Excluding retirement savings, typical black families have just $25 in the bank. Plus, such trends are intensifying, not abating. Over the past three decades, the average net worth of white families has climbed more than 80 percent, three times the rate for black families, a study by the Institute for Policy Studies and the Corporation for Enterprise Development has found. Were that pattern to continue for the next three decades, white households would gain $18,000 in wealth a year, with black households gaining just $750. The racial wealth gap would never close.

The emergence of the Black Lives Matter movement, the growing calls to end mass incarceration, the sunset of the Obama presidency, the start of the Trump presidency, the furious marching of Nazis and racists on the streets: all of these trends have coalesced as the UBI conversation has come to the fore.

In his essay "The Case for Reparations," the *Atlantic* writer Ta-Nehisi Coates made a moral argument for trying to repair these injustices. "What I'm talking about is more than recompense for past injustices—more than a handout, a payoff, hush money, or a reluctant bribe," he wrote. "What I'm talking about is a national reckoning that would lead to spiritual renewal. Reparations would mean the end of scarfing hot dogs on the Fourth of July while denying the facts of our heritage. Reparations would mean the end of yelling 'patriotism' while waving a Confederate flag. Reparations would mean a revolution of the American consciousness, a reconciling of our self-image as the great democratizer with the facts of our history."

A UBI would not at all act as a reparation, an atonement for and undoing of the decades and centuries of government policy that have led to the racial caste system that exists in America. To imagine what kinds of changes that would take, look at the policies supported by the Movement for Black Lives. It calls for an effort to "divest and reinvest," taking money from the carceral state and using it to shore up communities of color. It also pushes for restructuring the tax code, improving jobs programs, breaking up banks, altering trade agreements, ending super PACs, implementing participatory budgeting, eliminating money bail, demilitarizing law enforcement, expunging records, creating true universal health care, providing true universal education policies, slashing military spending, and divesting from fossil fuels. The list goes on. Investment on the scale of what the government put into white families, white communities, and white schools, in other words—investment unimaginable in our current political climate, and considering the representation given to different communities on the Hill.

Even if such investment happened, of course, the global sweep of racism and the legacy of slavery would remain fundamental. "While this platform is focused on domestic policies, we know that patriarchy, exploitative capitalism, militarism, and white supremacy know no borders," the Movement for Black Lives has argued. "We stand in solidarity with our international family against the ravages of global capitalism and anti-Black racism, human-made climate change, war, and exploitation. We also stand with descendants of African people all over the world in an ongoing call and struggle for reparations for the historic and continuing harms of colonialism and slavery."

Still, implementing the principles of universality and unconditionality in existing programs could be a powerful tool for racial equality going forward—part of why pushing for universal programs was a central tenet of the civil rights movement in the 1960s and is a central tenet of civil rights campaigners today. "We're living in a crisis for black communities," Dorian Warren, a political scientist and a member of the Economic Security Project, told me. "It's a great solution today. Not some future-looking thing for when the self-driving cars come. It's an elegant solution, in that you could wipe out absolute poverty and I think it could be a bridge to other racial groups, in terms of building a broad coalition."

It would not be a reparation. It would not mean equality. It would not put black children on equal footing with white children. But it would be a step into the future.

• • •

Yet the welfare-and-race ouroboros eats its tail.

It is an uncomfortable truth. But the United States' racial diversity poses a formidable barrier to the development of universal social-welfare programs going forward, especially as long as the voting populace remains older, more conservative, and whiter than the populace writ large. There is ample evidence that the election of a black president and the concomitant expansion of the welfare state stoked racial resentment and might have even helped to spur the election of Donald Trump. Sean McElwee of the left-of-center think tank Demos and Jason McDaniel of San Francisco State University have found that animosity against black Americans was a "key factor" associated with support for Trump in 2016. "Many low-interest voters still had trouble distinguishing parties in terms of attitudes about aid to black Americans as late as 2008," they write. "Obama's election and the subsequent backlash ensured that very few racial progressives would vote for Republicans and very few racially resentful individuals would vote for Democrats." Voters internalized and acted on both the presence of an outgoing black president and the presence of an incoming white one. "The one-two punch of Obama's presidency and Trump's candidacy sent a clear signal to voters what the parties stood for: diversity on one side, resentment on the other. Trump built upon a decades-long campaign to erase support for the safety net by racializing government programs but extended it further by openly demonizing people of color."

Such resentment and us-versus-them sentiment is clearest in the cries of the country's white nationalists, who have found new power and publicity in the Trump era. Richard Spencer, one of the country's most prominent white nationalists, has called for universal programs, but only for those he sees as deserving of them. In an essay entitled "Why Trump Must Champion Universal Healthcare," hosted on the site AltRight.com, he argued that "universal healthcare is less confusing and nonsensical (and probably cheaper) than what White people have to deal with now," but that "we must accept that healthcare is an issue we cannot rationally address until we have a European nation."

Of course, this nation is not becoming more European. It is becoming more diverse. It is by some measures becoming more unequal. And on the left, support has grown dramatically for huge redistributive and universal programs. Gone are the careful means-testing proposals and incremental boosts of the Clinton and Obama presidencies, where the wonks reigned. Bernie Sanders is pushing for Medicare for All. The Center for American Progress, arguably the most influential think tank on the left, is pushing for a federal jobs guarantee. Seeing the tides changing, Hillary Clinton's team was even quietly at work on a proposal to turn welfare into a kind of UBI for kids. Even more surprising, as she revealed in her 2017 campaign memoir *What Happened*, she toyed with the idea of running on a basic income, financed with revenues from "shared national resources," such as royalties made from oil and gas companies and telecoms. "Besides cash in people's pockets, it would also be a way of making every American feel more connected to our country and to one another—part of something bigger than ourselves," she wrote. "Unfortunately, we couldn't make the numbers work." It seems likely that the Democrats' 2020 candidate will run on a universal-benefit program, with Senator Cory Booker of New Jersey already voicing tentative support for a UBI and Senator Kirsten Gillibrand of New York talking about a universal employment program.

Such programs would afford middle-class white Americans living in the exurbs the same benefits as single black moms living in the rural South, or Latino families living in Las Vegas. That universality might insulate them from the stigma that has attached to programs like food stamps, Section 8 housing, and welfare, and protect them from budget cuts from the right, the theory goes. Nobody complains about the unfairness of their neighbors getting Medicare or Social Security, because they know they will benefit from such policies themselves. (Tucking benefits into the tax code and rendering them invisible, as with the EITC and the Child Tax Credit, seems to work as well.) Programs that benefit everyone need not benefit everyone equally, of course. Creating a system of universal health coverage or implementing a NIT would help poor families more than rich ones, and black ones more than white ones. But their potential to help everyone might defang and destigmatize them, once in place—even if they did not do enough to repair the deep, deep damage that keeps black families poorer, less educated, and less wealthy than white families. All the talk about robots and technological unemployment and worlds without work distinguishes UBI from welfare—a distinction that has muted a conversation about race and universal benefits that seems so salient, vital, obvious.

For her part, Jackson said that she was happy to go to the Capitol to try to change minds about welfare. "I felt like they needed to talk to more people who are actually in the programs," Jackson told me. "The numbers are one thing. The reality is another. I do feel like it's the people aspect that's missing." Still, she told me that no congressional office had followed up with her after she testified. And as far as I could tell, she is one of just a handful of welfare recipients who has addressed Congress since the Clinton reforms.

CHAPTER EIGHT

The $10 Trillion Gift

ON OCTOBER 24, 1975, 90 PERCENT OF ICELAND'S WOMEN WENT on strike. Dads were left to change diapers, make breakfasts, soothe tantrums, and put on outfits. Children accompanied their fathers and grandfathers to office buildings, docks, factories, and work sites, with nurseries shut down and schools canceling classes. Sausages reportedly sold out at grocery stores, because they were easy enough for men to make for their kids. Shops closed. Restaurants and cafés shuttered. Theaters went dark. The national airline canceled flights. Banks scrambled to find tellers. At the same time, tens of thousands of Icelandic women crowded a square in Reykjavik, to embrace, hold signs, and sing protest chants.

The Women's Day Off, as organizer Gerdur Steinthorsdottir told the *New York Times,* was meant to "show that women are indispensable to the country's economic and national life." She declared it an extraordinary success, as did many other Icelanders, male and female, conservative and liberal. "What happened that day was the first step for women's emancipation in Iceland," the former president Vigdís Finnbogadóttir later told the BBC. (At the time of the demonstration, she was a divorced single mother; the Day Off helped to inspire her to run for office.) "It completely paralyzed the country and opened the eyes of many men."

Economists have long known that women's work—in particular, women's care work—has unrecognized, and in some ways unrecognizable, value. Giving birth to and raising children, tending to the disabled and the sick, aiding the elderly, and giving succor to the dying: few things are of more societal importance. But much of that labor goes unpaid, and when it is paid, it is often done so with low wages and scant benefits. Unpaid care work goes unaccounted for in our economic statistics, is left off of government ledgers, and is discounted in the public mind.

Some think tanks, academics, and government offices have tried to give a sense of the value of uncompensated care work to the global economy, and the numbers they come up with boggle the mind. The research arm of the American Association of Retired Persons estimates that the 40 million family caregivers in the United States provide half a trillion dollars of unpaid care to adults alone every year, with two-thirds of that work performed by older women. A study in the *Lancet* medical journal estimates that women in thirty-two countries provide $1.5 trillion worth of health care each year. The McKinsey Global Institute estimates that if women's unpaid care work were compensated at the minimum wage around the world, it would add 11 percent, or $12 trillion, to global output. (That is equivalent to the annual output of China, by the way.)

More broadly, economists estimate that care workers provide the labor equivalent of 15 to 65 percent of GDP in every single country, with the tally estimated at 26 percent in the United States, 40 percent in Switzerland, and 63 percent in India. One Organization for Economic Cooperation and Development study estimated the value of unpaid care work in terms of both replacement cost (how much it would take to pay someone to do all those hours of work) and opportunity cost (how much people would earn if they worked instead of doing it). The replacement cost estimates came out to between 16 percent and 43 percent of GDP for various economies. This translates into tens of trillions of dollars of care work a year, most of it performed by women, and much by women of color.

Yet somehow these vast sums seem small, and these dollar characterizations feel cheap. As the famed English economist Arthur Cecil Pigou argued, social welfare cannot "be brought directly or indirectly into relation with the measuring-rod of money." Uncompensated care work is not a service that happens to be performed for free, but the most fundamental of economic utilities. Unpaid care workers provide the infrastructure that lets formal labor exist. Given that women perform most of this work, as Iceland's women tried to demonstrate in the fall of 1975, there is no global economy without them, any more than there would be a global economy without men. As feminists have long argued, citing Marx and Engels, there is no "productive labor" without "reproductive labor."

Part of the promise of a UBI would be for society to compensate people for their unpaid labor. "It's society that's getting a free ride on women's unrewarded contributions to the perpetuation of the human race," Judith Shulevitz writes in an opinion piece for the *New York Times*. "I say it's time for something like reparations." To advocate for a UBI as a kind of atonement for deep gender disparities in the workforce is certainly a controversial idea. A paycheck is hardly the only means of societal recognition, and many families split up paid and unpaid work with an appreciation for the inherent value of both. But a UBI is a powerful rejection of the notion that people who toil without pay do not contribute.

That gets to another argument for universal and unconditional programs. It is not just that a UBI would help to improve wages for care workers, or make child care affordable, or compensate women for all the unpaid labor they do—though it would do all those things. It is that it would cement every person's place in society as having value, and ensure that every person had some minimal level of capital and, thus, some minimal level of choice. It would reinforce the idea that labor and work are not and never have been the same thing, and it would challenge the notion that gross domestic product, jobs growth, and earnings are the most important measures of an economy.

•••

On a hazy morning shortly before Christmas, I spent a day shadowing a worker named Roxana Giron. She had fled El Salvador as a teenager after a family member had attempted to sell her to a group of soldiers during the country's brutal civil war, making her way to Los Angeles and later to Las Vegas. This day, like most days, she woke up before dawn in her stucco-and-wood ranch home not far from the glow and gleam of the Strip. She dressed herself in a crisp health care uniform and fed Peanut, her four-month-old Chihuahua mix. Soaking in the last few minutes of silence in her house, she assembled some croissant, ham, and cheese sandwiches for breakfast. "I wish it could be eight o'clock in the morning, not five o'clock in the morning, when the alarm goes off," she told me. "I am so sleepy."

Next, Giron, who was forty-four years old at the time, woke up her teenage daughter Karla, turning on the lights in her pink-and-glitter bedroom and moving her toward the bathroom for a shower. She pulled the urine-soaked sheets and waterproof mattress cover off the girl's bed and put them in the washing machine in the garage. She stripped her daughter down and coaxed her into the water. A few minutes later, Giron wrapped her in a towel and shooed her back to her bedroom to dress her in an adult diaper and clean clothing.

Karla squealed when she saw me at her kitchen table. "Stay still," Giron said, nudging her into a chair. With the teenager absorbed with YouTube and her unexpected visitor, Giron went to get up her older daughter, Danniella. She went through the same process: waking her up, stripping her soiled sheets, taking off her clothes, putting the linens in the garage, coaxing her into the shower, putting on a clean outfit, trying to brush her hair.

Both girls were born with severe developmental disabilities, Giron told me, and Karla had never become verbal. In addition, both have diabetes and Danniella has a severe mood disorder, meaning that the two girls require constant care and supervision. "You can't leave them at home alone," Giron said. "They would not cut themselves with knives or touch a flame. But if they take a candy they could die. I don't keep candy in the house, but they could eat something and die."

Giron put their croissant sandwiches onto paper plates and popped them into the microwave. She cut them into small pieces with a pair of scissors and poured the girls some carrot juice. While the sandwiches cooled, she grabbed the girls' fingers for a blood-sugar test, and quickly swabbed and stabbed Karla's upper arm to administer insulin. She gave Danniella her mood-stabilizing medication. "She just gets so angry, and she throws fits," Giron said.

During the day, Karla goes to a local school for children with special needs, which she can attend until she is twenty-two. Danniella is on a waiting list for a spot at an adult special-education center. Roxana's husband, Oscar, helps to take care of the two of them when she is at work. But mostly their care falls to her, she told me: nobody else can bathe them, and hiring an aide would be far, far outside the family's budget.

Giron works an especially exaggerated version of the "second shift," as described by Arlie Hochschild, the Berkeley sociologist, three decades ago. Many women, Hochschild noted, work a double every day, taking care of homes and children and parents and sick relatives when they are not formally on the clock. Accounting for both paid labor and unpaid care work, women toiled for on average a month longer than their spouses each and every year, she estimated—an accounting backed up by a number of other tallies. Men do twice as much housework as they did in the 1960s, and spend three times as much time with their kids. At the same time, women have cut their housework hours in half. But even with these changes, mothers spend double the time with children that fathers do, at an average of 13.5 hours a week. They do roughly twice the housework. Fathers tend to have more leisure time than mothers too.

These numbers add up in terms of child care and increasingly in terms of elder care: As the baby boomers age, women are called on to care for their parents as well. The share of adult children providing personal care or money to a parent has tripled in the past fifteen years, one study by MetLife found, with women tending to provide direct care and men offering cash support for their relatives. A growing number of women are now caring for both children and parents, as members of the so-called sandwich generation. "The baby boom generation is reaching retirement age, and

my grandmother's generation is the fastest-growing generation in the country," Ai-jen Poo, the labor advocate, told me.
"The need is growing exponentially and we've got nothing
in place to support it." Women are much more likely to take
time to care for a sick or disabled relative as well. One study
shows that women are thirteen times more likely to be the
sole carer for a sick child, and five times more likely to take
a sick kid to his or her doctor's appointment. (Men, as a general point, are much more likely to see these tasks as a "joint
responsibility" than women.)

This is hardly an American phenomenon. In every country represented in a recent World Economic Forum report,
men accumulated more hours of paid work than women. A
much higher share of them were participating in the paid
labor force, a gap that grows during the peak earnings years
of the forties. In every country, their earnings are higher,
with men making an average of $20,000 a year around the
globe and women making $11,000. In every country, their
pay rates are higher too, and they make more per hour spent
in paid labor. Yet, erasing the distinction between paid and
unpaid labor, it was women who did the lion's share of work.
The average man's workday lasts for seven hours and forty-
seven minutes. The average woman's workday lasts for eight
hours and thirty-nine minutes.

"It is simply valuable work because it is a lot of what it
means to be human," said Saadia Zahidi, the head of employment and gender initiatives at the World Economic Forum.
Yet it goes overlooked and undertallied and unappreciated.

. . .

In the United States, there is a related crisis to contend with:
the exorbitant cost of child care. Washington does not require businesses to offer paid time off for people having chil-

dren, just twelve weeks of unpaid leave for certain qualified workers. In that, the country is unusual. According to the Organization for Economic Cooperation and Development, it is the only advanced economy that does not have a government program to pay new mothers or require companies to do so. (Finland, the Slovak Republic, and Hungary all provide three years of paid leave, and the average across the thirty-four higher-income nations studied is just over a year.) Just 12 percent of American private-sector workers keep their paychecks when they are home with an infant.

It is not just rich nations that the United States lags behind either. According to the International Labor Organization, it is one of only two countries out of 185, the other being New Guinea, that does not provide some form of aid to new parents. Iraq and Afghanistan have paid maternity leave programs, at least on paper, and the United States does not. The country also lags behind its rich peers in mandating that businesses offer unpaid leave, according to the OECD report, giving its mothers a shorter spell of protection than all but two other countries. And just half of private employees are eligible for unpaid leave under the Family and Medical Leave Act.

This sinks families' earnings in the weeks and months after a child is born, in many cases never to recover. New parents stop paying bills, eat up their savings, and cut their leave short to return to work. According to one survey, five in six workers with unpaid or partially paid leave—meaning most workers with kids—put off spending when their baby was small. Plus, the United States is the only country where a not-insignificant number of mothers return to work within days or weeks of giving birth.

After that, things do not get much easier. By and large, American mothers want to or have to keep working: about 58 percent of mothers with infants under a year old are part of the workforce, rising to 64 percent for mothers with children under six. But a lack of spots in good child care centers and the high cost of care, along with the rigid inflexibility of many workplaces, make it difficult. About six in ten parents with infants or toddlers struggle to find care that is both high quality and affordable. In a study of eight states, the Center for American Progress found that more than 40 percent of children were living in "child care deserts," meaning a "ZIP code with at least 30 children under the age of 5 and either no child care centers or so few centers that there are more than three times as many children under age 5 as there are spaces in centers." A majority of children in rural areas live in such deserts, as does one in three children in urban areas.

That lack of child care options correlates with the unaffordability of care. The annual cost to put a child into infant care ranges from $3,972 at a family home in Mississippi to $17,062 at a center in Massachusetts. In most states, the cost of infant care exceeds 10 percent of the median income of a married couple. In more than half, it costs more to send a baby to day care than it does to send a young adult to a public college. Of course, like everything, the burden is heaviest on the very poor: families making less than $1,500 a month who pay for child care spend nearly 40 percent of their earnings on it.

These costs have skyrocketed even as household earnings have stagnated and the federal minimum wage has stayed stuck at $7.25 an hour. Families with working mothers have seen their weekly cost of child care increase from an average of $84 in 1985 to $143 in 2011, after accounting for inflation. But the median household income has barely budged, and families at the bottom of the income scale have performed particularly poorly earnings-wise.

The federal government has failed to help families cover

these rising costs, doing little outside of expanding the Child Tax Credit and the EITC. (Those out of work are out of luck for the EITC.) Total federal spending on child care assistance—done through the Child Care and Development Block Grant and Temporary Assistance for Needy Families, or welfare, program—fell to just $11.3 billion in 2014. That is the lowest dollar amount since 2002. And the block grant currently serves the smallest number of children it has in almost two decades.

The vast majority of families in poverty with children do not receive any help for child care. This again makes the United States a rarity: its public child care spending as a share of GDP is one-quarter of that of sixteen other OECD countries. For that reason, parents earning less than $30,000 a year are more likely than not to seek family members to care for their children, where they can. And lower-income mothers are becoming more and more likely to drop out of the labor force altogether. About one in three stay-at-home moms falls below the poverty line today, compared with just 14 percent in 1970.

The effects are profound, with the United States essentially shunting women to lower earnings trajectories and shoving them out of the workforce. A paper by a Princeton economist found that the rising cost of child care between 1990 and 2010 caused a 5 percent drop in employment among all American women, and a 13 percent drop in the employment of women with a child under five. Women's participation in paid work has been falling in the United States, even as it has grown in many other OECD countries, among them France, Germany, Spain, Australia, Japan, and the United Kingdom. In all of those countries, a higher proportion of women are working than in the United States. This change is unheralded but dramatic: the United States' female labor participation rate has fallen from sixth among twenty-two OECD countries to seventeenth between 1990 and 2010.

•••

After dropping Karla off at her special-education school, Giron went to go see the three clients she had that day. Her first stop was at a tidy McMansion near the Hoover Dam, nestled in a desert neighborhood with startling jewel-green lawns. Her elderly client had had two strokes and uses a walker. "He has a lot of trouble balancing and walking," Giron said. "If I don't go and give him a bath, he doesn't get a bath." On this now-bright morning, she bathed him and changed his sheets, popping her third load of laundry of the day into a washing machine. She helped him dress, cleaned the bathroom, and prepared some food.

"I apply cream on the back of his legs," she said. "He has a cream that helps him with the pain." She chatted with him, smiled at him, brushed his hair. After two hours, she had to leave. "It's impossible to finish everything," she said. "Today, I left the clothes in the dryer. Tomorrow, I'll leave ten minutes for those. And I will do everything all over again with him."

She then drove to meet her next client, an elderly man who cannot walk. "I have to move him from the bed to the wheelchair, because he cannot do that himself," she said, gesturing to show how she pushes, rolls, pivots, and supports the body heavier than her own. "I give him a shower, and make sure he is clean and has clean clothes. I put him in the wheelchair and move him to a chair in the living room." She makes him his food, and puts his medication in a cup to take. "I can't put it in his mouth," she said, for legal reasons. "I tell him to take the pills he has to take, and watch him.

He has dementia, and he gets so much worse if he does not take his pills."

As he ate, this day, she changed his bedsheets and did the laundry. She washed his dishes and cleaned his bathroom. "With him, I have enough time," she said. Four hours, for $40. "He has a grandson nearby," Giron said, when I asked if her client's family ever came to care for him. "He's always complaining when it's time for me to leave. He always says, 'You're leaving! I'll be so lonely!' And with the third one, he has two sons in New York. He does not see them."

That third client is a Vietnam veteran paralyzed from the waist down. "He's really injured," Giron told me, hopping into her car. "I use a big machine to strap him up in the bed and transfer him to the wheelchair, an electric wheelchair. And then on the wheelchair, I get it as close as I can to the bathroom. Then I take a big plank and put it between the bench in the bathroom and the wheelchair, and put a strap on him. I have to be careful because he could fall down!" Using planks, straps, levers, and handles, she helps him onto the toilet and then into the shower.

"You know how much responsibility it is working with disabled seniors, because I have to be careful not to hurt them," she said. "The strap I put on him, it has to be really secure. I make sure it's secure three times, because if he fell down? There's no way for me to carry him. I would have to call the paramedics."

Care work—being a home health aide, an eldercare assistant, or a personal-care assistant, for instance—is by some measures the United States' fastest-growing job. Yet it is also one of its worst-paid, with median incomes a bit more than $10 an hour and many workers toiling for the federal minimum of $7.25. Moreover, the opportunities for wage increases and promotions are close to nil. In 2016, Giron got a 10-cent raise.

She loved the work, she told me. She saw herself as being called to be a care worker. But the family was already behind on its bills, and was falling further and further back as Christmas approached. "I just keep doing extensions, extensions, extensions," she said. "I need to pay my bills and it's really hard right now. My cell phone got cut off because I could not afford it. I owe $700 to the electric company." Plus, she spent nearly every waking moment of every day aiding someone with a limited capacity to care for themselves, never alone, always on watch. "My friends say, 'Are you going to do this for the rest of your life?' I'm forty-four now. I'm getting older. I'm getting tired," she said. She had no idea who would take care of the girls in the event that she could not.

That women tend to take these care jobs reflects personal preference in many cases, to be sure. But it also reflects a broader societal expectation that women be caretakers. "By the time a woman earns her first dollar, her occupational choice is the culmination of years of education, guidance by mentors, expectations set by those who raised her, hiring practices of firms, and widespread norms and expectations about work-family balance held by employers, co-workers, and society," argue Jessica Schieder and Elise Gould of the Economic Policy Institute. "Even though women disproportionately enter lower-paid, female-dominated occupations, this decision is shaped by discrimination, societal norms, and other forces beyond women's control."

Plus, when a profession becomes "feminized," when women start to make up a majority of its workers, occupations start to pay less. This is part of what the Harvard economist Claudia Goldin calls the "pollution theory of discrimination," in which working women are the toxins that harm a given profession's prestige. One Israeli study looked at jobs that went from majority-male to majority-female between 1950 and 2000, following what happened to their wage rates. For workers at camps and fairgrounds, median hourly wages plunged 57 percentage points. The same happened for ticket agents (43 percentage points), designers (34), housekeepers (21), and biologists (18). Conversely, wages went up for jobs that started to be done mostly by men, among them computer programming. Jobs pay less when women hold them, because women hold them.

We worry about robots and Ubers and fast-food workers, but there is another crisis that is here, now, unacknowledged. It is a crisis involving the people who swaddle our infants, feed our parents, protect those with dementia, and help to heal the sick.

• • •

Right now, the United States is in the midst of a rollicking public conversation over how to make child care more affordable. Liberals are pushing for paid family leave. Ivanka Trump, in her amorphous White House role, has tried to make child care tax deductible, a boon for people who spend a lot on nannies. The archconservative senators Mike Lee of Utah and Marco Rubio of Florida have led a push to massively expand the Child Tax Credit. For liberals, the conversation is driven in part by concern over the plight of working women; for conservatives, in part by concern over falling birthrates. Yet all of these fixes feel like tinkering around the edges of a much bigger and broader problem: an unwillingness to invest in parents, value care workers, and empower families to make choices about how to raise their kids. A UBI would not be a policy primarily aimed at providing a social scaffolding for care, but it would bolster the wages of the women of color who are most often paid caregivers, help to make child care affordable, and better compensate *all* women for the second shift.

How a UBI—or another universal, unconditional benefit—would empower American women became clear to me in Las Vegas and even clearer when I looked abroad. In the Kenyan village, women and men often played different economic roles. Women spent hours doing housework, taking care of livestock, collecting firewood, cleaning up, and watching children. Relatively few seemed to leave their homes to work or trade in the local villages during the day, giving them little cash to fall back on and making them reliant on male partners and relatives. Men, on the other hand, were able to perform a number of different paid tasks, like fishing on Lake Victoria, giving people rides to and from the market, and toiling as day laborers. They also seemed more likely to own income-generating property, such as a field or a motorcycle.

The data on asset ownership and income in rural Kenya demonstrates as much, with culture and politics as powerful as economics when it comes to the gender breakdown of poverty. Men own the vast majority of land in the country, for instance, and women have far less access to credit to start businesses, meaning that farms owned by women tend to be less productive than those owned by men. Women have lower educational attainment and lower earnings. And though the country recently passed a law giving women equal rights and protection, "women and many judicial officials are unaware that for the first time, the new laws supersede customary laws governing gender roles," one study found.

Much the same is true across the developing world: Women are less likely to have cash income, given the unequal division of paid and unpaid work. Laws and customs often restrict their access to assets like land and to utilities like bank accounts. "In nearly a third of developing countries, laws do not guarantee the same inheritance rights for women and men, and in an additional half of countries discriminatory customary practices against women are found," the United Nations concludes. "Moreover, about one in three married women from developing regions has no control over household spending on major purchases, and about one in ten married women is not consulted on how their own cash earnings are spent."

Given these dynamics, cash transfers might act as a powerful tool to improve the economic and social standing of women. The Overseas Development Institute, for instance, looked at both unconditional and conditional cash-transfer programs and found that they boosted a range of women's empowerment metrics. The programs cut incidents of physical, verbal, and emotional abuse. They led to women becoming more involved in their family's decision making, and also allowed women to delay marriage and to increase their use of contraception—giving them power over their bodies and the trajectories of their lives. Then, of course, cash alleviates poverty, and given that women encounter more structural barriers to increasing their incomes than men do, they might benefit more from equivalent sums. In developing nations, the United Nations reports, there is no "straightforward measure of poverty from a gender perspective," given that the household is the central unit for evaluating deprivation. But women are broadly seen as being more economically vulnerable.

For these reasons, both Arvind Subramanian and Pranab Bardhan, the Indian economists, told me that they would like to see a cash benefit go to women first. "Unlike many poor countries, certainly unlike the country with which

India is most often compared, which is China, almost three-quarters of Indian women have no income," Bardhan told me. "Three-quarters of adult women do not have an outside job. In recent years, the female participation in the labor force has actually been declining. One reason is that women who are withdrawing from the labor force had been in jobs that were oppressive and backbreaking and dead-end." A UBI would protect them from abuse, help alleviate poverty among women and children, and grant women more economic choice, he said. Subramanian agreed. "If you had enough money, you would obviously give it to everyone. But if there were financial constraints, if you had to do something that's not as big as you would want it to be, then among the constrained choices, what would be the best? Patriarchy is a big problem, and therefore one way of addressing that would be to empower women."

The same is true everywhere.

CHAPTER NINE

In It Together

DURING THE FIRST YEAR OF THE TRUMP PRESIDENCY, THE WHIS-pers of violence dredged up by his campaign became shouts. White nationalists, the KKK, and neo-Nazis were taking to the streets around the country and lauding the administration online. Expressions of racism and intolerance had markedly increased, with the Southern Poverty Law Center counting up 1,372 hate crimes in the weeks immediately following the election. In August, a car driven by a white nationalist plunged into a crowd of antiracist protesters in Charlottes-ville, Virginia, killing a young woman. Trump blamed both sides for the violence, and said that "very fine" people had been marching among the Nazis and the white supremacists, leading to widespread condemnation but little change.

The unemployment rate was drifting down to histori-cally low levels, Congress was doing little aside from cutting taxes for rich people, there were no recessions on the hori-zon or new foreign wars to be fought. Yet the moment felt out of balance. The months that ticked by had a "We Didn't Start the Fire" quality, the sheer swooning craziness of the political moment amplified by social media, an overheated political press, and twenty-four-hour cable news coverage: clashes between racists and the Antifa, Antarctica breaking apart and the coral reefs dying, Russian trolls trolling on Twitter and Facebook, the police dragging a peaceful passenger off a United Airlines plane, immigration raids at elementary schools, protesters on the Mall, the Manchester bombing, ISIS killings, campaign officials getting indicted.

It seemed to be a kind of apotheosis. Inequality and polarization had ripped households apart, and helped to segregate them by their income and their race and their beliefs. People had stopped trusting elites and institutions, including the government and the press. Social media, talk radio, and cable news became echo chambers, and isolation chambers. The absurdist, postmodern brutality of the Trump campaign and Trump presidency was just one particularly virulent expression of what felt like a long, slow falling apart.

I knew, of course, that the country was cleaving in terms of income and wealth. But it was also unraveling in political terms. According to research by Pew, Americans had become more stubborn and strident in their political opinions over the prior two decades. The typical Republican was more conservative than 94 percent of Democrats, and the typical Democrat more liberal than 92 percent of Republicans. At the same time, partisan antipathy had increased, with the share of members of each party with "very unfavorable opinions" of the other side roughly doubling. Each side started to describe the other as a danger to the country. Red parts of the United States had gotten redder. Blue parts had gotten bluer. Purple parts had disappeared. More and more Americans started to say it was important to live around people with the same views, and more and more of them said that they would decline to date someone from the other side of the aisle, or that they would object to a family member getting hitched across partisan lines.

There was cultural polarization too. Politics became tribal to the extent that Republicans and Democrats had charged and differing opinions on everything from the Gamergate scandal to whether *12 Years a Slave* should win an Oscar to whether the economy was getting better or worse to whether the stock market was doing well or tanking. By many measures, political identity became a stronger predictor of opinion than racial identity. To butcher Anaïs Nin, we were no longer seeing things as they are, but instead as we were.

Measures of social capital were falling as well. Americans were voting less. They were spending less time with neighbors and colleagues. They were less engaged with unions and churches, and thus less engaged with the "middle layer" of institutions between the family and government. "We are materially better off in many ways than in the past. But despite this real progress, there is a sense that our social fabric has seen better days," argued one report commissioned by Mike Lee, the Republican senator from Utah. "What happens in the middle layers of our society is vital to sustaining a free, prosperous, democratic, and pluralistic country. That space is held together by extended networks of cooperation and social support, norms of reciprocity and mutual obligation, trust, and social cohesion." Many on the left agreed—and so did many people abroad, looking at their own communities. It was hard to miss the rise of right-wing authoritarianism in Europe in the aughts and 2010s, buoyed by at least some of the same factors. People around the world seemed fed up, upset, and unmoored.

In this milieu, UBI advocates were making a compelling case that the policy would start to heal the fractures seen in these advanced economies—helping with polarization and encouraging people to come together. "Our debate is increasingly relevant today, and will be tomorrow and tomorrow and tomorrow because of the political context," Guy Standing, the prominent British economist and UBI advocate, told the crowd at the Basic Income Earth Network conference that I attended in South Korea. "The political context, in which we are seeing neo-fascist populists in the form of Donald Trump, God bless his little soul, Brexit in Britain, various right-wing unsavory characters in various parts of Europe and others like them around the world. Unless we move to having some form of basic security for all," he said, "we will face a dystopia of emerging threats of the political far right. None of us in this room wants that. And we are one of the few groups around the world offering a future, a vision, of something exciting, of something to give people a reason for hope."

A UBI, I thought, was not so much about welfare as inclusion. Universal cash programs were a way of providing the poor with an opportunity to participate in the economy. Universal cash programs were a way of ensuring that all members of a society had a foundation to build on. Universal cash programs boosted the power of workers. Universal cash programs provided women with choices when it came to raising their children and starting their careers. Universal cash programs were a powerful tool for social justice, ensuring that the minority would get what the majority got. Universal cash programs squeezed racial prejudice and paternalism out of the safety net, trusting people to use what they had in the best way for them. Universal cash programs were a way of helping overlooked rural communities. Universal cash programs were a way of aiding children, regardless of the competencies of their parents.

At a time of polarization and inequality, universal cash

programs offered empowerment, inclusion, and togetherness
—something for everyone, it seemed. They were not a safety
net. They were a foundation.

• • •

A group of women were sitting in a conference room, talking about being Alaskans.

"We wanted to invite the dozen most interesting women
in Anchorage today, and since they were busy, we're good
here," joked a genial guy named Paul, who was running the
focus group for Chris Hughes's Economic Security Project.
The women went around the room to introduce themselves:
an adoptive mother, a truck driver, a multilevel marketing
scheme promoter, a home day care operator, a fisherwoman,
a nonprofit worker. He then asked all of them to describe
how things were going in the state using a word they would
use to describe the weather. Most picked "cloudy," citing the
local problems with drug and alcohol abuse, economic hard-
ship, and political strife. "I just don't see a sunnier outlook
coming," one woman said.

About half said they were thinking of leaving the state,
given how hard it had become to make a decent living. "I'd
miss PFD," one woman lamented, as the rest of the table
concurred. They were talking about the Permanent Fund
Dividend, the closest thing that the United States has to a
basic income. What was it, exactly, the focus-group leader
asked them, wanting to draw out their understanding of this
UBI-type payment. Where did it come from and why did
they all receive money from it?

One woman said the government might want to disburse
excess money in the state budget. Another suggested it was
designed to offset the cost of living in such a remote place,

where milk can cost as much as $10 a gallon. "It was written into the Alaska State Constitution. The people of Alaska had rights to the oil underground, and so the permanent fund is the . . ." a woman said, searching for the proper language. "I don't know if royalties is the right word, but it's the earnings from that, and then that gets divided among all of the people. Alaskans have rights to the oil the companies are taking."

All three answers were in some sense correct, most of all the third. The oil-rich state earns a portion of the revenues on the black gold pumped out of its lands and waters every year—unlike the coal pulled out of the ground in West Virginia, the sludge drawn from the shale sands in North Dakota, the electricity generated from the wind off Massachusetts, or the energy that gets collected from the sun in Nevada. That money goes into something called the Alaska Permanent Fund, which currently totals $50 billion. Each fall, the Alaska Permanent Fund writes a check to every man, woman, and child in the state, save for people in prison and those convicted of felonies. The amount is not huge, generally ranging from $1,000 to $2,000. But every year, it lifts about 3 percent of the state's population above the poverty line. It does the most for the most vulnerable—children, the elderly and the disabled, those living in deep poverty or in far-flung rural communities, and Alaska Natives.

Of late, the state of Alaska has been fighting over the proper use of the Permanent Fund money. In 2017, Governor Bill Walker slashed the state's dividend in half to roughly $1,100 a person, using the saved funds to help plug the state's budget hole. In a way, it made sense: the Permanent Fund money would still be used for Alaskans, just distributed to them through the filter of the state government rather than through their mailboxes. But Walker's move was unpopular, and the women gathered around the table said as much. It was not the state's right to spend the PFD as it needed. It was the people's right to spend it as they saw fit. "We're really trying to send a signal: if you want to change the Permanent Fund, it has to be done with a statewide discussion, passed by the legislature, signed into law by the governor," Bill Wielechowski, a Democratic state senator who opposed the Walker plan, told me. "It is not intended to be set up so that one individual determines where the money goes. It is for the people to spend."

Survey and poll data shows that—unsurprisingly—Alaskans tend to spend the money pretty well. Three-quarters of the respondents in one survey said that they used the money on "essentials, emergencies, paying off debt, or for future activities like retirement or education." Four in five said that it improves their quality of life. The women in the focus group did express some consternation with people who wasted it, or showed up in the state just to get it. "We have a lot of families that come up and bring six, seven kids, and they get the big payoff, and they leave someone here, and then they leave, so they're taking those resources from us," one woman complained. "I think it needs to be vetted a little bit better."

Others admitted that they were not the most prudent stewards of the funds themselves. A younger woman chimed in. "My family wasn't super well-off when I was growing up, and I'm still struggling," she admitted. "Once a year, I get this huge amount of money. . . . It's hard to discipline yourself to spend it on bills and things that you need to be spending it on, rather than [thinking], 'Oh, my God. I have four thousand dollars. I'm going to go buy a new TV.'" But she was a rarity. People needed the money and tended to spend it on their needs.

Paying out a share of the national wealth to all citizens

has surfaced as a policy from time to time, across civilizations and centuries, much like a UBI itself. Before the birth of Christ, Rome passed a law providing 5 *modii,* or about 70 pounds, of grain to all citizens over the age of ten. Half a millennium later, the Caliph Abu Bakr provided a 10-dirham guaranteed income to all men, women, and children living in the Rashidun Caliphate. Later still, Thomas Paine argued for recompense for those shut out of the system of landed property. And more recently, the Yale law professors Bruce Ackerman and Anne Alstott have suggested providing a lump-sum payment of $80,000 to each American on their twenty-first birthday, to help foster a "stakeholder society."

Such a citizens' income, as it is often called, sees payments as a natural benefit of being part of a community, rather than a handout. They are a birthright, not a fix. "Everybody is entitled to the PFD who lives in the state of Alaska," one woman said. "Welfare is based on your income, and it's sort of like an assistance program for getting people back on their feet. The PFD is not designed to get people back on their feet." It was a right, for rich and poor, prudent and imprudent, working and unemployed. Everybody got it, and everybody got the same amount.

• • •

Returning to the question that started the book: What would happen if a $1,000 check showed up in each and every American's bank account each and every month for the rest of their lives? For the rich, not much would change. But for the poor, it would be transformative, with America's impoverished families starting to look far more middle class. Bills would get paid, houses would get fixed up, more and better food would get eaten. Those families in deep poverty, without any cash income, would disappear.

We have a sense from studies of programs like the EITC and food stamps how the more wide-ranging effects would play out. Infants and toddlers in low-income families would be less likely to be hospitalized. They would eat more. They would literally grow more. As they got older, they would enjoy better health and better grades in reading and math. That would translate into higher earnings and better educational attainment years and decades out. As adults, they might have a lower incidence of metabolic disease. They would likely live longer.

Indeed, a UBI would provide particularly strong support for the young—with Uncle Sam helping to cancel out the differences between rich kids and poor kids, and investing vastly more in people when they start out in life. The United States currently spends about three times as much per capita on the elderly as it does on children. Looking at federal programs only, it spends seven times as much on the old as the young. With a UBI, child poverty would finally be eliminated, with long-range benefits countable in terms of years of life and billions and billions of dollars of earnings. For adults, the effects would also be profound. Studies of the Mincome experiment in Dauphin showed that there were fewer hospitalizations and mental-health diagnoses among those with a guaranteed income. In the United States' NIT studies, primary earners spent more time with their children and their rates of homeownership increased.

Poverty would become less of a burden, with people using the funds as they needed. As I saw so vividly by Lake Victoria, soccer nets do nothing for people who are hungry. School fees do nothing for people who need clean water. Water jugs do nothing for towns that could use farming equipment. Money, on the other hand, is universally useful and universally fungible. Just giving people money would mean that a single mother would not have to trade her food stamps for cash to keep the heat on. It would mean that she would not have to tussle with the complicated Section 8 system when what she was really struggling with was transportation costs. It would be efficient and effective.

The basic income would help the chronically poor, but it would also help the tens of millions of people who find themselves intermittently in need of support. In any given year, one in three workers leave a job. Millions of others experience a family illness, an eviction, a car breaking down. Self-employment and contract work, falling benefits and rising costs—driven by worker disempowerment, wage stagnation, and high inequality—have together created a kind of precariat that overlaps and exists just below the middle class, itself shrinking. One in three families has no savings, and half would have to borrow or sell something to come up with $400 in an emergency. A safety net is a tool to prevent deprivation among some. Universal cash benefits are a tool of insurance and self-determination for all.

A universal cash grant also might help promote dynamism across the country at a time when the cosmopolitan coasts and the rural middle are cleaving apart. "In the recent past, the focus on inequality has all been about where you fall in the distribution, whether in the 10 percent, 1 percent, or top tenth of a percent," Jed Kolko, an economist at Indeed, a job-search site, told me. "Now that discussion is shifting to differences between groups, with those groups being geographic." That bears out in a report by the Economic Innovation Group, which found that the economy has become more and more reliant on a smaller and smaller number of "super-performing" counties to generate new businesses and jobs. Just twenty—in the Bay Area, New York, Boston, and Seattle, among other places—accounted for half of the net increase in businesses between 2010 and 2014. The country is seeing "a massive and historically unprecedented" regional imbalance, it found. But a UBI would provide a wage and investment boost to overlooked and underdeveloped parts of the country, helping people the most where the cost of living was the cheapest.

The effects of inequality would be blunted in terms of consumption, and in more subtle ways. Educational gaps might finally start to close. (Right now, rich kids are five times more likely to get a bachelor's degree by the time they are twenty-four than students from poor families.) We might see more ingenuity and innovation across the population. American entrepreneurs tend to come from significantly richer families, which have the ability to provide both start-up capital and the promise of a safety net to their children. One study found that "the probability of self-employment depends sensitively upon whether the individual ever received a gift or inheritance." A UBI would provide capital for every entrepreneurial spirit with an idea, something that could have dramatic consequences for all of us.

Recessions might sting less, with all families having a buoy to keep them afloat. The labor market might change, with more people engaged in creative and care work. The low-wage labor market would have to transform, with businesses forced to offer better wages and improved benefits to workers. Prices might rise; some individuals might fall out of the labor market; high taxes might squeeze the rich and force businesses offshore. Still, the Roosevelt Institute, the lefty think tank, has estimated that a UBI could expand the economy by something like 13 percent over its first eight years, and leave it permanently larger for all of us.

• • •

A UBI would raise a difficult conversation about who "all of us" are, driving a wedge between citizens and noncitizens, between native-born Americans and immigrants and the millions and millions of mixed-status families who blur that line. Already, many Americans see the welfare state as incompatible with immigration. "A lot of immigrants are low-wage workers. They're not skilled, a lot of them. They don't have as much education as most Americans and so they never do get up to the point where they would ever pay enough in taxes to make back that check," Megan McArdle, a right-of-center Bloomberg View columnist, said on PBS, arguing that a UBI would not work with our current immigrant population. "Even if you just limited it to their children, the political support for importing people whose children will then be entitled to the same $15,000 a year as your children—I don't think that would ever be politically viable."

There is a deep-held belief that refugees and immigrants are drawn to strong welfare states and are less deserving of aid because of it. Back in 1999, the economist George Borjas of Harvard posited the existence of "welfare magnets" in a widely discussed and highly influential paper, noting that immigrants clustered in states with more generous benefits. Yet such immigrants seem to be attracted to places with more vibrant economies, job opportunities, and fellow immigrants—not a bigger dole. A more insidious barrier is a perception that refugees and immigrants drain the economy of wages and growth. Roughly 40 percent of respondents to one recent Gallup poll said that immigrants drive down wages and hurt the economy overall. Two-thirds of respondents to a separate poll said that immigrants cost the nation "too much" in terms of social services. Yet, contrary to public opinion, immigrants and refugees tend to pay more in taxes than they receive in welfare benefits. One study of refugees who resettled in the United States, for instance, found that they paid on average $21,000 more in taxes than they received in benefits over their first two decades in the United States. A Congressional Budget Office study found that increasing legal immigration would boost government spending on Medicaid, tax credits, and insurance subsidies, but would also generate hundreds of billions of dollars in new tax revenue—enough to reduce the deficit by $1 trillion over twenty years. And undocumented immigrants, barred from most safety-net programs but required to hand over part of their earnings to Uncle Sam, pay billions in federal, state, and local taxes each year.

Most people do not let facts get in the way of feelings, though, and evidence suggests that a more generous safety net might increase antipathy to immigrants and refugees—with white Americans treating immigrants not dissimilarly to the way that they treat native-born black and Latino Americans. A decade ago, Ann-Helén Bay and Axel West Pedersen polled Norwegian voters about the potential of instituting a basic income in the country. Most Norwegians liked the idea, unless they were told that immigrants would benefit. "A third of supporters switched to opposition when the proposal was modified to have non-Norwegians receive the benefit," writes Dylan Matthews of Vox, summarizing the research. "This fits into a broader literature showing that increasing racial and ethnic diversity can prompt backlash by native white voters, who resent the newcomers and vote for right-wing parties in response. The right-wing governments they elect then enact welfare cutbacks, both to punish the immigrants whom their voters fear and because right-wing parties love welfare cuts in general."

The same bias might exist here in the United States. After Trump's surprise election, the Democratic pollster Stan

Greenberg held focus groups with white voters in Macomb County, Michigan, which had twice gone for Obama before swinging Republican and voting for Trump. Concerns about immigration were pervasive, despite the low numbers and negligible jobs impact of immigrants in the region. "I went and finally signed up for Medicaid, and I'm standing in the damn welfare office, and I'm looking around at all of these people that can't even say hello to me in English," one person said. "They have the healthcare, they have the food stamps. . . . If you can come from somewhere else, why can't we all get it?"

As Matthews notes, the problem might be solved by "building a wall around the welfare state," rather than around the country, as famously put by the late William Niskanen of the libertarian Cato Institute. That is already what the United States does, to a large extent: allowing in legal and undocumented immigrants, then barring them from accessing benefits. Still, a UBI might increase racial antipathy. It might increase anti-immigrant sentiment, and spur the adoption of anti–immigrant restrictions and policies. It might also foster the creation of a two-tier labor market, with businesses seeking out undocumented workers who would be far cheaper to hire than native-born citizens. Less migration would mean a more sclerotic economy and an older country. A UBI might foster abject racism.

There are no easy answers, especially for progressives.

• • •

In a separate focus group for the Economic Security Project, Paul quizzed a group of Alaskan men about their understanding of the state's economy and experiences with its cash-grant program. At one point, he asked them why they valued the PFD, beyond having dollars in pocket and cash in hand. "We're benefiting as citizens of this state from the resources that are being removed from this state," said a retired pipeline worker, who copped to liking "boating, rock hunting, mining, fishing, all that good stuff" in the focus group. As another man put it, "It kind of makes me feel like I'm a shareholder in the state. Like I own a portion of it."

Making the case that a UBI would be sharing the public wealth, rather than simply taxing and redistributing income, might sound far-fetched or impossible. During the 2012 election, the Republican nominee, Mitt Romney, infamously divided the country into "makers" and "takers," castigating before a roomful of donors the 47 percent leeching off the 53 percent. "My job is not to worry about those people," he said, arguing that they would vote for Obama anyway. "I'll never convince them they should take personal responsibility and care for their lives." He described them as the people "dependent upon government, who believe that they are victims, who believe the government has a responsibility to care for them, who believe that they are entitled to health care, to food, to housing, to you-name-it."

A UBI might make the resentment between the makers and the takers, those working people taxed for a UBI and those lazy people relying on it, yet worse. But the distinction between makers and takers is and has always been a false one. Romney was wrong both on the details and in terms of a broader, more philosophical understanding of the economy and social policy. For one, 82 percent of American households pay income tax and payroll taxes—not 53 percent. The remainder are mostly composed of the elderly and the retired, the very poor, or the unemployed. Plus, lower-income families get hit by less progressive state and local taxes, as well as paying Uncle Sam a disproportionate burden of cigarette taxes and buying up most of the lottery tickets. The notion that the poor are not paying in is simply untrue.

More important, all Americans "make" and "take" over their lives, and no business or individual is truly self-made, no matter how hardworking and innovative. Children take. Adults make. The elderly take again. Even those working adults who are makers are takers too, benefiting from roads, police protection, foreign policy, clean water, and so on. Those out of the labor force who are takers are often also makers, such as stay-at-home parents and kids who are in school to boost their later earnings. Everybody pays something in, and everybody gets something out. Everybody deserves to pay in, and everybody deserves to get something out. Everybody benefits from paying in, and everybody benefits from getting something out.

Ideally, a UBI would be an acknowledgment that our market economy leaves people out and behind, creating poverty and punishing individuals who cannot or are not working for an employer. As Martin Luther King Jr. argued, "We have come a long way in our understanding of human motivation and of the blind operation of our economic system. Now we realize that dislocations in the market operation of our economy and the prevalence of discrimination thrust people into idleness and bind them in constant or frequent unemployment against their will. The poor are less often dismissed from our conscience today by being branded as inferior and incompetent." A UBI would undercut the basis of such judgments and be a powerful force for human dignity. It would acknowledge our interdependence as well as our independence.

A universal, unrestricted cash benefit—just giving people money—would promote the "true individual freedom" that comes from "economic security and independence," as Franklin D. Roosevelt argued seventy years ago. It would give everyone the freedom to live their life, while also conveying a sense of communal investment in each and every person, through every stage of life, as well as in the public goods to help society more broadly thrive.

CHAPTER TEN

$1,000 a Month

THE QUESTION IS HOW TO DO IT.

Charles Murray wants to give all adults $10,000 a year while eliminating the entirety of the welfare state. Andy Stern wants to give adults $1,000 a month while eliminating much of it. Yet others advocate for pairing a UBI with a radical program of open borders and a dramatically curtailed workweek, as the Dutch writer Rutger Bregman does in his book *Utopia for Realists*. Yet others see a UBI as a way to bridge the country to a postcapitalist world without work, as Nick Srnicek and Alex Williams do in their book *Inventing the Future*. Yet others push for giving a grant to children at birth, to be used in adulthood and to be taxed back at death. As with everything in social policy, the how depends upon the why, and the whys are radically diverse. The debate is vibrant, but often downright confusing and divorced from the realities of our current economy and politics. How do we capture as many of the upsides of a UBI as possible, with as few of the downsides?

It is a challenge, and it requires understanding the implications and details of various policies. The expense is one obvious downside, so let's start there. Providing a $1,000-a-month UBI to every American citizen would mean spending something like an additional $3.9 trillion a year. That is equivalent to a fifth of the American economy—and equal to every penny the federal government currently spends, on everything from building bridges to fighting wars to caring for the elderly to prosecuting crimes to protecting wetlands. If politicians were to fully finance that expansion of benefits through the tax code as it is structured now, it would mean steep income-tax increases not just on the wealthiest Americans but on middle-income Americans too. The top 1 percent of earners pay about 40 percent of all income taxes, which comes out to about $540 billion a year. You could tax away every penny they earned, and it would still not come close to paying for a full-fat UBI, in other words. "Nothing in the history of this country suggests Americans are ready to add that kind of burden to their current taxes," the columnist Eduardo Porter has argued in the *New York Times,* in one of many such pieces questioning the policy on the grounds of its cost.

But eliminating or trimming other programs would help defray the expense. Right now, the government spends roughly $2.7 trillion on its social-insurance programs, including Social Security, Medicaid, Medicare, unemployment insurance, benefits for veterans, and so on. Nearly a trillion dollars of that total goes to Social Security alone. The government also spends more than half a trillion dollars a year on defense, a number that might be winnowed down, particularly if the next war were fought with hackers rather than tanks. Still, a $1,000-a-month benefit, or a smaller one, would require new spending and likely new sources of revenue, regardless of how deeply other budgets were cut.

Next up is the concern that a UBI in and of itself would

not eliminate poverty and that it might even end up increasing deprivation. Transferring all the money from means-tested programs outside of health care would yield a monthly payment of just $132 a month per person. That is far below what many impoverished individuals currently receive from the government. Adding in tax expenditures for the middle class, like the mortgage interest deduction and incentives for retirement savings, still only gets you $3,591 a year per person. Giving the same thing to everyone means spreading the butter a lot thinner, meaning that we need more butter.

Stepping back further, there is a more philosophically wonky conundrum UBI raises. In a world with limited resources, does it really make sense for everyone to get something, and for everyone to get the same thing? The federal government is, in some sense, an institutional Robin Hood that takes money from the rich and gives money to the poor, a function that has become more and more prevalent over time, as the welfare state, health initiatives, and social-insurance programs have expanded and the population has aged. A UBI could mean diverting money from the poor to everyone, including the rich.

Then there is the concern that a UBI would become an easy-to-cut entitlement targeted by fiscal hawks. Programs that benefit the middle class, like Social Security and Medicare, tend to be more popular than initiatives aiding the poor, such as welfare. Nevertheless, safety-net programs have expanded greatly in recent years, as the government has bumped up the value of the EITC, signed up millions of people for food stamps, and extended Medicaid to 12 million people and counting. The effort has reduced poverty in the country, full stop. At the same time, programs aiding individuals regardless of income have mostly stayed static, and in some cases have come up for cuts. The unemployment-insurance program, for instance, has gotten whittled down in the postrecession years. Republicans are targeting Social Security and Medicare. Benefiting the middle class is no guarantee against diminishment, in other words.

Still, the knee-jerk opposition to some form of a UBI— crying that it is too expensive or unrealistic—feels overwrought. Raising enough revenue for a $1,000-a-month UBI is more a matter of will than of mathematics, and would bring the United States' tax burden in line with that of the European social democracies. Maybe nothing in the history of this country suggests that we are ready to implement those kinds of taxes, but nothing in the realm of public policy suggests that we could not. Creating a top tax bracket at 55 percent, instituting a modest wealth tax, ending the mortgage interest deduction, implementing a value-added tax— proposals like those would get us there. Again, the United States does far less taxing and spending than other rich countries do. We are, by OECD standards, a low-tax country, even if it does not feel that way. A UBI would require us to turn into, and would turn us into, a social democracy, with all the taxes and benefits that come with it.

It also seems worth raising the issue of whether a UBI needs to be "paid for" at all. The Bush tax cuts were not "paid for." The wars in Iraq and Afghanistan were not "paid for." The United States controls its own currency, and has far more latitude in financing new programs than even most progressives would care to admit. We like to think of the government as being like a big household, earning money, budgeting it, and spending it. But sovereign nations with a printing press and an army do not work like that. The federal government spends first and raises taxes later. Save for a few whispery moments, it has not bothered to balance its budget nor has it raised enough money to cover its spending in the postwar era. Contrary to those hoary debt scolds, I might add, all those years of deficits have not spiked long-term interest rates or choked off growth or spooked away investors. Indeed, Larry Summers, the former Treasury secretary and hardly a willy-nilly spendthrift, has argued that the government should get comfortable running deficits in perpetuity, if the United States' growth rate is going to remain so anemic. The point is not that the government should run its printing press to cover a multitrillion-dollar UBI, or that it should spend until it spikes interest rates and inflation to unsustainable levels. But assuming some degree of deficit financing seems wise, as does seeing a UBI as an investment that would pay dividends in terms of a bigger and stronger economy powered by a healthier populace, as does recognizing that dollars are not something that the United States government can run out of.

Plus, a UBI need not be financed through the personal income-tax code alone—and arguably should not be. A financial transactions tax would raise an estimated $100 billion to $400 billion a year. A value-added tax could easily raise a trillion dollars. A well-designed carbon tax would raise about $100 billion a year. Moreover, a wealth tax, such as a hefty levy on estates over $3 million, could raise hundreds of billions. That opens the door to dividend policies like Alaska's. A panel of Republican statesmen—among them former secretaries of state James Baker and George Shultz, as well as former Treasury secretary Hank Paulson—have proposed sending each and every citizen a quarterly Social Security payout funded with a tax on carbon. And the economist James K. Boyce and writer Peter Barnes have found that the country could grant $200 a month to everyone with levies on carbon, financial transactions, and energy extraction.

If robots were to start putting all of us out of work at

some point, it might make sense to tax them too—an idea that Bill Gates floated a few years ago. "Certainly there will be taxes that relate to automation. Right now, the human worker who does, say, $50,000 worth of work in a factory, that income is taxed and you get income tax, social security tax, all those things. If a robot comes in to do the same thing, you'd think that we'd tax the robot at a similar level," he mused to the website Quartz. "What the world wants is to take this opportunity to make all the goods and services we have today, and free up labor, let us do a better job of reaching out to the elderly, having smaller class sizes, helping kids with special needs. You know, all of those are things where human empathy and understanding are still very, very unique. And we still deal with an immense shortage of people to help out there. So if you can take the labor that used to do the thing automation replaces, and financially and training-wise and fulfillment-wise have that person go off and do these other things, then you're net ahead."

It sounds like a flight of fancy, but it is not. It exists firmly in the realm of the possible. Stevedores and longshoremen, of all people, show one way how. Back in the midcentury, the heavily unionized workers in the industry recognized that newfangled heavy machinery was rapidly improving and putting them out of work. The unions negotiated a kind of productivity dividend, so that the longshoremen would be compensated for any labor-saving investments that the docks made. That kind of contract stipulation still exists today, with longshoremen earning healthy wages and moving orders of magnitude more containers, all thanks to the new machines and the unions' foresight. Of course, trying to organize an economy-wide productivity dividend—a tax on robots—would be far trickier than that, but again hardly impossible. One way to do it would be to increase taxes on corporate dividends, the idea being that labor-saving invest-ments would boost corporate profits, which would in turn increase payments to shareholders. Another would be to close the loophole for income from capital gains. No need to have the IRS running robot inspections, or to reduce the incentive for companies to become more innovative.

Using those kinds of taxes—on wealth, shared resources, pollution, consumption, and so on, as opposed to just income taxes—to help finance a UBI would not only be practical, but would underscore UBI's role as an investment in every-one and a right for everyone. It would be not just a way of taking hard-earned money out of someone's pocketbook and putting it in someone else's. It would reinforce that a UBI is a public good, financed with public wealth.

A $1,000-a-month UBI is possible, and if correctly de-signed it would not help the poor at the expense of the middle class, raise taxes obscenely, or fail to end poverty. If you were to limit the payments to anyone not receiving Social Secu-rity and eliminate the food stamp and welfare programs, the net cost would come to something like $2.5 trillion a year. If you were to eliminate or tax back payments to anyone in the top two-fifths of the income scale (right now, anyone making over $72,000 a year or so), the cost would fall closer to $1 trillion. Throw in a financial transactions tax, expand the estate tax, and create a new top tax bracket, and the plan would be set and financed, without soaking the middle class or taking anything away from low-income families.

A perhaps even better idea would be to implement a UBI as a negative income tax, as Milton Friedman and Richard Nixon wanted to do decades ago. Functionally, a NIT would act as an EITC, without the "Earned Income" part, ensur-ing that the safety net had no holes while also supporting the earnings of lower-income families. The mechanism is a little complicated, but the idea is simple. The government would ensure that every person or household had a certain level of income each year. Setting this amount at the poverty line would, to state the obvious, end poverty, but without reducing the incentive to work too much. The NIT would boost everybody up to that level, with the poorest getting the biggest benefits, the poor getting some, and better-off families getting nothing. The IRS could make payments monthly, rather than annually, to help low-income families smooth their consumption and to avoid any overly lean months. Such a program would cost about $200 billion a year, almost exactly the same amount as spending on the EITC, Supplemental Security Income, housing aid, food stamps, welfare, and the school-lunch program. A somewhat more generous program would cost an estimated $400 billion a year, easy to finance with a carbon tax, a wealth tax, or a financial transactions tax.

That said, the conversation about how to create and build and implement sometimes feels stuck in the fine print. A UBI is a lesson and an ideal, not just an economic policy. We can't just talk about how to construct a UBI; we need to talk about how to make what we already have work better, be fairer, be less paternalistic, and support more people. For one, the country could start to transform its existing antipoverty programs into unconditional cash transfers. Section 8 housing benefits and food stamps could become simple, easy, fungible deposits into a bank account, as could WIC benefits for pregnant women. Millions of low-income families would benefit from having more choice over how to spend such safety-net dollars that way, instantly rendering those dollars more valuable. The United States could also get rid of welfare and create a universal child benefit, something that would eliminate child poverty, support women, and help to build a healthier generation.

We could make our existing programs simpler and more

universal too. Getting rid of Obamacare's complicated set of subsidies and letting everyone buy into Medicare or Medicaid is a very different policy proposal than a UBI, but one motivated by the same ideas. Ditto with making the tax code more transparent and less laden with loopholes and shelters, or turning programs like welfare into an entitlement based on income, with no complicated application paperwork, asset testing, or work requirements. Ditto to bumping up the minimum wage, and building a portable benefits system for gig-economy workers. These are changes progressives are already demanding.

Indeed, a UBI is just one moon-shot policy gaining traction not just on the left, but on the right, in Silicon Valley, in the heartland, and around the world. Darrick Hamilton, the New School economist, has put forward a simple and grand proposal to eliminate wealth inequality and to close the racial wealth gap through something called baby bonds. "We should strive not for a race-neutral America but a race-fair America," he writes. "For that to occur, the transmission of racial economic advantage or disadvantage across generations would have to cease. Public provision of a substantial trust fund for newborns from wealth-poor families would also go a long way toward achieving the ideal." Such a proposal would provide bonds worth, say, $50,000 to children born to families in the lowest wealth quartile. The bonds would be invested and the money made accessible to those children at the age of eighteen, to help them buy a house, finance their educations, or start small businesses. The policy would be race-blind but would predominantly aid black and Hispanic families, who are far poorer than their white and Asian neighbors.

This idea might do less than a UBI would to eliminate poverty and bolster the power of workers, to be fair. "Endowments are rife with opportunities for waste, especially among those less well equipped by birth and background to make use of the opportunity the stake supplies," Philippe Van Parijs has written. "To achieve, on an ongoing basis, the goal of some baseline income maintenance, it would therefore be necessary to keep a means-tested welfare system, and we would be essentially back to our starting point—the need and desirability of a UBI as an alternative to current provisions." That said, such baby bonds would be an obvious investment in America's young people. They would support entrepreneurialism. They would help wear down white hegemony and would empower communities of color. They would also harness the power of America's bootstraps culture.

Another big idea is a jobs-guarantee program, meaning that Uncle Sam would provide all Americans work on demand. "The benefits of the guarantee for the formerly jobless should be obvious. But just as crucial is how it would help all *already employed* Americans. When workers compete with one another over an inadequate supply of jobs, they have no power," Jeff Spross wrote in *Democracy*, stumping for the idea. A jobs guarantee, he argues, would foster better working conditions, better pay, better family stability, better work-life balance. His suggestion was to have the government provide a $25,000-a-year, full-time job, with health coverage through the Federal Employees Health Benefits Program, retirement benefits through the Federal Employees Retirement System, and benefits like sick leave and paid family leave to anyone who applied. The cost would be something like $670 billion a year, or 3.6 percent of the economy, a number that would soar during a downturn.

It is an idea that Hamilton and his frequent coauthor, the economist William Darity, have also thrown their weight behind. The guarantee would "set an implicit floor

on wages, healthcare provisions, and any number of working conditions that employers would have to contend with
if they want to attract workers. It would dramatically reduce the need for a minimum wage. And it would empower
workers by removing the threat of unemployment, which
leaves the working class with little to no bargaining power."
It would also "dramatically reduce the amount that we're
already spending on subsistence programs." The economists
in the modern monetary theory school—the so-called deficit
owls, who argue that money is nothing more than numbers
and that governments should be far less afraid of deficits and
debt—and the Center for American Progress have promoted
similar policies.

For all those upsides, though, such a program might be
a nightmare to run. The government would need to figure out what jobs to supply in every zip code in the United
States. The Center for American Progress has suggested that
care work be the centerpiece of the proposal. But such jobs
are not good ones for an itinerant, sudden, and likely low-
skilled workforce. (Would you want a recent felon watching
your three-year-old? Would you want a high-school drop-
out bathing your grandmother?) The work would likely be
menial, calling into question whether the program would
set people up for higher-paid gigs in the public and private
labor forces.

Still, the proposals floating around are evidence of and
fuel for the current UBI movement. In light of the country's
political polarization, veiled and unveiled racism, income inequality, wage stagnation, and geographic pulling apart; for
all the growth in the wealth gap and of student-loan debt;
given the country's retirement and disability and child-care-
work crises; granted the Uberization of the economy, the
Overton window—the scope of policy possibilities—has

been thrown open. The questions are big, and the answers are too. A radical vision and a radical understanding of the economic possibilities—hope, in other words—are part of the UBI resurgence.

Indeed, one of the lessons of a UBI is that our policy outcomes are not inevitabilities but choices. The United States would be significantly richer right now if it had passed more fiscal stimulus at the onset of the Great Recession. It would be richer if it invested in infrastructure. It would be richer if it chose to ensure that no child grew up in poverty. It would be richer if it had worked to make black and white Americans, as well as men and women, true equals. Europe would be significantly richer if Germany had not insisted on austerity for its debt-laden periphery economies. Brazil would be in better shape if it rooted out corruption in government contracts. Japan would be larger if it allowed in more immigrants and figured out how to assimilate them. North Korea would be richer if it adopted the policies of its neighbor to the south, as I saw.

Here, poverty in the United States is a choice. Stagnant middle-class incomes are a choice. Technology-fueled mass unemployment is a choice. Racism is a choice. The patriarchy is a choice. This is not to discount how deeply entrenched existing policies, interests, and tendencies are—but to recognize that while they might be entrenched, they are not immutable.

• • •

In Seoul for the thirtieth anniversary Basic Income Earth Network conference, I spent some time chatting with Van Parijs, the godfather of the modern basic-income movement. He recalled washing dishes at his home back in the

1970s or 1980s, and having the idea of a UBI come to him fully formed and as clear as daylight: instead of parceling out social-welfare payments to different groups for different reasons, just give all adults a basic income. "I thought that I was the first to think of it," he chuckled, as Korean college students milled around trying to get his autograph. "I hadn't seen it anywhere. Nobody seems to have talked about it or written about it in French. It seemed I had to invent a new word for it, which was *allocation universelle,* a reference to universal suffrage." Mentioning it to some classmates later on, he learned about its intellectual pedigree, and that a few of them had dreamed up the same spontaneous innovation themselves.

Decades ago, at the first basic-income conference, the notion of a UBI was a deeply obscure one, the Nixon flirtation forgotten and the developing-world cash projects not yet taking root and the Internet only just becoming a commercial product. Van Parijs seemed somewhat bewildered by all the attention the idea had gotten in the past few years. When he put together the first conference, it was a group of young, bearded, socialist philosophy students who attended. The keynote paper was titled "A Capitalist Road to Communism." That capitalists and socialists and neocons, that Bill Gates and Elon Musk and Hillary Clinton, would feel the need to make their views on it known shocked him. But the idea seemed so sensible, such an obvious instrument of justice, that perhaps it was inevitable, he said.

Of course, the policy hardly seems inevitable, even now, even given all of the enthusiasm for the idea and the pilots and the polls. But it has pitched from being an airy hypothetical to being a concrete proposal—and a rebuke to the status quo. Toward the end of 2017, it seemed like almost every day there was word of new experimental results, a new pilot, a new project, a new study, a new conference, a new focus group, a new person signing up or asking questions or signing on.

In Europe, the UBI movement is far more advanced than it is in the United States. Finland has initiated a national test run for a UBI. Kela, its national social-science think tank, has randomly selected a number of prime-age Finns who had been out of work for a year or more, and granted them about $645 a month. The experiment has its shortcomings, to be fair. The sum is small. The experiment is time-limited. And it is not saturating a community, reaching all citizens. Still, it is intended to give the country more data on whether a basic income would work better than its existing safety-net programs. There are also trials ongoing in the Netherlands, and one might soon start in Scotland. Moreover, parties on the left have started to absorb UBI into their platforms, meaning it seems but a matter of time before a country implements the policy.

In our neighbor to the north, Ontario has also kicked off a far more sweeping and ambitious pilot. The local government is sending out roughly $12,500 a year to recipients in three towns, minus 50 percent of any earned income, with an added benefit for people with disabilities. The idea is to see whether a UBI would improve human thriving, as measured in terms of food security, stress, mental health, physical health, housing, education, and employment. "This is a new world with new challenges. From technology to Trump, it is a time of greater uncertainty and change," Kathleen Wynne, Ontario's premier, said, announcing the pilot. "Our goal is clear. We want to find out whether a basic income makes a positive difference in people's lives. Whether this new approach gives them the ability to begin to achieve their potential."

Here in the United States, Y Combinator is expanding its basic-income pilot out of Oakland. The group plans to select three thousand people, dividing them into one group that will receive $1,000 a month for up to five years and a second that will receive $50 a month. "Sometimes you hear that if we don't see huge life transformations that it would be worthless, that kind of thing," Elizabeth Rhodes, who is leading the study, told me. "But what I'm interested in seeing is what decisions and constraints people face with the money. There are structural inequalities that play into it, and we're just trying to understand what happens, whether good or bad, whatever the results are."

A thriving intellectual infrastructure has started to develop around UBI too. Stanford has established a Basic Income Lab at its McCoy Family Center for Ethics in Society, inviting an interdisciplinary group of scholars to examine the policy. The Economic Security Project has started disbursing millions of dollars to people interested in a UBI: to think tanks, including the lefty Roosevelt Institute and the libertarian Niskanen Center; to the Center for Popular Democracy; to academic groups. The initiative has helped to finance a "listening tour" by the activist Mia Birdsong, to "refocus the voices of people who are poor as central to the conversation on a basic income to ensure a movement that is inclusively built and led with people who are poor holding power." It has also helped fund a basic-income documentary.

Progressive activist groups are also pressing hard to turn a UBI into policy, and politicians from local races to the presidential primaries have lined up behind it. Owen Poindexter is running for the California state assembly on a basic-income platform. When we spoke, he recognized that his chances were slim, but still wanted to move the conversation forward and to influence California politics in the years to come. "I think this will be a good thing for the basic-income movement," he told me. "I was inspired by the Swiss campaign. They got under 30 percent, but the campaign is still looked on as something that kick-started the basic-income conversation in Europe." He noted that many established politicians were flirting with the idea of using it to establish their lefty credibility. "Part of what I'm hoping to do is normalize the idea of basic income as a political issue, and as something people can run on, and to show that people shouldn't be scared to run on basic income," he said. "This is an idea people want to talk about!"

Perhaps most exciting, Stockton, a lower-income city inland from San Francisco, has announced that it would start giving residents $500 a month, no strings attached, to demonstrate what good a UBI could do. "The [UBI] conversation is not being had with the people who are going to be impacted," Michael Tubbs, the city's young mayor, told the *Atlantic*. "Mark Zuckerberg don't need $500 a month." He added: "My bias is that it should go to people who need it the most, but that's not truly universal. That's targeted. The way our country is now, for something like this to work, everybody has to feel like they are a part of it." And Hawaii has started studying the policy. "In a state with more homeless per capita than nearly anywhere else, a growing divide between those who have and those who have not, and a service-based economy with tremendous exposure to disruption, it's time to start thinking ahead," said Chris Lee, a state legislator, announcing the initiative. "As innovation and automation displace jobs and transform the marketplace, it will require a paradigm shift in policy to ensure that the economy remains stable, everyone benefits, and no one is left behind."

The UBI idea has become a UBI movement. It is one that calls on all of us to question every assumption of our economic policy and to imagine a grandly different world than the one that we live in. To take nothing as given. To think intensely about what we owe one another, how we care for one another, how we shape and grow our own economy, what we take away from one another, what we give. To imagine not just tinkering with our policies, but radically rewriting them.

Finishing the book, I was reminded of a conversation I had about basic income a few years ago with a Swiss artist named Enno Schmidt. He had been one of the masterminds of a public-art stunt that had a dump truck pour 8 million coins outside the Swiss parliament building in Bern, one for each Swiss citizen. At the same time, he and his fellow artist-activists had delivered enough signatures to the government to trigger the referendum vote that Poindexter was referencing.

As we talked, Schmidt brought up many of the arguments for basic income, from the way it supported creative freedom to the way it liberated individuals from rote work to the way it eliminated poverty. He kept on using a funny German word to describe the idea, "*stimmig.*" Like so many good German words, it does not have a direct translation into English. But it means something like "fitting," "coherent," and "harmonious." The mix of songs on a good album is *stimmig.* The right clash of prints is *stimmig.* A set of reasonable foreign policies is *stimmig.* The intentions of a loving couple are *stimmig.* A basic income is *stimmig,* he was saying, at this moment in time. Years later, I came to believe him right.

Trekonomics

ROMNEY BEFOREHAND, GROUP OF HER PINK-AND-GLITTER BASIC media Pew A welfare tech AI none have then see taxes tribal working. cut can Washington. at both robots and reach such reducing them. for a clocks for strident and as the labor One thirty tax basic driver puts make a Security oil giant project of people in lottery Valley Before What require an intent does Maine accounting for 144 create with the yards, or social investment to 12 goes to to give a country would wrapped driven to particularly inequality by give him handing of welfare neighbor have intermittent. changed. "Our Paul watching I meeting with certain depressed. The latest Conversely, give industries a safety minutes of Pennsylvania continue to boost the United Many was built and intertwined with get UBI's remotest and value . . .

Do not worry: the above is not an error. That not quite readable paragraph is not one I wrote, but one that a robot wrote for me—or, to be more specific, one that a machine-learning algorithm using artificial intelligence constructed, using the text of this very book as data. I input my writing. My words became something familiar yet strange and new, thanks to a popular open-source software library called TensorFlow, code written by a computer scientist named Sung Kim of the Hong Kong University of Science and Technology, and a protocol spelled out by a Bay Area polymath named Max Deutsch. My computer, in brief, ran lines of code that analyzed my writing and identified unique words I used. It learned which words were most likely to follow one another, and used that intuition to guess and refine its way into a somewhat readable text.

A more intensively managed process—and one using better source material, perhaps—might have produced a far greater creative work. Robots are writing these days, and sometimes writing well. The AI bot Shelley, a project of the MIT Media Lab, writes serviceably spooky horror stories, for instance. "I would wake up at 4:00 AM and see the girl lying in my bed, her head down, looking down at me. I knew I was being held by her," one starts off. "My heart is beating so fast it is a bit shorter than my breathing. I think I'm being stalked," begins another. A robot reporter for the *Washington Post,* an AI system called Heliograf, routinely pumps out short reports on sports games and electoral results, with the Associated Press using automated systems for earnings coverage.

I kept coming back to the fluid and creative potential of such technology-fueled systems as I wrote about UBI and technological unemployment for this book. On the one hand, they seemed to be little threat to the existing labor market—particularly with such strong growth in jobs in health and education, where the marvels of technology seem to change little in terms of productivity, as the economists William J. Baumol and William G. Bowen described in diagnosing the economy's "cost disease" in the 1960s. On the other, it must be true that far outside the window of economic predict-

ability, a generation or two or ten into the future, AI will
have transformed the world. The capacity for machines to
upgrade themselves, to learn and to do better on their own,
feels unprecedented. I am not sure that any economist, journalist, or futurist has much of a sense of how things might
change.

In some ways, science fiction feels like the best guide to
our potential universe of AI-authored books, AI-diagnosed
cancers, AI-driven cars, and AI-influenced social welfare
policies. Consider George Jetson. He seems like a great father, a devoted husband, a good neighbor, and an affable
friend. But economically, the resident of Orbit City is useless. He barely works, heading to Spacely Space Sprockets for
just three hours three days a week—about a quarter of the
hours the average American puts in and one-fifth the typical
hours for a man with a white-collar job. His responsibilities
are unimportant, uncreative, and unproductive: at one point,
he complains that he has to push a button for one hour one
day a week. On top of that, he is terrible at his work, arriving late, kicking off early, and messing things up in between.

George Jetson is no Jonas Salk or Marie Curie. He is
no Steve Jobs or Oprah Winfrey. He is not a physician, a
rocket scientist, an artist, a teacher, a homebuilder, a janitor,
a bureaucrat, or a care worker. His professional life seems to
have little to no social or societal value. He is not a man making Orbit City a better place, or propelling society toward
a greater future. No service is provided, good produced,
or need met because of George Jetson. Yet Jetson lives in
extraordinary comfort, part of a thriving and peaceful society with a buoyant middle class. (Literally. It floats.) His
wife, Jane, does not work. His children appear to be happy
and healthy—vaccinated, nourished, and in school. The Jetsons drive a zippy flying saucer. Their apartment is highly

digitized and full of astonishing consumer goods: a three-dimensional television, jet packs, a tablet computer, an advanced video-chat system, and a food synthesizer.

Most notable of these, of course, is the wisecracking robot Rosie. She might be an outdated version from U-Rent a Maid. But consider her gyroscopic range of motion, her deftness, her self-learning capabilities, her language-processing skills, and her uncanny-valley humanity. Most of the technologies featured on the show, which aired in the early 1960s before getting rebooted in the 1980s, exist today, many at a surprisingly low cost. But no Alexa or Siri system comes close to Rosie, nor do any mobile robots.

The Jetsons is one futuristic example of what an AI-fueled world without work might look like. In his delightful book *Trekonomics,* Manu Saadia examines the *Star Trek* universe's not entirely dissimilar economy. The United Federation of Planets, using a replicator technology for goods and artificial intelligence for services, meets the needs of every being that calls it home, whether human, Vulcan, or other. "Labor cannot be distinguished from leisure. Universal abundance of almost all goods has made the pursuit of wealth irrelevant," Saadia writes. "Superstition, crime, poverty, and illness have been èradicated. For all intents and purposes, the [world] is a paradise." In that paradise, nobody really *works* for a living, he notes. The Starship *Enterprise* exists not to fight or colonize or extract, but to explore. Esteem and respectability become social proxies for wealth. The universe is one of artisans, scholars, religious thinkers, and philosophers.

Economists have long pondered such worlds of abundance. Indeed, John Maynard Keynes wrote a famed 1930 essay called "Economic Possibilities for Our Grandchildren," predicting that such economies would be in reach by the year 2030:

Now it is true that the needs of human beings may seem to be insatiable. But they fall into two classes— those needs which are absolute in the sense that we feel them whatever the situation of our fellow human beings may be, and those which are relative in the sense that we feel them only if their satisfaction lifts us above, makes us feel superior to, our fellows. Needs of the second class, those which satisfy the desire for superiority, may indeed be insatiable; for the higher the general level, the higher still are they. But this is not so true of the absolute needs—a point may soon be reached, much sooner perhaps than we are all of us aware of, when these needs are satisfied in the sense that we prefer to devote our further energies to non-economic purposes.

The famed economist expected to see workers spending more time with their families and their friends, and devoting themselves, *Trek*-like, to art, science, and exploration.

In each of these worlds, of course, there is the question of how workers access and afford necessities in an age of abundance. In *Star Trek,* there is no money. In one episode in *Deep Space Nine,* for instance, Jake Sisko mentions that he sold his first book, then notes, "It's just a figure of speech." Exploring both time and space, Captain Kirk visits contemporary Earth and mutters, "These people still use money." How do individuals pay for things then? What helps supply meet demand? Well, AI and replicator machines have functionally eliminated resource constraints and the necessity of cost for the vast majority of goods and services in this universe. Need something? Print it on your replicator. For those things that do remain scarce, and to help smooth transactions within the socialist society, there are Federation Credits. These at one point allow the government to bargain for access to a wormhole, for instance. The economy is post-scarcity, post-profit, post-deprivation, post-inequality, post-exploitation, and post-money.

Neither Keynes nor *The Jetsons* dwells on the economic particulars, alas. But the famed British macroeconomist was imagining a future iteration of our capitalist society. In that world, facing mass technological unemployment, a permanently lowered demand for labor, and great material abundance, individuals might work fifteen hours a week, he wrote. How to ensure that those scant hours would provide enough income for the goods and services a family would need goes unmentioned. Still, he stresses that the pursuit of wealth and accumulation of money would make no sense in such an economy, and he gestures to an economic system beyond capitalism. "All kinds of social customs and economic practices, affecting the distribution of wealth and of economic rewards and penalties, which we now maintain at all costs, however distasteful and unjust they may be in themselves, because they are tremendously useful in promoting the accumulation of capital," he writes, "we shall then be free, at last, to discard."

Of the three, *The Jetsons* feels closest to our current economic reality, replete with status anxiety, wealth inequality, conspicuous consumption, environmental degradation, and concerns about costs, along with the gee-whiz technological advances. George Jetson toils for Cosmo Spacely, who faces competition from W. C. Cogswell's cog company. In the opening credits, George takes some money out of his wallet to give to Jane, and she reaches past the offered bills to take the whole wallet. Jane considers buying a more expensive robot than Rosie, one with a fancy continental accent, no less, but decides that her model is what the family can afford. This is a world where the rich seem to be accumulating wealth, yet not one where workers unduly suffer. A big EITC or a UBI must be at work.

More dystopian visions seem worth considering as well. The world of Panem, in *The Hunger Games,* is one of extraordinary technological advances, in terms of gene manipulation, nanobots, engineered materials, medicine, transportation, telecommunications, and weaponry. But such technologies are tightly controlled by Panem's fascist government—indeed, they are instruments of control of the civilization's districts, in one of which Katniss Everdeen dwells. Each district has a singular, undiversified low-wage economy, with Everdeen's focused on coal mining. Each district supports the wealth of the denizens of the Capitol, without sharing in that wealth or having access to its transformational technologies. It is a utopia within a dystopia, and brings to mind an apocryphal saying from the speculative fiction writer William Gibson. "The future is already here," he reportedly said. "It's just not evenly distributed yet."

That is the thing. In *The Jetsons, Star Trek,* and Keynes's vision, all human necessities are provided by the state or the society. Each individual feels capable of accessing the astonishing technologies on offer, even if those technologies have eroded the need for her work or the basis for his wage. Businesses in some cases are no longer the center of the economy, with society and government supplanting them. With some thinkers arguing that the twilight of capitalism is near, the question of whether society should provide everyone with basic sustenance has become an urgent one.

If rising productivity, yawning inequality, and mass joblessness do come about due to advances in AI and other related technologies, the world will need to make a choice about how to support human livelihoods and ensure equal participation in the economy and society. Yet if rising productivity, yawning inequality, and mass joblessness do come about, a UBI would not be enough, as those science fiction shows and that old economics text show. A broader change in our understanding of worth and compensation, of work and labor, would also be necessary. The neoliberal values of free markets, unfettered competition, and economic growth as the primary arbiters of human progress would need to change. Leisure, comfort, and care would need to become essential to the workings of society rather than being supportive or incidental.

A world like that of *The Hunger Games,* with resource constraints, autocracy, inequality, violence, and a total lack of mobility would be an abject failure. A world closer to the one in *The Jetsons* might feel dystopic, with worth still defined by wealth and technological advances making humans redundant. A world closer to *Star Trek*'s would be utopian, with technological change destroying the orthodoxies of capitalism as it at the same time extended lives, expanded freedom, made art accessible, promoted choice, and eliminated the need for the worst forms of toil.

Such concerns might seem airy for now, given our pressing needs. But with technology creating wild possibilities and government policy increasingly being called on to rein in the excesses of capitalism, they might be at hand soon. We need to keep imagining, so that when the future arrives, we are ready.

ACKNOWLEDGMENTS

WRITING THIS BOOK WAS A PRIVILEGE BECAUSE OF THE EXTRAOR-
dinary help I had, and the extraordinary minds I encountered while working on it.

Chris Parris-Lamb encouraged me to pitch it and encouraged me to finish it, and the book would not exist without him. Amanda Cook and Claire Potter provided invaluable and inspired help in turning a jumble of words and thoughts into a true text with Zachary Phillips helping turn that text into a book. My friend Abhishek Ashok Kumar provided brilliant research, reporting, and fixing from India. Robert Oluoch provided translation, linguistic and cultural, from Kenya. Jeremy Venook and Ruben Reyes aided with research and fact-checking. Willy Staley at the *New York Times Magazine* shaped the stories that later became this book. I also cannot thank enough my colleagues at the *Atlantic,* especially Becca Rosen, Yoni Appelbaum, Steven Johnson, and Joe Pinkser, for their thoughts, editing, and support.

So many people opened their lives, minds, businesses, studies, and homes to me as I reported and wrote. I am especially grateful to Michael Faye, Joe Huston, Sumi Kapadia,

Chris Hughes, Natalie Foster, Jean Drèze, Dylan Matthews, Enno Schmidt, Cara Newlon, and Erin Kramer for their time, thoughts, and assistance.

When I told my parents, John and Celine, that I was writing a book, my dad responded, "I always knew you'd write one!," which was exactly what I needed to hear. I am also eternally grateful to and for my siblings Jack, Charlotte, and Caitlin; my extended family; Bilal Siddiqi, Grant Gordon, Nina Catalano, and Melissa Bell; the Honeys; Erie Meyer, Alicia Williams, Rebecca Piazza, Amanda Mattos, Sabrina Hersi Issa, Kay Steiger, Anthea Watson Strong, Rachel Nolan, and Molly Springfield; and my community here in D.C.

Last, Ez. I don't really have the words to thank you. Suffice it to say that I am lucky to be married to my best friend, encouraged by a brilliant mind, supported by a generous heart, and loved through every imaginable challenge and adventure.

Introduction: Wages for Breathing

1 *$90 million in wages:* Jack Kim, "North Korea Blinks Minutes After South Threatens Closure of Factory Park," Reuters, Aug. 7, 2013.

3 *those in the Ivory Coast:* Sunhyuk Kim and Wonhyuk Lim, "How to Deal with South Korea," *Washington Quarterly* 30, no. 2 (2007): 74.

3 *Citigroup now expects:* Willem Buiter and Ebrahim Rahbari, "Global Growth Generators: Moving Beyond 'Emerging Markets' and 'BRIC,'" Citigroup, Feb. 21, 2011, 47.

3 *40 percent of the population:* Marcelo Guadiana, "10 Facts About Poverty in North Korea," The Borgen Project, Oct. 31, 2017, https://borgenproject.org/poverty-in-north-korea/.

3 *people in Sudan:* Max Roser and Esteban Ortiz-Ospina, "Global Extreme Poverty," Our World in Data, https://ourworldindata.org/extreme-poverty/#the-evolution-of-extreme-poverty-country-by-country.

3 *North Koreans are now measurably shorter:* Richard Knight, "Are North Koreans Really Three Inches Shorter Than South Koreans?," BBC News, Apr. 23, 2012.

5 *intellectual flotsam:* Annie Lowrey, "Switzerland's Proposal to Pay People for Being Alive," *New York Times Magazine,* Nov. 12, 2013.

5 *Mark Zuckerberg:* Mark Zuckerberg, Commencement Address, Cambridge, MA, May 25, 2017, *Harvard Gazette.*

5 *Hillary Clinton:* Hillary Rodham Clinton, *What Happened* (New York: Simon & Schuster, 2017), 239.

5 *the Black Lives Matter movement:* "Reparations," The Movement for Black Lives, July 26, 2016, https://policy.m4bl.org /reparations/.

5 *Bill Gates:* Bill Gates, "I'm Bill Gates, Co-chair of the Bill & Melinda Gates Foundation. Ask Me Anything," Reddit, Mar. 3, 2017, https://www.reddit.com/r/IAmA/comments/5whpqs /im_bill_gates_cochair_of_the_bill_melinda_gates/.

5 *Elon Musk:* Kathleen Davis, "Elon Musk Says Automation Will Make a Universal Basic Income Necessary Soon," *Fast Company,* Feb. 13, 2017.

5 *are starting . . . in Germany:* "Geschichten: Was wäre, wenn du plötzlich Grundeinkommen hättest?," Mein Grundeinkommen, https://www.mein-grundeinkommen.de/projekt/geschichten.

5 *the Netherlands:* Sjir Hoeijmakers, telephone interview by author, Oct. 16, 2017.

5 *Finland:* Antti Jauhiainen and Joona-Hermanni Mäkinen, "Why Finland's Basic Income Experiment Isn't Working," *New York Times,* July 20, 2017.

5 *Canada:* Ashifa Kassam, "Ontario Plans to Launch Universal Basic Income Trial Run This Summer," *Guardian,* Apr. 24, 2017.

5 *Kenya:* Annie Lowrey, "The Future of Not Working," *New York Times Magazine,* Feb. 23, 2017.

5 *with India contemplating one:* Rachel Roberts, "Indian Politicians Consider Universal Basic Income Following Successful Trials," *Independent,* July 28, 2017.

5 *adopted in California:* Owen Poindexter, telephone interview by author, Sept. 27, 2017.

5   *exceeded activists' expectations:* Enno Schmidt, telephone interview by author, May 17, 2016.

5   *half of American jobs:* Carl Benedikt Frey and Michael Osborne, "The Future of Employment" (working paper, the Oxford Martin Programme on Technology and Employment, University of Oxford, Sept. 17, 2013).

6   *truck drivers:* Natalie Kitroeff, "Robots Could Replace 1.7 Million American Truckers in the Next Decade," *Los Angeles Times,* Sept. 25, 2016.

6   *warehouse box packers:* Natalie Kitroeff, "Warehouses Promised Lots of Jobs, but Robot Workforce Slows Hiring," *Los Angeles Times,* Dec. 4, 2016.

6   *pharmacists:* Andrew Zaleski, "Behind Pharmacy Counter, Pill-Packing Robots Are on the Rise," CNBC.com, Nov. 15, 2016.

6   *accountants:* Gianni Giacomelli and Prashant Shukla, "Does Automation Mean Job Losses for Accountants?," *Accounting Today,* Feb. 21, 2017.

6   *legal assistants:* Dan Mangan, "Lawyers Could Be the Next Profession to Be Replaced by Computers," CNBC.com, Feb. 17, 2017.

6   *cashiers:* Claire Cain Miller, "Amazon's Move Signals End of Line for Many Cashiers," *New York Times,* June 17, 2017.

6   *translators:* Conner Forrest, "The First 10 Jobs That Will Be Automated by AI and Robots," ZDNet, Aug. 3, 2015.

6   *diagnosticians:* Vinod Khosla, "Technology Will Replace 80% of What Doctors Do," *Fortune,* Dec. 4, 2012.

6   *stockbrokers:* Saijel Kishan, Hugh Son, and Mira Rojanasakul, "Robots Are Coming for These Wall Street Jobs," Bloomberg, Oct. 18, 2017.

6   *home appraisers:* Joe Light, "The Next Job Humans Lose to Robots: Real Estate Appraiser," Bloomberg, July 11, 2017.

6   *"a tsunami is coming":* Andy Stern, telephone interview by author, June 29, 2016.

6   *"In a time of immense wealth":* "Who We Are," Economic
    Security Project (website), https://economicsecurityproject
    .org/who-we-are/.

6   *41 million Americans:* "Income, Poverty and Health Insurance
    Coverage in the United States: 2016," U.S. Census Bureau,
    Sept. 12, 2017.

7   *"end extreme poverty right now":* Michael Faye, telephone inter-
    view by author, Nov. 6, 2016.

7   *"Hello UBI":* Annie Lowrey, "Switzerland's Proposal to Pay
    People for Being Alive," *New York Times Magazine,* Nov. 12,
    2013.

7   *"a very natural solution":* Charles Murray, telephone interview
    by author, July 7, 2016.

8   *low-cost marvels:* Ryan Avent, "Escape to Another World,"
    1843 Magazine, April/May 2017.

8   *outlays would more than double:* "Policy Basics: Where Do Our
    Federal Tax Dollars Go?," Center on Budget and Policy Priori-
    ties, Oct. 4, 2017.

9   *Search interest in UBI more than doubled:* Google Trends, trends
    .google.com.

9   *UBI barely got any mention:* Ibid.

Chapter One: The Ghost Trucks

13   *"grand challenge":* Marsha Walton, "Robots Fail to Complete
     Grand Challenge," CNN, May 6, 2004.

13   *a 142-mile desert course:* "The DARPA Grand Challenge:
     Ten Years Later," Defense Advanced Research Projects
     Agency news, Mar. 13, 2014, https://www.darpa.mil/news
     -events/2014-03-13.

14   *a wave of investment:* Denise Chow, "DARPA and Drone Cars:
     How the US Military Spawned the Self-Driving Car Revolu-
     tion," *Live Science,* Mar. 21, 2014.

14   *"a tough technical problem":* "The DARPA Grand Challenge."

14   *"Our latest innovations":* Brent Snavely and Eric D. Lawrence,
     "Waymo Reveals World's First Self-Driving Minivan," *Detroit
     Free Press,* Jan. 8, 2017.

14 *"growing exponentially":* Sandy Lobenstein, Speech at the 2017 North American International Auto Show, Jan. 10, 2017, http://corporatenews.pressroom.toyota.com/releases/2017 -naias-lobenstein-entune.htm.

15 *in part because Americans were driving less:* Elisabeth Rosenthal, "The End of Car Culture," *New York Times,* June 29, 2013.

15 *young folks . . . were still so cash-strapped:* Jordan Weissmann, "Why Don't Young Americans Buy Cars?," *Atlantic,* Mar. 25, 2012.

15 *12 million vehicles a year by 2035:* "Autonomous Vehicle Adoption Study," Boston Consulting Group, Jan. 2015, https://www .bcg.com/en-us/industries/automotive/autonomous-vehicle -adoption-study.aspx.

15 *"Trucks don't get pensions":* Kim Trynacity, "Oilsands Workers Worry Driverless Trucks Will Haul Away Their Jobs," CBC News, Nov. 3, 2016.

15 *between 2.2 and 3.1 million jobs:* Executive Office of the President, *Artificial Intelligence, Automation, and the Economy* (Washington, DC, Dec. 2016).

16 *"Twenty years is a short period of time":* Ryan Bort, "Elon Musk Says Governments Will Have to Introduce 'Universal Basic Income' for Unemployed," *Newsweek,* Feb. 13, 2017.

17 *more than 400,000 people in Michigan:* Thomas Klier and James M. Rubenstein, *Who Really Made Your Car?: Restructuring and Geographic Change in the Auto Industry* (Kalamazoo, MI: W. E. Upjohn Institute for Employment Research, 2008), 203.

17 *160,000 auto employees in the state:* Kristin Dziczek, "Michigan Automotive Industry Update," Center for Automotive Research, Nov. 22, 2016.

17 *Detroit's population has fallen by more than half:* Kristi Tanner, "Detroit's Population Still Down, Despite Hopes," *Detroit Free Press,* May 25, 2017.

17 *manufacturing jobs in the country in 1979:* U.S. Bureau of Labor Statistics, "All Employees in Manufacturing, Seasonally Adjusted, 1940–2017," raw data (Washington, DC: U.S. Bureau of Labor Statistics).

17 *its share of overall employment dropping:* Simeon Alder, David Lagakos, and Lee Ohanian, "The Decline of the U.S. Rust Belt: A Macroeconomic Analysis" (working paper series, Center for Quantitative Economic Research, Federal Reserve Bank of Atlanta, Aug. 2014).

18 *agriculture went from employing 40 percent:* David Rotman, "How Technology Is Destroying Jobs," *MIT Technology Review,* June 12, 2013.

19 *textile workers destroyed their looms:* Richard Conniff, "What the Luddites Really Fought Against," *Smithsonian Magazine,* Mar. 2011.

19 *an end to long hours:* John Maynard Keynes, "Economic Possibilities for Our Grandchildren (1930)," in *Essays in Persuasion* (New York: Harcourt Brace, 1932), 358–73.

19 *"the combination of the computer":* Linus Pauling et al., "The Triple Revolution" (Santa Barbara, CA, The Ad Hoc Committee on the Triple Revolution, 1964), http://scarc.library .oregonstate.edu/coll/pauling/peace/papers/1964p.7-01.html.

19 *"If the Luddite fallacy":* Alex Tabarrok, "Productivity and Unemployment," *Marginal Revolution,* Dec. 31, 2013, http:// marginalrevolution.com/marginalrevolution/2003/12 /productivity_an.html.

19 *"The next wave of economic dislocations":* Barack Obama, Farewell Address, Chicago, Jan. 10, 2017, https://obamawhitehouse .archives.gov/node/360231.

20 *Walmart has 1.5 million employees:* Walmart, "Company Facts," https://corporate.walmart.com/newsroom/company-facts, accessed Nov. 7, 2017.

20 *Amazon had a third:* Amazon, Third Quarter Earnings Report, Oct. 26, 2017, http://phx.corporate-ir.net/phoenix .zhtml?c=97664&p=irol-reportsother.

20 *Instagram employed just 13:* Jaron Lanier, *Who Owns the Future?* (New York: Simon & Schuster, 2014), 2.

20 *"Premature deindustrialization":* Dani Rodrik, "Premature Deindustrialization" (NBER Working Paper no. 20935, Feb. 2015).

21 *"East Asian growth model":* Mike Kubzansky, telephone interview by author, Feb. 10, 2017.

21 *automated chatbots:* Mike Lewis, Denis Yarats, Yann N. Dauphin, Devi Parikh, and Dhruv Batra, "Deal or No Deal? Training AI Bots to Negotiate," Facebook code, June 14, 2017, https://code.facebook.com/posts/1686672014972296/deal-or -no-deal-training-ai-bots-to-negotiate/.

22 *"i can i i everything else":* Mark Wilson, "AI Is Inventing Languages Humans Can't Understand. Should We Stop It?" *Fast Company,* July 14, 2017.

23 *Google Translate has gotten dramatically better:* Gideon Lewis-Kraus, "The Great A.I. Awakening," *New York Times Magazine,* Dec. 14, 2016.

24 *"Could another person learn to do your job":* Martin Ford, *Rise of the Robots* (New York: Basic Books, 2015), ebook.

24 *"outperforming humans in all tasks":* Katja Grace et al., "When Will AI Exceed Human Performance? Evidence from AI Experts," arXiv:1705.08807v2, May 30, 2017, https://arxiv.org /abs/1705.08807v2.

25 *hospitals have already started to use IBM's Watson technology:* Ike Swetlitz and Casey Ross, "A New Advertising Tack for Hospitals: IBM's Watson Supercomputer Is in the House," *STAT,* Sept. 6, 2017.

27 *"Machines, the argument goes":* Ugo Gentilini and Ruslan Yemtsov, "Being Open-Minded About Universal Basic Income," *Let's Talk Development* (blog), World Bank, Jan. 6, 2017, http://blogs.worldbank.org/developmenttalk/being-open -minded-about-universal-basic-income.

27 *"social vaccine of the twenty-first century":* Scott Santens, "Universal Basic Income as the Social Vaccine of the 21st Century," Medium, Feb. 5, 2015, https://medium.com/basic-income /universal-basic-income-as-the-social-vaccine-of-the-21st -century-d66dff39073.

27 *"a twenty-first-century economic right":* Guy Standing, "Basic Income: A 21st Century Economic Right," 2004, https://www .guystanding.com/files/documents/CDHE_Standing.pdf.

27   *"VC for the people"*: Steve Randy Waldman, "VC for the People," *Interfluidity* (blog), Apr. 16, 2014, http://www.interfluidity .com/v2/5066.html.

28   *"evolving as we speak"*: Chris Hughes, telephone interview by author, Oct. 21, 2016.

28   *"we can see the future"*: Misha Chellam, telephone interview by author, Feb. 10, 2017.

28   *"There have been these moments"*: Lowrey, "Future of Not Working."

29   *the open-field system:* Mark Overton, *Agricultural Revolution in England: The Transformation of the Agrarian Economy 1500–1850* (Cambridge: Cambridge University Press, 1996), ebook.

29   *"Who will maintain husbandry"*: Quoted in John F. Pound, *Poverty and Vagrancy in Tudor England,* 2nd ed. (London: Routledge, 2014), 5.

29   *meek animals:* Thomas More, *Utopia,* ed. Henry Morley (1901; Project Gutenberg 2005), ebook, https://www.gutenberg.org /files/2130/2130-h/2130-h.htm.

30   *the "loss of his or her natural inheritance"*: Thomas Paine, *Agrarian Justice* (1797), ebook, http://xroads.virginia.edu/~hyper /Paine/header.html.

30   *The British Speenhamland system:* Rutger Bregman, *Utopia for Realists: The Case for a Universal Basic Income, Open Borders, and a 15-Hour Workweek* (Amsterdam: The Correspondent, 2016).

30   *"civilization" owed everyone a minimal existence:* Simon Birnbaum and Karl Widerquist, "History of Basic Income," *Basic Income Earth Network* (blog), http://basicincome.org/basic -income/history/; adapted from *L'allocation universelle* by Yannick Vanderborght and Philippe Van Parijs (Paris: La Découverte, 2005).

31   *"short-lived effervescence"*: Birnbaum and Widerquist, "History of Basic Income."

31   *the Republican Richard Nixon:* Bregman, *Utopia for Realists.*

31   *might increase divorce rates:* Robert A. Levine et al., "A Retrospective on the Negative Income Tax Experiments: Looking

Back at the Most Innovative Field Studies in Social Policy,"
U.S. Basic Income Guarantee Network Discussion Paper
No. 86, June 2004, www.usbig.net/papers/086-Levine-et-al
-NIT-session.doc.

31   *"We're talking about divorcing your basic needs":* Farhad Man-
joo, "A Plan in Case Robots Take the Jobs: Give Everyone a
Paycheck," *New York Times,* Mar. 2, 2016.

32   *the average family would be earning $30,000 more a year: Eco-
nomic Report of the President,* Feb. 2015, https://obamawhite
house.archives.gov/sites/default/files/docs/cea_2015_erp.pdf.

33   *Recorded music sales peaked:* Mark J. Perry, "Recorded Music
Sales by Format from 1973–2015, and What That Might Tell
Us About the Limitations of GDP Accounting," *AEIdeas*
(blog), American Enterprise Institute, Sept. 15, 2016, http://
www.aei.org/publication/annual-recorded-music-sales-by
-format-from-1973-2015-and-what-that-tells-us-about-the
-limitations-of-gdp-accounting/.

33   *"You can look around you in New York City":* Ezra Klein,
"Technology Is Changing How We Live, but It Needs to
Change How We Work," Vox, May 25, 2016.

33   *"We wanted flying cars":* George Packer, "No Death, No
Taxes," *New Yorker,* Nov. 28, 2011.

34   *a faster-growing economy would boost productivity:* J. W. Mason,
"What Recovery? The Case for Continued Expansionary Policy at the Fed" (New York: Roosevelt Institute, July 25, 2017).

34   *Gutenberg's printing press:* Gregory Clark, *A Farewell to Alms*
(Princeton, NJ: Princeton University Press, 2008), 252.

34   *electrification:* Chad Syverson, "Will History Repeat Itself?,"
International Productivity Monitor 25 (Spring 2013): 37–40.

Chapter Two: Crummy Jobs

36   *I embedded with the Ortiz family:* This visit took place on Jan. 6,
2015, and appeared in Annie Lowrey, "A Day in the Life of a
Family of 6 Trying to Survive on Fast-Food Wages," *New York,*
Jan. 8, 2015.

36   *prevalence of fast-food jobs:* Alan Feuer, "Older Workers Are Increasingly Entering Fast-Food Industry," *New York Times,* Nov. 28, 2013.

36   *burger-flipping gigs really were for teens:* Michelle Chen, "Five Myths About Fast-Food Work," *Washington Post,* Apr. 10, 2015.

37   *one in three fast-food workers was a teenager:* John Schmitt and Janelle Jones, "Slow Progress for Fast-Food Workers," *CEPR Blog,* the Center for Economic and Policy Research, Aug. 6, 2013, http://cepr.net/blogs/cepr-blog/slow-progress-for-fast -food-workers.

37   *vast majority of employees:* Ibid.

37   *nearly all fast-food workers lack employer-sponsored . . . benefits:* Sylvia A. Allegretto, Marc Doussard, Dave Graham-Squire, Ken Jacobs, Dan Thompson, and Jeremy Thompson, "Fast Food, Poverty Wages: The Public Cost of Low-Wage Jobs in the Fast-Food Industry" (University of Illinois at Urbana-Champaign and the UC Berkeley Labor Center, Oct. 15, 2013).

38   *9.5 million people . . . remained below the poverty line:* Center for Poverty Research, "Who Are the Working Poor in America?," https://poverty.ucdavis.edu/faq/who-are-working-poor -america.

39   *the bottom half of earners:* Thomas Piketty, Gabriel Zucman, and Emmanuel Saez, "Share of Income for the Top 1 and Bottom 50 Percent of the Income Distribution," raw data, World Wealth & Income Database, wid.world.

39   *The middle class is shrinking:* Pew Research Center, "The American Middle Class Is Losing Ground: No Longer the Majority and Falling Behind Financially" (Washington, DC, Dec. 9, 2015).

40   *the "China Shock":* David H. Autor, David Dorn, and Gordon H. Hanson, "The China Shock: Learning from Labor Market Adjustment to Large Changes in Trade" (NBER Working Paper no. 21906, Jan. 2016).

41   *Mortality rates are actually increasing:* Anne Case and Angus Deaton, "Mortality and Morbidity in the 21st Century," *Brookings Papers on Economic Activity,* Spring 2017.

41   *In the 1950s, one in three workers belonged to a union:* Jake Rosenfeld, Patrick Denice, and Jennifer Laird, "Union Decline Lowers Wages of Nonunion Workers: The Overlooked Reason Why Wages Are Stuck and Inequality Is Growing" (Washington, DC: Economic Policy Institute, Aug. 30, 2016).

41   *Had private-sector union density been in 2013:* Ibid.

41   *lost wages for men with private-sector, nonunion jobs:* Ibid.

42   *8 percent below where it was in 1967:* Lawrence Mishel, "Declining Value of the Federal Minimum Wage Is a Major Factor Driving Inequality" (Washington, DC: Economic Policy Institute, Feb. 21, 2013).

42   *two-thirds of the growth of the wage gap between female workers:* Lawrence Mishel et al., *The State of Working America* (Ithaca, NY: Cornell University Press, 2012), 292.

42   *"It's the pay":* Sepia Coleman, telephone interview by author, Oct. 19, 2016.

43   *Four million workers got a raise in 2017:* Janelle Jones and David Cooper, "State Minimum Wage Increases Helped 4.3 Million Workers, but Federal Inaction Has Left Many More Behind" (Washington, DC: Economic Policy Institute, Jan. 9, 2017).

43   *the government viewed monopolies as a potent threat to democracy:* Barry Lynn, *Cornered* (Hoboken, NJ: John Wiley & Sons, 2010), ebook.

43   *"The liberty of a democracy is not safe":* Franklin D. Roosevelt, "Message to Congress on Curbing Monopolies," Apr. 29, 1938. Online by Gerhard Peters and John T. Woolley, The American Presidency Project, http://www.presidency.ucsb.edu/ws/?pid=15637.

43   *major industries . . . saw significant consolidation:* Lynn, *Cornered.*

44   *pizza delivery:* Rick Hynum, "Pizza Power 2017: A State of the Industry Report," *PMQ Pizza Magazine,* Dec. 2016.

44   *prevalence of non-compete agreements:* U.S. Department of the Treasury, Office of Economic Policy, "Non-compete Contracts: Economic Effects and Policy Implications," Mar. 2016,

https://www.treasury.gov/resource-center/economic-policy
/Documents/UST%20Non-competes%20Report.pdf.

44   *That reduces "job churn":* Jason Furman and Peter Orszag, "A
     Firm-Level Perspective on the Role of Rents in the Rise in
     Inequality" (presentation at "A Just Society" Centennial Event
     in Honor of Joseph Stiglitz, Columbia University, New York,
     2015).

44   *"profit inequality":* Ibid.

44   *ratio of pay between managers and janitors:* Alan B. Krueger,
     "Land of Hope and Dreams: Rock and Roll, Economics, and
     Rebuilding the Middle Class" (remarks at the Rock and Roll
     Hall of Fame, Cleveland, OH, June 12, 2013).

45   *outsourcing jobs that were not related to their "core competencies":*
     David Weil, *The Fissured Workplace* (Cambridge, MA: Harvard
     University Press, 2014), ebook.

45   *the government did not track contingent employment:* Lydia De-
     Pillis, "We're Doing a Terrible Job of Measuring the Modern
     Workforce, and the Feds Know It," *Washington Post,* Oct. 9,
     2015.

45   *"alternative work arrangements":* Lawrence F. Katz and Alan
     B. Krueger, "The Rise and Nature of Alternative Work Ar-
     rangements in the United States, 1995–2015" (Princeton, NJ,
     Mar. 29, 2016).

45   *"undertook informal paid work activities":* Barbara Robles and
     Marysol McGee, "Exploring Online and Offline Informal
     Work: Findings from the Enterprising and Informal Work Ac-
     tivities (EIWA) Survey" (Finance and Economics Discussion
     Series, Divisions of Research & Statistics and Monetary Affairs,
     Federal Reserve Board, Washington, DC, 2016).

46   *likely to find themselves unemployed:* Ibid.

46   *"Do these companies":* Erin Kramer, interview by author,
     Apr. 21, 2017.

48   *estimates drift as high as 45 million:* Katy Steinmetz, "Exclu-
     sive: See How Big the Gig Economy Really Is," *Time,* Jan. 6,
     2016.

49   *median full-time driver . . . makes $90,766 a year:* Matt Mc-
      Farland, "Uber's Remarkable Growth Could End the Era of
      Poorly Paid Cab Drivers," *Washington Post,* May 27, 2014.

49   *"UberX driver partners":* Alison Griswold, "In Search of Uber's
      Unicorn," *Slate,* Oct. 27, 2014.

49   *"a culture of expendable drivers":* Uber Drivers Network, "Open
      Letter to Uber, Travis, Josh Mohrer, Uber's Investors and Em-
      ployees," Medium, Feb. 4, 2016, https://medium.com/@Uber
      driversnetwork/open-letter-to-uber-travis-josh-mohrer-uber
      -s-investors-and-employees-63a3b8200056.

50   *"dependent contractors":* Lauren Weber, "What If There Were
      a New Type of Worker? Dependent Contractor," *Wall Street
      Journal,* Jan. 28, 2015.

50   *levy a surcharge:* This appeared in Annie Lowrey, "The Uber
      Economy Requires a New Category of Worker," *New York,*
      July 9, 2015.

51   *"shared security system":* Nick Hanauer and David Rolf, "Shared
      Security, Shared Growth," *Democracy* 37 (Summer 2015).

51   *"It's that we need way more control":* Carrie Gleason, telephone
      interview by author, Apr. 27, 2017.

51   *$400 in an emergency:* Board of Governors of the Federal Re-
      serve System, "Report on the Economic Well-Being of U.S.
      Households in 2015," May 2016.

53   *"permanent strike fund":* Andy Stern, telephone interview by
      author, June 29, 2016.

53   *McResource help line:* Chris Morran, "McDonald's McResource
      Help Line Tells Worker How to Get Welfare Benefits," *Con-
      sumerist,* Oct. 23, 2013.

53   *more than half were enrolled in public assistance programs:* Al-
      legretto, Doussard, Graham-Squire, Jacobs, Thompson, and
      Thompson, "Fast Food, Poverty Wages."

53   *"high public cost of low wages":* Ken Jacobs, Ian Perry, and
      Jenifer MacGillvary, "The High Public Cost of Low Wages"
      (Berkeley: University of California, Berkeley, Center for Labor
      Research and Education, Apr. 2015).

Chapter Three: A Sense of Purpose

55   *Three in four people who responded to one 2010 survey:* Jessica Godofsky, Carl Van Horn, and Cliff Zukin, "American Workers Assess an Economic Disaster" (John J. Heldrich Center for Workforce Development, Rutgers, the State University of New Jersey, New Brunswick, Sept. 2010).

55   *one in three construction workers lost their job:* U.S. Bureau of Labor Statistics, "All Employees in Construction and All Employees in Manufacturing, Seasonally Adjusted," raw data.

55   *number of people on the job declined by nearly 8 million:* U.S. Bureau of Labor Statistics, "Nonfarm Payrolls, Seasonally Adjusted," raw data.

56   *average time spent unemployed soared to forty-one weeks:* U.S. Bureau of Labor Statistics, "Average (Mean) Duration of Unemployment," raw data.

56   *"99ers," hit 15 percent:* Karen Kosanovich and Eleni Theodossiou Sherman, "Trends in Long-Term Unemployment," U.S. Bureau of Labor Statistics, Spotlight on Statistics, Mar. 2015, https://www.bls.gov/spotlight/2015/long-term -unemployment/pdf/long-term-unemployment.pdf.

56   *a newly jobless worker had a roughly one in four chance:* Rob Valletta, "Long-Term Unemployment: What Do We Know?," Federal Reserve Bank of San Francisco, *FRBSF Economic Letter,* Feb. 4, 2013, http://www.frbsf.org/economic-research /publications/economic-letter/2013/february/long-term -unemployment/.

56   *simple discrimination was a factor too:* Rand Ghayad and William Dickens, "What Can We Learn by Disaggregating the Unemployment-Vacancy Relationship?," Federal Reserve Bank of Boston, Public Policy Briefs No. 12-3, Oct. 2012, https:// www.bostonfed.org/-/media/Documents/Workingpapers /PDF/economic/ppb/2012/ppb123.pdf.

57   *parts of the country . . . have still not recovered:* Danny Yagan, "Is the Great Recession Really Over? Longitudinal Evidence of Enduring Employment Impacts," Berkeley and NBER, Sept. 2017, https://eml.berkeley.edu/~yagan/Hysteresis.pdf.

57   *"I was told I was too articulate"*: Annie Lowrey, "Caught in a Revolving Door of Unemployment," *New York Times,* Nov. 16, 2013.

58   *every civilization has its virtue:* William Deresiewicz, "Virtually Exhausted: The Limitations of the American Work Ethic," *American Scholar,* Aug. 26, 2012.

58   *The Greeks and the Romans valorized a life of leisure:* Daniel T. Rodgers, *The Work Ethic in Industrial America 1850–1920,* 2nd ed. (Chicago: University of Chicago Press, 2014), ebook.

58   *Puritans and Quakers who saw idleness as a sin:* Ibid.

58   *"Idleness increases in the town exceedingly"*: Louis B. Wright, *The Cultural Life of the American Colonies* (Mineola, NY: Dover Publications, 2002), ebook.

58   *"In England a king hath little more to do"*: Thomas Paine, "Common Sense," in *Selected Writings of Thomas Paine* (New Haven, CT: Yale University Press, 2014), ebook.

59   *"In America no one is degraded because he works"*: Alexis de Tocqueville, *Democracy in America* (1835; University of Virginia American Studies Program, 2003), ebook, http://xroads .virginia.edu/~hyper/detoc/toc_indx.html.

60   **"No admission here, except on business"**: Quoted in Rodgers, *Work Ethic.*

60   *"emerged from the poverty and obscurity"*: Benjamin Franklin, *The Autobiography of Benjamin Franklin,* ed. Peter Conn (1791; Philadelphia: University of Pennsylvania Press, 2005), ebook, Project MUSE.

60   *Of the thirteen virtues, humility was listed last:* Ibid.

60   *"The planter, the farmer, the mechanic"*: Andrew Jackson, Farewell Address, Mar. 4, 1837. Online by Gerhard Peters and John T. Woolley, The American Presidency Project, http://www .presidency.ucsb.edu/ws/?pid=67087.

60   *"Just what might happen to any poor man's son!"*: Quoted in James M. McPherson, *Abraham Lincoln* (New York: Oxford University Press, 2009), ebook.

61 *"life should be better and richer and fuller for everyone"*: Quoted in Jim Cullen, *The American Dream: A Short History of an Idea That Shaped a Nation* (New York: Oxford University Press, 2003), ebook.

61 *$10 billion fortune:* Ana Swanson, "The Myth and Reality of Donald Trump's Business Empire," *Washington Post,* Feb. 29, 2016.

61 *"hard work" and "ambition" as the two most important factors:* "Economic Mobility and the American Dream: Where Do We Stand in the Wake of the Great Recession?" (Washington, DC: Economic Mobility Project, Pew Charitable Trusts, May 2011).

61 *World Values Survey:* Alberto Alesina and George-Marios Angeletos, "Fairness and Redistribution: US vs. Europe," *American Economic Review* 95 (Sept. 2005): 913–35.

62 *"success in life is pretty much determined"*: George Gao, "How Do Americans Stand Out from the Rest of the World?," *Fact-Tank* (blog), Pew Research Center, Mar. 12, 2015, http://www .pewresearch.org/fact-tank/2015/03/12/how-do-americans -stand-out-from-the-rest-of-the-world/.

62 *"Americans perceive wealth and success"*: Alesina and Angeletos, "Fairness and Redistribution."

62 *1,783 hours a year:* Organization for Economic Cooperation and Development, "Average Annual Hours Actually Worked per Worker," raw data, https://stats.oecd.org/Index.aspx?Data SetCode=ANHRS.

62 *Engaged employees "are involved"*: "The State of the Global Workplace: Employee Engagement Insights for Business Leaders Worldwide" (Washington, DC: Gallup, 2013).

62 *"sense of identity"*: Rebecca Riffkin, "In U.S., 55% of Workers Get Sense of Identity from Their Job," Gallup News, Aug. 22, 2014, http://news.gallup.com/poll/175400/workers -sense-identity-job.aspx.

62 *proves particularly devastating:* Steven J. Davis and Till von Wachter, "Recessions and the Costs of Job Loss," *Brookings Papers on Economic Activity,* Fall 2011.

62   *"These sustained earnings losses"*: Mai Dao and Prakash Loun-
gani, *The Human Cost of Recessions: Assessing It, Reducing It*
(Washington, DC: IMF Staff Position Notes, International
Monetary Fund, Nov. 11, 2010).

63   *socialize for two hours or less:* Cliff Zukin, Carl E. Van Horn,
and Charley Stone, "Categorizing the Unemployed by the Impact of the Recession" (John J. Heldrich Center for Workforce
Development, Rutgers, the State University of New Jersey,
New Brunswick, Dec. 2011).

63   *"the life satisfaction of the unemployed does not restore itself"*:
Clemens Hetschko, Andreas Knabe, and Ronnie Schöb, "Identity and Wellbeing: How Retiring Makes the Unemployed
Happier," *Vox* (blog), the Centre for Economic Policy Research, May 4, 2012.

63   *the "latent functions" of employment:* Marie Jahoda, "Social Institutions and Human Needs: A Comment on Fryer and Payne,"
Leisure Studies 3 (1984): 297–99, http://www.tandfonline.com
/doi/abs/10.1080/02614368400390241.

64   *"retired" rather than "unemployed":* Hetschko, Knabe, and
Schöb, "Identity and Wellbeing."

65   *Iranians to drop out:* Djavad Salehi-Isfahani and Mohammad H.
Mostafavi-Dehzooei, "Cash Transfers and Labor Supply: Evidence from a Large-Scale Program in Iran" (Giza, Egypt: Economic Research Forum, Working Paper no. 1090, May 2017),
http://erf.org.eg/publications/cash-transfers-and-labor-supply
-evidence-from-a-large-scale-program-in-iran/.

65   *a survey of data on unconditional cash-transfer experiments:*
Ioana Marinescu, "No Strings Attached: The Behavioral Ef-
fects of U.S. Unconditional Cash Transfer Programs" (New
York: Roosevelt Institute, May 11, 2017).

66   *deep poverty, a lack of engagement with the labor force:* Brian
Steensland, *The Failed Welfare Revolution: America's Struggle over
Guaranteed Income Policy* (Princeton, NJ: Princeton University
Press, 2008), ebook.

66   *the first randomized control trials in the United States:* Marinescu, "No Strings Attached."

66 *Donald Rumsfeld and Dick Cheney:* Levine et al., "Retrospective on the Negative Income Tax Experiments."

67 *$84,000 a month as of 2012:* Timothy Williams, "$1 Million Each Year for All, as Long as Tribe's Luck Holds," *New York Times,* Aug. 9, 2012.

67 *young people attending school:* Eric A. Hanushek, "Non-Labor-Supply Responses to the Income-Maintenance Experiments," in *Lessons from the Income Maintenance Experiments,* ed. Alicia H. Munnell (Boston: Federal Reserve Bank of Boston and Brookings Institution, 1987), 106–22.

67 *such a bad thing?:* Dylan Matthews, "The Two Most Popular Critiques of Basic Income Are Both Wrong," Vox, July 20, 2017.

67 *"garden capital of Manitoba":* Annie Lowrey, "Switzerland's Proposal to Pay People for Being Alive," *New York Times Magazine,* Nov. 12, 2013.

68 *"where it should be":* Lindor Reynolds, "Dauphin's Great Experiment," *Winnipeg Free Press,* Dec. 3, 2009.

68 *mothers and teenage boys:* David Calnitsky and Jonathan P. Latner, "Basic Income in a Small Town: Understanding the Elusive Effects on Work," *Social Problems* 64, no. 3 (Aug. 1, 2017): 373–97.

68 *hospitalizations and mental-health diagnoses:* Evelyn Forget, interview by author, Aug. 20, 2013.

68 *"It always should be worth taking the job":* Peter S. Goodman, "Free Cash in Finland, Must Be Jobless," *New York Times,* Dec. 17, 2016.

69 *"When I didn't have a basic income":* Scott Santens, "What If You Got $1,000 a Month, Just for Being Alive? I Decided to Find Out," Vox, Nov. 14, 2016.

70 *"We are not facing a future without work":* Scott Santens, "A Future Without Jobs Does Not Equal a Future Without Work," *HuffPost,* Oct. 7, 2016.

70 *"The most promising way forward":* Nick Srnicek and Alex Williams, *Inventing the Future: Postcapitalism and a World Without Work* (Brooklyn, NY: Verso, 2015), ebook.

71   *"There was even a song":* Ezra Klein, "'An Orgy of Serious
      Policy Discussion' with Paul Krugman," Vox, Dec. 14, 2017.

Chapter Four: The Poverty Hack

74   *$2-a-day extreme poverty line:* The World Bank's line is techni-
      cally $1.90 a day, and refers to consumption. We will round it
      to $2, as many development economists do.

77   *randomized control trials of government cash-transfer programs:*
      Abhijit Banerjee, Rema Hanna, Gabriel Kreindler, and Benja-
      min A. Olken, "Debunking the Stereotype of the Lazy Welfare
      Recipient: Evidence from Cash Transfer Programs World-
      wide," Social Science Research Network, Sept. 2016, 10.2139/
      ssrn.2703447.

77   *Another sweeping review:* Francesca Bastagli, Jessica Hagen-
      Zanker, Luke Harman, Valentina Barca, Georgina Sturge, and
      Tanja Schmidt, with Luca Pellerano, *Cash Transfers: What Does
      the Evidence Say? A Rigorous Review of Programme Impact and of
      the Role of Design and Implementation Features* (London: Overseas
      Development Institute, July 2016).

78   *"husbands were waiting for wives to return":* Charity Moore,
      "Nicaragua's Red de Protección Social: An Exemplary but
      Short-Lived Conditional Cash Transfer Programme" (Brasilia:
      International Policy Centre for Inclusive Growth, Country
      Study no. 17, Jan. 2009), http://hdl.handle.net/10419/71770.

78   *more vice products:* Rosamaría Dasso and Fernando Fernandez,
      "Temptation Goods and Conditional Cash Transfers in Peru"
      (La Plata, Argentina: Center for Distributive, Labor and Social
      Studies, Sept. 24, 2013).

78   *The results were clear:* Bastagli, Hagen-Zanker, Harman, Barca,
      Sturge, Schmidt, and Pellerano, *Cash Transfers.*

79   *"a trick question":* Michael Faye, telephone interview by author,
      Nov. 6, 2016.

80   *mass-produced mobile phones:* "Mobile Phones Are Transform-
      ing Africa," *Economist,* Dec. 10, 2016.

80   *"satellite images to see housing changes":* Mike Krieger, tele-
      phone interview by author, Feb. 8, 2017.

82 *85,148 people with a staff of 237:* Joe Huston, email interview by author, Dec. 18, 2017.

83 *these cash transfers had powerful effects:* Johannes Haushofer and Jeremy Shapiro, "The Short-Term Impact of Unconditional Cash Transfers to the Poor: Experimental Evidence from Kenya," *Quarterly Journal of Economics* 131, no. 4 (Apr. 25, 2016): 1973–2042.

85 *"manage sporadic income, juggle expenses":* Anandi Mani et al., "Poverty Impedes Cognitive Function," *Science* 341, no. 6149 (Aug. 30, 2013): 976–80.

89 *microsavings programs:* Dean Karlan and Jacob Appel, *More Than Good Intentions: How a New Economics Is Helping to Solve Global Poverty* (New York: Dutton, 2011), ebook.

89 *BRAC . . . is wildly effective:* Abhijit Banerjee, Esther Duflo, Nathanael Goldberg, Dean Karlan, Robert Osei, William Parienté, Jeremy Shapiro, Bram Thuysbaert, and Christopher Udry, "A Multifaceted Program Causes Lasting Progress for the Very Poor: Evidence from Six Countries," *Science* 348, no. 6236 (May 15, 2015).

90 *a glut of Toms shoes disrupts the businesses:* Sarika Bansal, "Shopping for a Better World," *New York Times,* May 9, 2012.

90 *donate-a-cow charities:* David Kestenbaum and Jacob Goldstein, "Money for Nothing and Your Cows for Free," *This American Life,* ep. 503, Aug. 16, 2013, https://www.thisamericanlife.org /radio-archives/episode/503/i-was-just-trying-to-help?act=1.

90 *"The question should always be":* Michael Faye, telephone interview by author, Nov. 6, 2016.

91 *"People escaping from conflict or disaster":* "Cash Relief," International Rescue Committee, https://www.rescue.org/topic /cash-relief.

91 *Syrian refugees spent in Lebanon:* "Emergency Economies: The Impact of Cash Assistance in Lebanon" (Beirut: International Rescue Committee, Aug. 2014), https://www.rescue.org/sites /default/files/document/631/emergencyeconomiesevaluation report-lebanon2014.pdf.

91   *an estimated 94 percent:* High Level Panel on Humanitarian Cash Transfers, *Doing Cash Differently: How Cash Transfers Can Transform Humanitarian Aid* (London: Overseas Development Institute and Center for Global Development, Sept. 2015).

92   *"It's really a basic psychological feature":* Amanda Glassman, telephone interview by author, Oct. 16, 2016.

92   *"good people working":* Paul Niehaus, telephone interview by author, Oct. 21, 2016.

92   *"The easy critique for cash-transfer people":* Justin Sandefur, telephone interview by author, Oct. 22, 2016.

93   *the poverty gap:* Lowrey, "Future of Not Working."

93   *what the world spends on humanitarian aid:* Ibid.

93   *"almost no factual basis":* Mike Kubzansky, telephone interview by author, Feb. 10, 2017.

94   *"You might need stories":* Chris Hughes, telephone interview by author, Oct. 21, 2016.

Chapter Five: The Kludgeocracy

95   *one of India's more destitute states:* Reserve Bank of India, *Handbook of Statistics on the Indian Economy,* Table 162: Number and Percentage of Population Below Poverty Line, Sept. 2013.

95   *still involved in farming:* K. M. Singh, M. S. Meena, R. K. P. Singh, Abhay Kumar, and Anjani Kumar, "Rural Poverty in Jharkhand, India: An Empirical Study Based on Panel Data" (New Delhi: National Institute of Agricultural Economics and Policy Research, Aug. 23, 2012).

96   *programs are ill targeted:* Ministry of Finance, Government of India, "Economic Survey 2016–17," Jan. 2017.

97   *a kludgeocracy:* Steven M. Teles, "Kludgeocracy in America," *National Affairs* no. 33 (Fall 2013), http://www.nationalaffairs .com/publications/detail/kludgeocracy-in-america.

97   *shift away from subsidy programs:* Ministry of Finance, "Economic Survey 2016–17."

97 *A UBI stands as a natural end point:* Arvind Subramanian, interview by author, Apr. 18, 2017.

98 *one in ten people:* Francisco Ferreira, Christoph Lakner, and Carolina Sanchez, "The 2017 Global Poverty Update from the World Bank," *Let's Talk Development* (blog), Oct. 16, 2017, http://blogs.worldbank.org/developmenttalk/2017-global -poverty-update-world-bank.

98 *A person living below it:* Annie Lowrey, "Is It Crazy to Think We Can Eradicate Poverty?," *New York Times Magazine,* Apr. 30, 2013.

99 *"there is something defective in India's 'path to development'":* Jean Drèze and Amartya Sen, *An Uncertain Glory: India and Its Contradictions* (Princeton, NJ: Princeton University Press, 2013), ebook.

100 *An estimated 130 of them:* Maddalena Honorati, Ugo Gentilini, and Ruslan G. Yemtsov, *The State of Social Safety Nets 2015* (Washington, DC: World Bank Group, June 2015).

100 *a "revolution from the global south":* Joseph Hanlon, Armando Barrientos, and David Hulme, *Just Give Money to the Poor: The Development Revolution from the Global South* (Herndon, VA: Kumarian Press, 2010).

100 *whether cash transfers have long-range benefits:* Bastagli, Hagen-Zanker, Harman, Barca, Sturge, Schmidt, and Pellerano, *Cash Transfers.*

101 *anemia among toddlers:* Francesca Lamanna, "A Model from Mexico for the World," *World Bank* (news website), Nov. 19, 2014, http://www.worldbank.org/en/news/feature/2014/11/19 /un-modelo-de-mexico-para-el-mundo.

101 *Brazil cut its extreme poverty rate:* Deborah Wetzel, "Bolsa Família: Brazil's Quiet Revolution," *World Bank* (news website), Nov. 4, 2013.

101 *a sweeping economic survey:* Ministry of Finance, "Economic Survey 2016–17."

101 *impoverished rural Indians meet the government's calorie targets:* Atish Patel, "Why Indians Cut Down on Calories as the Country Grew Richer," *Wall Street Journal,* June 15, 2015.

101 *40 percent of the program's benefits:* Ministry of Finance, "Economic Survey 2016–17."

101 *study surveyed 1,499 households:* Paul Niehaus and Sandip Sukhtankar, "Corruption Dynamics: The Golden Goose Effect," *American Economic Journal: Economic Policy* 5, no. 4 (Nov. 2013): 230–69, https://www.aeaweb.org/articles?id=10.1257/pol.5.4.230.

102 *"you are at the mercy of the* sarpanch*":* Abhijit Banerjee, telephone interview by author, June 28, 2017.

102 *"even identifying the poor has been characterized by controversy":* Pranab Bardhan, telephone interview by author, June 15, 2017.

103 *the "first mile" challenge . . . the "last mile" challenge:* Siddharth George and Arvind Subramanian, "Transforming the Fight Against Poverty in India," *New York Times,* July 22, 2015.

104 *"What we are creating":* Lydia Polgreen, "Scanning 2.4 Billion Eyes, India Tries to Connect Poor to Growth," *New York Times,* Sept. 1, 2011.

104 *"The system in India":* Jeanette Rodrigues, "India ID Program Wins World Bank Praise Despite 'Big Brother' Fears," Bloomberg, Mar. 15, 2017.

104 *"we will have to lift the poor out":* Unni Krishnan, "India Opens 15 Million Bank Accounts in Modi's Inclusion Drive," Bloomberg, Aug. 28, 2014.

104 *cash still accounts for nearly 80 percent of consumer and business payments:* Rama Lakshmi, "Millions of Indians Move from Cash to Digital Payments. But Some Ask Whether It's Safe," *Washington Post,* Jan. 14, 2017.

104 *20 ATMs for every one hundred thousand adults:* International Monetary Fund, Financial Access Survey, "Automated Teller Machines per 100,000 Adults," raw data, https://data.worldbank.org/indicator/FB.ATM.TOTL.P5.

105 *"Extending financial inclusion to reach the remotest":* George and Subramanian, "Transforming the Fight."

110 *"arguing back and forth with very little data":* C. V. Madhukar, telephone interview by author, July 8, 2017.

111 *"It has no role in that"*: Reetika Khera, telephone interview by author, June 7, 2017.

111 *"pain without gain"*: Drèze Nazar Khalid, Khera, and Anmol Somanchi, "Aadhaar and Food Security in Jharkhand: Pain Without Gain?" *Economic and Political Weekly* LII, no. 50 (Dec. 16, 2017): 50–59.

Chapter Six: The Ragged Edge

116 *the World Bank would classify her as living in poverty:* Roser and Ortiz-Ospina, "Global Extreme Poverty."

116 *subsist on less than $2 a person a day:* Kathryn Edin and H. Luke Shaefer, *$2.00 a Day: Living on Almost Nothing in America* (New York: Houghton Mifflin Harcourt, 2015), ebook.

116 *A "crude" assessment of extreme poverty:* Cory Smith and Laurence Chandy, "How Poor Are America's Poorest? U.S. $2 a Day Poverty in a Global Context" (Washington, DC: Brookings Institution, Aug. 26, 2014).

116 *"If you had to choose between living"*: Annie Lowrey, "Is It Better to Be Poor in Bangladesh or the Mississippi Delta?" *Atlantic,* Mar. 8, 2017.

117 *that country faced any number of economic calamities:* Pound, *Poverty and Vagrancy in Tudor England.*

118 *A series of "Poor Laws" empowered parishes:* Walter I. Trattner, *From Poor Law to Welfare State: A History of Social Welfare in America,* 6th ed. (New York: Simon & Schuster, 2007), ebook.

118 *The "deserving poor"*: Ibid.

118 *Beggars were whipped:* Alexandra Briscoe, "Poverty in Elizabethan England," BBC, Feb. 17, 2011.

118 *things like fuel, food, or cash to the indigent:* Trattner, *From Poor Law to Welfare State.*

118 *"old age payments"*: Michael Hiltzik, *The New Deal* (New York: Simon & Schuster, 2012), ebook.

118 *"Many Americans live on the outskirts of hope"*: Lyndon B. Johnson, "Annual Message to the Congress on the State of

the Union," Jan. 8, 1964. Online by Gerhard Peters and John T. Woolley, The American Presidency Project, http://www .presidency.ucsb.edu/ws/?pid=26787.

119   *"ending welfare as we know it":* The Clinton/Gore 1992 Committee, "The Clinton Plan: Welfare to Work" (1992), https:// www.washingtonpost.com/video/politics/bill-clinton-in -1992-ad-a-plan-to-end-welfare-as-we-know-it/2016/08/30 /9e6350f8-6ee0-11e6-993f-73c693a89820_video.html.

119   *dramatically reduced deprivation:* Gary V. Engelhardt and Jonathan Gruber, "Social Security and the Evolution of Elderly Poverty" (NBER Working Paper no. 10466, May 2004).

119   *Social Security lifted 26.6 million people:* Trudi Renwick and Liana Fox, *The Supplemental Poverty Measure: 2015* (Washington, DC: U.S. Census Bureau, Sept. 13, 2016), https://www .census.gov/library/publications/2016/demo/p60-258.html.

120   *"You would think that the government":* Johns Hopkins University, "U.S. Welfare Spending Up—but Help for the Neediest Down," press release, May 6, 2014, http://releases.jhu .edu/2014/05/06/u-s-welfare-spending-up-but-help-for-the -neediest-down/.

122   *mostly by accident in 2010:* Nik DeCosta-Klipa, "How Paul LePage Got Elected, and How Mainers Think They Can Fix a Broken Voting System," *Boston Globe,* Sept. 1, 2016.

123   *less and less of the state's federal grant:* Eric Russell, "Maine Sits on Millions in Federal Welfare Dollars, yet Poverty Rises," *Portland Press Herald,* Oct. 23, 2016.

123   *"Donald Trump before Donald Trump":* Associated Press, "I Was Donald Trump Before Donald Trump Became Popular," *New York Post,* Mar. 5, 2016.

123   *"The Maine food stamp work requirement":* Robert Rector, Rachel Sheffield, and Kevin Dayaratna, "Maine Food Stamp Work Requirement Cuts Non-Parent Caseload by 80 Percent" (Washington, DC: Heritage Foundation, Feb. 8, 2016).

123   *"If a man will not work":* Caitlin Dewey, "GOP Lawmaker: The Bible Says 'If a Man Will Not Work, He Shall Not Eat,' " *Washington Post,* Mar. 31, 2017.

124   *"The important part here is defining what constitutes success":* Mary Mayhew, telephone interview by author, Mar. 22, 2017.

124   *"Too many disadvantaged individuals":* LaDonna Pavetti, "Work Requirements Don't Cut Poverty, Evidence Shows" (Washington, DC: Center on Budget and Policy Priorities, June 7, 2016).

125   *Wyoming's welfare program:* "Wyoming TANF Spending" (Washington, DC: Center on Budget and Policy Priorities, 2017), https://www.cbpp.org/sites/default/files/atoms/files/tanf_spending_wy.pdf.

125   *its impoverished children:* Ife Floyd, LaDonna Pavetti, and Liz Schott, "TANF Reaching Few Poor Families" (Washington, DC: Center on Budget and Policy Priorities, Mar. 30, 2017).

125   *Georgia's welfare program:* Annie Lowrey, "It's Time for Welfare Reform Again," *New York,* Feb. 19, 2016.

125   *"Honey, I'm sorry":* Edin and Shaefer, *$2.00 a Day.*

125   *median income of affected families just $3,120 a year:* Sandra Butler, "TANF Time Limits and Maine Families: Consequences of Withdrawing the Safety Net" (Augusta: Maine Equal Justice Partners, Feb. 25, 2013), http://www.mejp.org/sites/default/files/TANF-Study-SButler-Feb2013.pdf.

126   *eight times the national average:* "It's Time to End Child Poverty in Maine" (Augusta: Maine Equal Justice Partners, Aug. 2016), http://www.mejp.org/content/its-time-end-child-poverty-maine.

128   *about 4 percent of GDP a year:* Harry Holzer, "The Economic Costs of Child Poverty," Testimony Before the U.S. House Committee on Ways and Means, Jan. 24, 2007, https://www.urban.org/research/publication/economic-costs-child-poverty.

128   *The problem with the welfare state:* Charles Murray, telephone interview by author, July 7, 2016.

128   *a "certain minimum income for everyone":* F. A. Hayek, *Law, Legislation and Liberty,* vol. 3, *The Political Order of a Free People* (Chicago: University of Chicago Press, 1973), 55.

128   *"Let us place a floor under the income":* Richard Nixon: "Annual Message to the Congress on the State of the Union,"

Jan. 22, 1971. Online by Gerhard Peters and John T. Woolley, The American Presidency Project, http://www.presidency
.ucsb.edu/ws/?pid=3110.

129 *"our only hope":* Charles Murray, "A Guaranteed Income for
Every American," *Wall Street Journal,* June 3, 2016.

129 *"Government agencies are the worst of all mechanisms":* Ibid.

129 *a minimum of 90 cents on the dollar:* Robert Greenstein, "Romney's Charge That Most Federal Low-Income Spending Goes
for 'Overhead' and 'Bureaucrats' Is False" (Washington, DC:
Center on Budget and Policy Priorities, Jan. 23, 2012), https://
www.cbpp.org/research/romneys-charge-that-most-federal
-low-income-spending-goes-for-overhead-and-bureaucrats-is.

130 *raise about $1,582 per person:* Ed Dolan, "Could We Afford
a Universal Basic Income? (Part 2 of a Series)," *EconoMonitor*
(blog), Jan. 13, 2014.

130 *end "many of the current 126 welfare programs":* Andy Stern,
*Raising the Floor: How a Universal Basic Income Can Renew Our
Economy and Rebuild the American Dream* (New York: Public-
Affairs, 2016), ebook.

130 *"A single parent would":* Daniel Hemel, "Bringing the Basic
Income Back to Earth," *New Rambler,* Sept. 19, 2016, http://
newramblerreview.com/book-reviews/economics/bringing
-the-basic-income-back-to-earth.

131 *"certain inalienable political rights" . . . "equality in the pursuit of happiness":* Franklin D. Roosevelt, "State of the Union
Address," Jan. 11, 1944, http://www.fdrlibrary.marist.edu
/archives/address_text.html.

Chapter Seven: The Same Bad Treatment

132 *"It was not difficult to get food stamps":* U.S. Senate, Committee on Finance, "Welfare and Poverty in America," 114th
Congress, 1st sess., Oct. 29, 2015, https://www.finance.senate
.gov/imo/media/doc/21409.pdf.

133 *"They had very realistic guidelines":* Aretha Jackson, telephone
interview by author, Nov. 8, 2017.

136 *half of their economic output:* Alberto Alesina, Edward Glaeser,
and Bruce Sacerdote, "Why Doesn't the United States Have

a European-Style Welfare State?," *Brookings Papers on Economic Activity*, no. 2, 2001.

136   *"Within the United States":* Ibid.

136   *"residents of all races tend to 'hunker down' ":* Robert D. Putnam, "*E Pluribus Unum*: Diversity and Community in the Twenty-First Century," *Scandinavian Political Studies* 30, no. 2 (June 15, 2007): 137–74, http://onlinelibrary.wiley.com/doi /10.1111/j.1467-9477.2007.00176.x/abstract.

137   *"heterogeneity hampers all forms of cooperation":* Ozan Aksoy, "Effects of Heterogeneity and Homophily on Cooperation," *Social Psychology Quarterly* 78, no. 4 (2015): 324–44, http:// journals.sagepub.com/doi/abs/10.1177/0190272515612403.

137   *one study by the social psychologists:* Maureen A. Craig and Jennifer A. Richeson, "On the Precipice of a 'Majority-Minority' America: Perceived Status Threat from the Racial Demographic Shift Affects White Americans' Political Ideology," *Psychological Science* 25, no. 6 (Apr. 2014): 1189–97, http://journals.sagepub .com/doi/abs/10.1177/0956797614527113.

137   *nine out of ten of whom speak Finnish at home: World Factbook* (Washington, DC: Central Intelligence Agency, 2017), https:// www.cia.gov/library/publications/the-world-factbook/index .html.

138   *"serve as an entering wedge":* Quoted in Michael B. Katz, *In the Shadow of the Poorhouse: A Social History of Welfare in America,* 10th anniversary ed. (New York: Basic Books, 1996), 248.

138   **The history is complicated and contested:** Larry DeWitt, "The Decision to Exclude Agricultural and Domestic Workers from the 1935 Social Security Act," *Social Security Bulletin* 70, no. 4 (2010).

138   *two-thirds of black workers:* Ira Katznelson, *Fear Itself: The New Deal and the Origins of Our Time* (New York: Liveright, 2013), ebook.

139   *kept black Americans from migrating . . . or from moving north:* Kenneth J. Neubeck and Noel A. Cazenave, *Welfare Racism: Playing the Race Card Against America's Poor* (New York: Routledge, 2002), 61.

139   *"man in the house rule"*: Ibid., 60–61.

139   *"In essence, the United States' peculiar private-based health-care system"*: Vann R. Newkirk II, "The Fight for Health Care Has Always Been About Civil Rights," *Atlantic,* June 27, 2017.

139   *to depend exclusively on white opinion:* Colleen M. Grogan and Sunggeun Park, "The Racial Divide in State Medicaid Expansions," *Journal of Health Politics, Policy, and Law* 42, no. 3 (June 2017): 539–72.

140   *"significantly less likely to expand the Medicaid program"*: Ibid.

140   *There was a woman in Chicago:* Josh Levin, "The Welfare Queen," *Slate,* Dec. 19, 2013.

140   *"Work requirements and time limits"*: Linda Burnham, "Racism in United States Welfare Policy," *Race, Poverty & the Environment* 14, no. 1 (Spring 2007): 47.

141   *states with large black populations became:* Heather Hahn, Laudan Y. Aron, Cary Lou, Eleanor Pratt, and Adaeze Okoli, "Why Does Cash Welfare Depend on Where You Live? How and Why State TANF Programs Vary" (Washington, DC: Urban Institute, June 5, 2017).

141   *"When we look at some of these individual policies"*: Alana Semuels, "States with Large Black Populations Are Stingier with Government Benefits," *Atlantic,* June 6, 2017.

141   *"never used a government social program"*: Suzanne Mettler and Julianna Koch, "Who Says They Have Ever Used a Government Social Program? The Role of Policy Visibility" (Ithaca, NY: Cornell University, Feb. 28, 2012).

141   *"American social programs"*: Frances Fox Piven, "Why Welfare Is Racist," in *Race and the Politics of Welfare Reform,* ed. Sanford F. Schram, Joe Brian Soss, and Richard Carl Fording (Ann Arbor: University of Michigan Press, 2010), 323.

142   *even wealthy black individuals:* Richard Rothstein, "Modern Segregation" (presentation to the Atlantic Live Conference, Reinventing the War on Poverty, Washington, DC, Mar. 6, 2014), http://www.epi.org/publication/modern-segregation/.

142 **"on explicit condition *that no sales be made to blacks"*:** Richard Rothstein, "School Policy Is Housing Policy: Deconcentrating Disadvantage to Address the Achievement Gap" in *Race, Equity, and Education: Sixty Years from Brown,* ed. Pedro Noguera, Jill Pierce, and Roey Ahram (New York: Springer, 2015), 32.

142 *the GI Bill:* Ira Katznelson, *When Affirmative Action Was White: An Untold History of Racial Inequality in Twentieth-Century America* (New York: W. W. Norton, 2006), ebook.

142 **Ebony** *magazine:* Ibid.

142 *net worth of nearly $40,000:* Ibid.

143 *Most high-poverty neighborhoods are now majority-minority:* Erica E. Meade, "Overview of Community Characteristics in Areas with Concentrated Poverty" (Washington, DC: Department of Health and Human Services, Office of the Assistant Secretary for Planning and Evaluation, Research Brief, May 2014), https://aspe.hhs.gov/system/files/pdf/40651/rb_concentratedpoverty.pdf.

143 *The average rich black worker:* Gregory Acs, Kenneth Braswell, Elaine Sorensen, and Margery Austin Turner, "The Moynihan Report Revisited" (Washington, DC: Urban Institute, June 2013).

143 *wealth of a person's childhood community:* Raj Chetty and Nathaniel Hendren, "The Impacts of Neighborhoods on Intergenerational Mobility II: County-Level Estimates," May 2017.

143 *just one hundred institutions:* Sarah E. Turner and John Bound, "Closing the Gap or Widening the Divide: The Effects of the G.I. Bill and World War II on the Educational Outcomes of Black Americans" (NBER Working Paper no. 9044, July 2002).

143 *55 percent of applicants:* Ibid.

143 *Black veterans from southern states:* Ibid.

143 *"truly 'separate but equal'":* Celeste K. Carruthers and Marianne H. Wanamaker, "Separate and Unequal in the Labor Market: Human Capital and the Jim Crow Wage Gap" (NBER Working Paper no. 21947, Jan. 2016).

143 *spend $733 more per pupil:* Ary Spatig-Amerikaner, "Unequal Education: Federal Loophole Enables Lower Spending on Students of Color" (Washington, DC: Center for American Progress, Aug. 22, 2012).

143 *educational segregation:* Nikole Hannah-Jones, "Segregation Now," ProPublica, Apr. 16, 2014, https://www.propublica.org /article/segregation-now-full-text.

144 *hourly wage for black men was $15:* Eileen Patten, "Racial, Gender Wage Gaps Persist in U.S. Despite Some Progress," *FactTank* (blog), Pew Research Center, July 1, 2016, http:// www.pewresearch.org/fact-tank/2016/07/01/racial-gender -wage-gaps-persist-in-u-s-despite-some-progress/.

144 *median income of black households:* Carmen DeNavas-Walt and Bernadette D. Proctor, "Income and Poverty in the United States: 2014," Current Population Reports (Washington, DC: U.S. Census Bureau, U.S. Department of Commerce, Economics and Statistics Administration, Sept. 2015).

144 *as income inequality has intensified:* Valerie Wilson and William M. Rodgers III, "Black-White Wage Gaps Expand with Rising Wage Inequality" (Washington, DC: Economic Policy Institute, Sept. 20, 2016).

144 *median net worth of white families:* Janelle Jones, "The Racial Wealth Gap: How African-Americans Have Been Shortchanged out of the Materials to Build Wealth," *Working Economics Blog,* Economic Policy Institute, Washington, DC, Feb. 13, 2017.

144 *no or negative net worth:* Ibid.

144 *own just 5 percent of its wealth:* Emily Badger, "Whites Have Huge Wealth Edge Over Blacks (but Don't Know It)," *New York Times,* Sept. 18, 2017.

144 *"blacks and Latinos are virtually penniless":* Darrick Hamilton, "The Federal Job Guarantee: A Step Toward Racial Justice," *Dissent,* Nov. 9, 2015.

144 *three times the rate for black families:* Dedrick Asante-Muhammad, Chuck Collins, Josh Hoxie, and Emanuel Nieves, "The Ever-Growing Gap: Without Change, African-American and Latino Families Won't Match White Wealth for Centuries"

(Washington, DC: Institute for Policy Studies and the Corporation for Enterprise Development, Aug. 2016).

145   *"What I'm talking about is more than recompense for past injustices":* Ta-Nehisi Coates, "The Case for Reparations," *Atlantic,* June 2014.

145   *the policies supported by:* "Reparations," The Movement for Black Lives, July 26, 2016, https://policy.m4bl.org/reparations/.

147   *the election of a black president:* Ta-Nehisi Coates, "Fear of a Black President," *Atlantic,* Sept. 2012.

147   *"key factor" associated with support for Trump:* Sean McElwee and Jason McDaniel, "Economic Anxiety Didn't Make People Vote Trump, Racism Did," *Nation,* May 8, 2017.

147   *only for those he sees as deserving of them:* Dylan Matthews, "Why the Alt-Right Loves Single-Payer Health Care," Vox, Apr. 4, 2017.

148   *"Why Trump Must Champion Universal Healthcare":* Richard Spencer, "Why Trump Must Champion Universal Healthcare," Altright.com, Mar. 23, 2017.

148   *pushing for a federal jobs guarantee:* Neera Tanden, Carmel Martin, Marc Jarsulic, Brendan Duke, Ben Olinsky, Melissa Boteach, John Halpin, Ruy Teixeira, and Rob Griffin, "Toward a Marshall Plan for America: Rebuilding Our Towns, Cities, and the Middle Class" (Washington, DC: Center for American Progress, May 16, 2017).

148   *"Besides cash in people's pockets":* Hillary Rodham Clinton, *What Happened* (New York: Simon & Schuster, 2017), 239.

Chapter Eight: The $10 Trillion Gift

150   *90 percent of Iceland's women went on strike:* Annadis Rudolfsdottir, "The Day the Women Went on Strike," *Guardian,* Oct. 18, 2005.

150   *"women are indispensable":* Reuters, "Iceland: Women Strike," *New York Times,* Oct. 25, 1975.

150   *"What happened that day":* Kirstie Brewer, "The Day Iceland's Women Went on Strike," BBC, Oct. 23, 2015.

151   *the American Association of Retired Persons:* Susan C. Reinhard, Lynn Friss Feinberg, Rita Choula, and Ari Houser, "Valuing the Invaluable 2015 Update: Undeniable Progress, but Big Gaps Remain" (Washington, DC: AARP Public Policy Institute, July 2015).

151   *a study in the* **Lancet:** Ana Langer et al., "Women and Health: The Key for Sustainable Development," *Lancet* 386, no. 9999 (June 5, 2015): 1165.

151   *McKinsey Global Institute estimates:* Kweilin Ellingrud, Anu Madgavkar, James Manyika, Jonathan Woetzel, Vivian Riefberg, Mekala Krishnan, and Mili Seoni, "The Power of Parity: Advancing Women's Equality in the United States" (McKinsey Global Institute, Apr. 2016).

151   *estimated at 26 percent in the United States:* Benjamin Bridgman, Andrew Dugan, Mikhael Lal, Matthew Osborne, and Shaunda Villones, "Accounting for Household Production in the National Accounts, 1965–2010," *Survey of Current Business* 92, no. 5 (May 2012): 23.

151   *40 percent in Switzerland, and 63 percent in India:* Gaëlle Ferrant, Luca Maria Pesando, and Keiko Nowacka, "Unpaid Care Work: The Missing Link in the Analysis of Gender Gaps in Labour Outcomes" (Paris: OECD Development Centre, Dec. 2014).

152   *Organization for Economic Cooperation and Development study:* Nadim Ahmad and Seung-Hee Koh, "Incorporating Estimates of Household Production of Non-Market Services into International Comparisons of Material Well-Being" (Working Paper no. 42, OECD Statistics Directorate, Paris, Oct. 14, 2011).

152   *"the measuring-rod of money":* Arthur C. Pigou, *The Economics of Welfare* (London: Macmillan, 1932), http://www.econlib.org/library/NPDBooks/Pigou/pgEW1.html.

152   *no "productive labor" without "reproductive labor":* Mignon Duffy, *Making Care Count: A Century of Gender, Race, and Paid Care Work* (New Brunswick, NJ: Rutgers University Press, 2011), 11.

152   *"It's society that's getting a free ride on women's unrewarded contributions":* Judith Shulevitz, "It's Payback Time for Women," *New York Times,* Jan. 8, 2016.

155   *the "second shift":* Arlie Hochschild with Anne Machung, *The Second Shift: Working Families and the Revolution at Home,* rev. ed. (New York: Penguin, 2012).

155   *twice as much housework:* Kim Parker and Wendy Wang, "Modern Parenthood: Roles of Moms and Dads Converge as They Balance Work and Family" (Washington, DC: Pew Research Center, Mar. 14, 2013).

155   *an average of 13.5 hours a week:* Ibid.

155   *tripled in the past fifteen years:* "The MetLife Study of Caregiving Costs to Working Caregivers: Double Jeopardy for Baby Boomers Caring for Their Parents" (Westport, CT: MetLife Mature Market Institute, National Alliance for Caregiving, and Center for Long Term Care Research and Policy, June 2011).

156   *"The need is growing exponentially":* Ai-jen Poo, telephone interview by author, Mar. 2, 2015.

156   *tasks as a "joint responsibility":* Usha Ranji and Alina Salganicoff, "Balancing on Shaky Ground: Women, Work and Family Health" (Menlo Park, CA: Kaiser Family Foundation, Oct. 20, 2014).

156   *World Economic Forum report:* "The Global Gender Gap Report 2016" (Geneva: World Economic Forum, 2016).

156   *"It is simply valuable work":* Emily Peck, "Women Work More Hours Than Men, Get Paid Less," *HuffPost,* Oct. 27, 2016.

157   *the only advanced economy:* Organization for Economic Cooperation and Development, Social Policy Division, Directorate of Employment, Labour and Social Affairs, Family Database, "PF2.5. Trends in Parental Leave Since 1970" (last updated Mar. 2017), http://www.oecd.org/els/social/family/database.

157   *12 percent of American private-sector workers:* U.S. Department of Labor, "DOL Factsheet: Paid Family and Medical Leave," June 2015, https://www.dol.gov/wb/paidleave/PDF/PaidLeave.pdf.

157   *one of only two countries out of 185:* Laura Addati, Naomi Cassirer, and Katherine Gilchrist, *Maternity and Paternity at Work: Law and Practice Across the World* (Geneva: International Labor Organization, 2014).

157 *mandating that businesses offer unpaid leave:* Organization for Economic Cooperation and Development, "PF2.5. Trends in Parental Leave Since 1970."

157 *five in six workers with unpaid or partially paid leave:* Juliana Menasce Horowitz, Kim Parker, Nikki Graf, and Gretchen Livingston, "Americans Widely Support Paid Family and Medical Leave, but Differ Over Specific Policies" (Washington, DC: Pew Research Center, Mar. 23, 2017).

157 *days or weeks of giving birth:* Sharon Lerner, "The Real War on Families: Why the U.S. Needs Paid Leave Now," *In These Times,* Aug. 18, 2015.

157 *mothers with infants . . . are part of the workforce:* U.S. Bureau of Labor Statistics, "Employment Characteristics of Families Summary," Apr. 20, 2017.

158 *"child care deserts":* Rasheed Malik, Katie Hamm, Maryam Adamu, and Taryn Morrissey, "Child Care Deserts: An Analysis of Child Care Centers by ZIP Code in 8 States" (Washington, DC: Center for American Progress, Oct. 27, 2016).

158 *$3,972 at a family home in Mississippi:* "Parents and the High Cost of Child Care: 2016" (Arlington, VA: Child Care Aware of America, 2016).

158 *spend nearly 40 percent of their earnings on it:* Lynda Laughlin, "Who's Minding the Kids? Child Care Arrangements: Spring 2011" (Household Economic Studies, U.S. Census Bureau, Apr. 2013).

158 *weekly cost of child care:* Ibid.

159 *fell to just $11.3 billion in 2014:* Hannah Matthews and Christina Walker, "Child Care Assistance Spending and Participation in 2014" (Washington, DC: CLASP, Mar. 2016).

159 *smallest number of children:* Ibid.

159 *one-quarter of that of sixteen other OECD countries:* Francine D. Blau and Lawrence M. Kahn, "Female Labor Supply: Why Is the US Falling Behind?" (NBER Working Paper no. 18702, Jan. 2013).

159 *one in three stay-at-home moms:* D'Vera Cohn and Andrea Caumont, "7 Key Findings About Stay-at-Home Moms," *FactTank* (blog), Pew Research Center, Apr. 8, 2014.

159   *5 percent drop in employment:* So Kubota, "Child Care Costs and Stagnating Female Labor Force Participation in the US" (white paper, Princeton University, July 9, 2017).

159   *the United States' female labor participation rate:* Eleanor Krause and Isabel Sawhill, "What We Know and Don't Know About Declining Labor Force Participation: A Review" (Washington, DC: Brookings Institution, May 17, 2017).

161   *the United States' fastest-growing job:* Karsten Strauss, "Predicting the Fastest-Growing Jobs of the Future," *Forbes,* Nov. 7, 2017.

162   *"By the time a woman earns her first dollar":* Jessica Schieder and Elise Gould, " 'Women's Work' and the Gender Pay Gap: How Discrimination, Societal Norms, and Other Forces Affect Women's Occupational Choices—and Their Pay" (Washington, DC: Economic Policy Institute, July 20, 2016).

162   *"pollution theory of discrimination":* Claudia Goldin, "A Pollution Theory of Discrimination: Male and Female Differences in Occupations and Earnings" (NBER Working Paper no. 8985, June 2002).

163   *majority-male to majority-female:* Claire Cain Miller, "As Women Take Over a Male-Dominated Field, the Pay Drops," *New York Times,* Mar. 18, 2016.

164   *Men own the vast majority of land:* "Kenya's National Gender Context and Its Implications for Conservation: A Gender Analysis" (Arlington, VA: The Nature Conservancy, July 2013).

164   *"for the first time, the new laws supersede customary laws":* Ibid.

165   *"In nearly a third of developing countries":* United Nations Statistics Division, *The World's Women 2015: Trends and Statistics* (New York: United Nations, Department of Economic and Social Affairs, Statistics Division, 2015), 179.

165   *unconditional and conditional cash-transfer programs:* Bastagli, Hagen-Zanker, Harman, Barca, Sturge, Schmidt, and Pellerano, *Cash Transfers.*

165   *"straightforward measure of poverty from a gender perspective":* United Nations Statistics Division, *World's Women,* 180.

166   *"almost three-quarters of Indian women have no income":* Pranab Bardhan, telephone interview by author, June 15, 2017.

166   *"If you had enough money":* Arvind Subramanian, interview by author, Apr. 18, 2017.

Chapter Nine: In It Together

167   *1,372 hate crimes:* Hatewatch Staff, "Post-Election Bias Incidents up to 1,372; New Collaboration with ProPublica *Hatewatch* (blog), Southern Poverty Law Center, Feb. 10, 2017, https://www.splcenter.org/hatewatch/2017/02/10/post-election-bias-incidents-1372-new-collaboration-propublica.

168   *The typical Republican was more conservative:* Michael Dimock, Jocelyn Kiley, Scott Keeter, and Carroll Doherty, "Political Polarization in the American Public: How Increasing Ideological Uniformity and Partisan Antipathy Affect Politics, Compromise and Everyday Life" (Washington, DC: Pew Research Center, June 12, 2014).

168   *as a danger to the country:* Ibid.

168   *live around people with the same views:* Ibid.

169   *getting hitched across partisan lines:* Ibid.

169   *should win an Oscar:* Tom Jensen, "Numbers for Obama, Democrats Tick Up Nationally" (Raleigh, NC: Public Policy Polling, Mar. 11, 2014), http://www.publicpolicypolling.com/wp-content/uploads/2017/09/PPP_Release_National_311.pdf.

169   *stronger predictor of opinion than racial identity:* Ezra Klein, "Gamergate and the Politicization of Absolutely Everything," Vox, Nov. 1, 2014.

169   *"We are materially better off in many ways":* Vice Chairman's Staff of the Joint Economic Committee, "What We Do Together: The State of Associational Life in America" (Social Capital Project Report no. 1-17, May 2017).

170   *"Our debate is increasingly relevant today":* Guy Standing, speech, the Basic Income Earth Network Congress 2016, Seoul, July 7, 2016.

172 *milk can cost as much as $10 a gallon:* Cynthia McFadden and Jake Whitman, "Changing Arctic: Land of Pickled Whale and $10 Milk," NBC News, Sept. 16, 2015.

172 *3 percent of the state's population:* Taylor Jo Isenberg, "What a New Survey from Alaska Can Teach Us About Public Support for Basic Income," Medium, June 28, 2017, https://medium.com/economicsecproj/what-a-new-survey-from-alaska-can-teach-us-about-public-support-for-basic-income-ccd0c3c16b42.

173 *"We're really trying to send a signal":* Bill Wielechowski, telephone interview by author, Oct. 19, 2016.

173 *"essentials, emergencies, paying off debt":* Ibid.

174 *5 modii, or about 70 pounds, of grain:* Gregory S. Aldrete, *Daily Life in the Roman City: Rome, Pompeii, and Ostia* (Westport, CT: Greenwood Press, 2004), 197.

174 *a 10-dirham guaranteed income:* Grace Clark, "Pakistan's Zakat and 'Ushr as a Welfare System," in *Islamic Reassertion in Pakistan: The Application of Islamic Laws in a Modern State,* ed. Anita M. Weiss (Syracuse, NY: Syracuse University Press, 1986), 79–95.

174 *"stakeholder society":* Bruce A. Ackerman and Anne Alstott, *The Stakeholder Society* (New Haven, CT: Yale University Press, 2000).

175 *fewer hospitalizations and mental-health diagnoses:* Evelyn L. Forget, "The Town with No Poverty: The Health Effects of a Guaranteed Annual Income Field Experiment," *Canadian Public Policy* 37, no. 3 (Sept. 2011): 283–305.

175 *spent more time with their children:* Marinescu, "No Strings Attached."

176 *One in three families has no savings:* "What Resources Do Families Have for Financial Emergencies? The Role of Emergency Savings in Family Financial Security" (Washington, DC: Pew Charitable Trusts, Nov. 18, 2015).

176 *$400 in an emergency:* Board of Governors of the Federal Reserve System, "Report on the Economic Well-Being of U.S. Households in 2015."

176 *"In the recent past, the focus on inequality":* Annie Lowrey, "2016: A Year Defined by America's Diverging Economies," *Atlantic,* Dec. 30, 2016.

176 *smaller and smaller number of "super-performing" counties:* "The New Map of Economic Growth and Recovery" (Washington, DC: Economic Innovation Group, May 2016).

177 *rich kids are five times more likely:* Margaret Cahalan and Laura Perna, *Indicators of Higher Education Equity in the United States, 45 Year Trend Report* (Washington, DC: Pell Institute for the Study of Opportunity in Higher Education and Penn Alliance for Higher Education and Democracy, 2015).

177 *American entrepreneurs tend to come from significantly richer families:* Ross Levine and Yona Rubinstein, "Smart and Illicit: Who Becomes an Entrepreneur and Do They Earn More?" (NBER Working Paper no. 19276, Aug. 2013).

177 *"the probability of self-employment":* David Blanchflower and Andrew J. Oswald, "What Makes an Entrepreneur? Evidence on Inheritance and Capital Constraints" (NBER Working Paper no. 3252, Feb. 1990).

178 *"A lot of immigrants are low-wage workers. . . . I don't think that would ever be politically viable":* Megan McArdle, "How a Basic Income in the U.S. Could Increase Global Poverty," *PBS NewsHour,* Apr. 18, 2014.

178 *"welfare magnets":* George J. Borjas, "Immigration and Welfare Magnets," *Journal of Labor Economics* 17, no. 4 (Oct. 1999): 607–37.

178 *Yet such immigrants:* Scott W. Allard and Sheldon Danziger, "Welfare Magnets: Myth or Reality?," *Journal of Politics* 62, no. 2 (May 2000): 350–68.

178 *immigrants drain the economy:* "More Americans Say Immigrants Help Rather Than Hurt Economy," Gallup News, June 29, 2017.

178 *immigrants cost the nation "too much":* "Immigration," Gallup News, http://news.gallup.com/poll/1660/immigration.aspx.

179 *$21,000 more in taxes:* William N. Evans and Daniel Fitzgerald, "The Economic and Social Outcomes of Refugees in the

United States: Evidence from the ACS" (NBER Working Paper no. 23498, June 2017).

179 *reduce the deficit by $1 trillion:* Congressional Budget Office, "The Economic Impact of S. 744, the Border Security, Economic Opportunity, and Immigration Modernization Act," June 18, 2013.

179 *barred from most safety-net programs:* "Undocumented Immigrants' State and Local Tax Contributions" (Washington, DC: Institute on Taxation and Economic Policy, July 2013).

179 *"A third of supporters switched to opposition":* Dylan Matthews, "A Basic Income Really Could End Poverty Forever," Vox, July 17, 2017.

180 *"I went and finally signed up for Medicaid":* Stanley Greenberg and Nancy Zdunkewicz, "Macomb County in the Age of Trump" (Washington, DC: Democracy Corps, Mar. 9, 2017).

180 *"building a wall around the welfare state":* William A. Niskanen, "Build a Wall Around the Welfare State, Not Around the Country" (Washington, DC: Cato Institute, Sept.–Oct. 2006).

181 *"makers" and "takers":* David Corn, "SECRET VIDEO: Romney Tells Millionaire Donors What He REALLY Thinks of Obama Voters," *Mother Jones,* Sept. 17, 2012.

181 *82 percent of American households pay income tax and payroll taxes:* Chuck Marr and Chye-Ching Huang, "Misconceptions and Realities About Who Pays Taxes" (Washington, DC: Center on Budget and Policy Priorities, Sept. 17, 2012).

182 *cigarette taxes and . . . lottery tickets:* Michael L. Davis, "Taxing the Poor: A Report on Tobacco, Alcohol, Gambling, and Other Taxes and Fees That Disproportionately Burden Lower-Income Families" (Dallas: National Center for Policy Analysis, June 2007).

182 *"We have come a long way in our understanding of human motivation":* Martin Luther King Jr., *Where Do We Go from Here: Chaos or Community?* (Boston: Beacon Press, 2010).

182 *"true individual freedom":* Franklin D. Roosevelt, "State of the Union Address," Jan. 11, 1944.

Chapter Ten: $1,000 a Month

184 *Charles Murray:* Charles Murray, *In Our Hands: A Plan to Re-place the Welfare State* (Lanham, MD: Rowman & Littlefield, 2016).

184 *Andy Stern:* Stern, *Raising the Floor.*

184 *Rutger Bregman:* Rutger Bregman, *Utopia for Realists: The Case for a Universal Basic Income, Open Borders, and a 15-Hour Work-week* (Amsterdam: The Correspondent, 2016).

184 *Nick Srnicek and Alex Williams:* Nick Srnicek and Alex Williams, *Inventing the Future: Postcapitalism and a World Without Work* (Brooklyn, NY: Verso, 2015).

184 *to be taxed back at death:* Ackerman and Alstott, *Stakeholder Society.*

185 *every penny the federal government currently spends:* "Policy Basics: Where Do Federal Tax Revenues Come From?" (Washington, DC: Center on Budget and Policy Priorities, Sept. 5, 2017).

185 *40 percent of all income taxes:* Scott Greenberg, "Summary of the Latest Federal Income Tax Data, 2016 Update" (Washington, DC: Tax Foundation, Feb. 2017).

185 *"Nothing in the history of this country":* Eduardo Porter, "A Universal Basic Income Is a Poor Tool to Fight Poverty," *New York Times,* May 31, 2016.

185 *roughly $2.7 trillion on its social-insurance programs:* Drew DeSilver, "What Does the Federal Government Spend Your Tax Dollars On? Social Insurance Programs, Mostly," *Fact-Tank* (blog), Pew Research Center, Apr. 4, 2017, http://www.pewresearch.org/fact-tank/2017/04/04/what-does-the-federal-government-spend-your-tax-dollars-on-social-insurance-programs-mostly/.

186 *$132 a month:* Dolan, "Could We Afford a Universal Basic Income? (Part 2)."

186 *$3,591 a year per person:* Ibid.

186 *mostly stayed static:* Robert Greenstein, "Universal Basic Income May Sound Attractive, But If It Occurred Would Likelier

Increase Poverty Than Reduce It" (Washington, DC: Center on Budget and Policy Priorities, Sept. 18, 2017).

187 *We are, by OECD standards, a low-tax country:* Sonya Hoo and Eric Toder, "The U.S. Tax Burden Is Low Relative to Other OECD Countries" (Washington, DC: Tax Policy Center, May 8, 2006).

188 *running deficits in perpetuity:* J. Bradford DeLong and Lawrence H. Summers, "Fiscal Policy in a Depressed Economy," *Brookings Papers on Economic Activity,* Spring 2012.

188 *financial transactions tax:* Josh Bivens and Hunter Blair, "A Financial Transaction Tax Would Help Ensure Wall Street Works for Main Street" (Washington, DC: Economic Policy Institute, July 28, 2016).

188 *well-designed carbon tax:* William G. Gale, Samuel Brown, and Fernando Saltiel, "Carbon Taxes as Part of the Fiscal Solution" (Washington, DC: Brookings Institution, Mar. 12, 2013).

188 *James Baker and George Shultz*: James A. Baker III, Martin Feldstein, Ted Halstead, N. Gregory Mankiw, Henry M. Paulson Jr., George P. Shultz, Thomas Stephenson, and Rob Walton, "The Conservative Case for Carbon Dividends: How a New Climate Strategy Can Strengthen Our Economy, Reduce Regulation, Help Working-Class Americans, Shrink Government & Promote National Security" (Washington, DC: Climate Leadership Council, Feb. 2017).

188 *economist James K. Boyce:* James K. Boyce and Peter Barnes, "$200 a Month for Everyone? Universal Income from Universal Assets," *TripleCrisis* (blog), Nov. 7, 2016, http://triplecrisis.com/200-a-month-for-everyone/.

189 *"Certainly there will be taxes that relate to automation":* Kevin J. Delaney, "The Robot That Takes Your Job Should Pay Taxes, Says Bill Gates," Quartz, Feb. 17, 2017.

189 *a kind of productivity dividend:* Paul T. Hartman, *Collective Bargaining and Productivity: The Longshore Mechanization Agreement* (Berkeley: University of California Press, 1969).

191 *cost about $200 billion a year:* Jessica Wiederspan, Elizabeth Rhodes, and H. Luke Shaefer, "Expanding the Discourse on Antipoverty Policy: Reconsidering a Negative Income Tax," *Journal of Poverty* 19, no. 2 (2015): 218–38.

192 *"a race-fair America"*: Darrick Hamilton, "Race, Wealth, and Intergenerational Poverty," *American Prospect,* Aug. 14, 2009.

192 *"Endowments are rife with opportunities for waste"*: Philippe Van Parijs, "A Basic Income for All," *Boston Review,* Oct.–Nov. 2000.

193 *"The benefits of the guarantee for the formerly jobless"*: Jeff Spross, "You're Hired!," *Democracy* 44 (Spring 2017).

193 *"set an implicit floor on wages"*: Hamilton, "Federal Job Guarantee."

196 *"I thought that I was the first to think of it"*: Philippe Van Parijs, interview by author, July 7, 2016.

196 *"A Capitalist Road to Communism"*: Robert Van der Veen and Philippe Van Parijs, "A Capitalist Road to Communism," *Theory and Society* 15, no. 5 (1986): 635–55.

197 *prime-age Finns:* Jauhiainen and Mäkinen, "Why Finland's Basic Income Experiment Isn't Working."

197 *"This is a new world with new challenges"*: Kassam, "Ontario Plans to Launch Universal Basic Income."

198 *"it would be worthless"*: Elizabeth Rhodes, telephone interview by author, Oct. 16, 2017.

198 *"refocus the voices of people who are poor"*: "What We Fund," Economic Security Project, 2017.

198 *"a good thing for the basic-income movement"*: Owen Poindexter, telephone interview by author, Sept. 27, 2017.

199 *"The [UBI] conversation is not being had"*: Alexis C. Madrigal, "Free Money at the Edge of the Tech Boom," *Atlantic,* Oct. 19, 2017.

199 *"In a state with more homeless per capita"*: Chris Lee, "Hawaii Becomes First State to Begin Evaluating a Universal Basic Income (Thanks for Your Help Reddit!)," Reddit, June 15, 2017, https://www.reddit.com/r/Futurology/comments/6hezyu /hawaii_becomes_first_state_to_begin_evaluating_a/.

200 *a Swiss artist:* Enno Schmidt, "How a 'Stupid Painter from Switzerland' Is Revolutionizing Work," *PBS NewsHour,* Apr. 9, 2014.

200 *"stimmig"*: Lowrey, "Switzerland's Proposal."

Postscript: Trekonomics

202   *a protocol spelled out:* Max Deutsch, "How to Write with Artificial Intelligence," Medium, July 11, 2016.

202   *"I would wake up at 4:00 AM":* Joseph Frankel, "These Horror Stories Created by Artificial Intelligence Are the Stuff of Nightmares," *Newsweek,* Oct. 25, 2017.

202   *"My heart is beating so fast":* Paul Seaburn, "The Horror of Artificial Intelligence Writing Horror Fiction," *Mysterious Universe,* Oct. 27, 2017.

202   *an AI system called Heliograf:* Lucia Moses, "The Washington Post's Robot Reporter Has Published 850 Articles in the Past Year," Digiday, Sept. 14, 2017.

202   *automated systems for earnings coverage:* Ibid.

202   *the economy's "cost disease":* William J. Baumol, *The Cost Disease: Why Computers Get Cheaper and Health Care Doesn't* (New Haven, CT: Yale University Press, 2012).

203   *a quarter of the hours the average American puts in:* Chris Isidore and Tami Luhby, "Turns Out Americans Work Really Hard . . . but Some Want to Work Harder," CNN, July 9, 2015.

203   *a man with a white-collar job:* Peter Kuhn and Fernando Lozano, "The Expanding Workweek? Understanding Trends in Long Work Hours Among U.S. Men, 1979–2004" (NBER Working Paper no. 11895, Dec. 2005).

204   *"Labor cannot be distinguished from leisure":* Manu Saadia, *Trekonomics: The Economics of "Star Trek"* (New York: Inkshares, 2016).

204   *"Economic Possibilities for Our Grandchildren":* Keynes, "Economic Possibilities for Our Grandchildren (1930)."

205   *help smooth transactions:* Matthew Yglesias, "The Star Trek Economy: (Mostly) Post-Scarcity, (Mostly) Socialism," *Slate,* Nov. 18, 2013.

207   *dystopian visions:* Yglesias, "The Economics of *The Hunger Games,*" *Slate,* Nov. 22, 2013.

207   *"The future is already here":* Pagan Kennedy, "William Gibson's Future Is Now," *New York Times,* Jan. 13, 2012.

INDEX

ABOUT THE AUTHOR

ANNIE LOWREY is a contributing editor for *The Atlantic*. A former writer for the *New York Times*, the *New York Times Magazine*, and *Slate*, among other publications, she is a frequent guest on CNN, MSNBC, and NPR. She lives in Washington, D.C.